HOWARD ZINN is a graduate of New York University and received his M.A. and Ph.D. degrees from Columbia University. He has taught at Upsala and Brooklyn Colleges, and at Spelman College, Atlanta, where he was professor of history and chairman of the department of history and social sciences. He is now with the department of government at Boston University.

LaGuardia in Congress won Honorable Mention in the Beveridge Award of the American Historical Association.

LaGuardia in Congress

BY HOWARD ZINN

The Norton Library
W · W · NORTON & COMPANY · INC ·
NEW YORK

Books That Live
The Norton imprint on a book means that in the publisher's
estimation it is a book not for a single season but for the years.
W. W. Norton & Company, Inc.

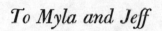

To Myla and Jeff

* Preface *

FIORELLO LAGUARDIA is known best as the tempestuous mayor of New York City in the days when Franklin D. Roosevelt sat in the White House. During that time he was New York's most colorful citizen, but no one city could contain his spirit, and he became a national figure, alternating between low-level comedy and high-minded reform, endearing himself to many Americans, outraging others.

There had been, however, an earlier time, which matched his mayoralty years in sheer drama and perhaps surpassed them in lasting achievement—LaGuardia's years in Congress. He was in the House of Representatives almost continuously from 1917 to 1933. There were two brief interruptions: once to fly with the American forces in Italy during World War I; then to serve during 1920 and 1921 as president of the New York City Board of Aldermen. But in 1923 he came back into Congress and during the next ten years conducted his own bustling side show for reform.

He attracted only a small audience. This was the decade of Harding, Coolidge, and Hoover, of scandal and revelry and unbounded prosperity. Or so it seemed until 1929. Then, sitting among the ruins, historians began their sober recalculation, a process unfinished even today, though the debris of depression has since been covered by the ashes of another war, and these too are now being buried under a new and greater "normalcy."

Upon reappraisal, the twenties take on a different aspect. The scenes of Babylon still predominate—short skirts and speakeasies, booming real estate and a rocketing stock market. But it is now beginning to be understood that these were only scenes; when the audience left the theater, it went home, not to Babylon but to Middletown, not to wild parties but to "the long arm of the job." For while in the twenties the spotlight was occupied by "Daddy" Browning and Al Capone, Charles Lindbergh and J. P. Morgan, there were many others, obscure and ordinary people, farmers and small businessmen, white-collar workers and manual laborers, who beheld the glittering spectacle but were never quite part of it. This basic fact about the twenties was understood and acted upon by only a small number of political leaders—men like Robert La Follette, George Norris, James Frear, and Fiorello La-Guardia.

Virtually all the congressional progressives of the twenties came from the prairie and mountain states of the trans-Mississippi region, but LaGuardia represented a slum district in East Harlem. In his district, Italians, Jews, Puerto Ricans, and a dozen other national groups lived in firetraps during the same years when statesmen, under white-domed palaces, thanked God for the blessings of prosperity. On 110th Street, mothers pondered anxiously the price of bread even while brokers downtown pored, just as anxiously, over the market quotations.

Like his fellow progressives, LaGuardia represented, in a sense, the conscience of the twenties. As Democrats and Republicans cavorted like rehearsed wrestlers in the center of the political ring, LaGuardia stalked the front rows and bellowed for real action. While Ku Klux Klan membership reached the millions and Congress tried to legislate the nation toward racial "purity," LaGuardia demanded that immigration bars be let down to Italians, Jews, and others. When self-styled patriots sought to make the Caribbean an American lake, LaGuardia called for the removal of marines from Nicaragua. Above the clatter of ticker-tape machines sounding their jubilant message, LaGuardia tried to tell the nation about striking miners in Pennsylvania.

The progressives of the twenties and early thirties, however, did not merely complain; they offered remedies, again and again. Congressional archives are filled with their rejected legislation, and LaGuardia's name reappears there continually. Most of the later New Deal legislation was anticipated by LaGuardia, Norris, Wagner, Costigan, and others both before and after the 1929 crash so that, when Franklin D. Roosevelt took his oath of office, a great deal of initial work had already been done.

Roosevelt once compared himself to a quarterback making up the plays as he went along. But even before he came out on the playing field, experienced teammates had piled up impressive yardage, had experimented with new plays, and were ready to join in the spirited offensive against economic crisis which we call the New Deal. LaGuardia, it appears, was an important link between two periods of reform, picking up the progressive football upon entering Congress in early 1917 and finally handing it over to Roosevelt in early 1933. In the years between, he battled in his own dogged fashion, under difficult conditions and almost alone, just to keep the ball in play.

It is necessary to make clear that LaGuardia was not a "big wheel" on Capitol Hill. He was a cog who refused to stay in place. Barred from important committee posts because of his political independence, and thus unable to play a direct role in lawmaking, he used the floor of the House of Representatives to bombard with his voice the fetishes of his time. He was not in a position, except for several brief moments of triumph in the last days of his congressional career, methodically to follow a bill through to victory. The necessity of insurgent politics made him a floor man rather than a committee man, and from this vantage point, which he used more than any other congressman in his day, he acted as tireless goad to the Babbitts, the Coolidges, the Mellons, and all the other guardians of the age of sham.

Permission to quote has been kindly granted by Caroline F. Ware, author of *Greenwich Village 1920–1930*, published by Houghton Mifflin Company, and by Harcourt, Brace and Company, publishers of *Middletown* by Robert S. and Helen Merrell Lynd.

A number of persons deserve my thanks in connection with this book. Professor William E. Leuchtenburg of Columbia University offered painstaking criticism of the first drafts, and Professor Richard Hofstadter of Columbia University was kind enough to advise me in the final stages of the manuscript. Mr. James Katsaros and Mr. Martin Schiller of the Municipal Archives in New York City were extremely helpful during the many months I spent with the LaGuardia Papers there. Valuable assistance in locating manuscript material was given by Mr. Herman Kahn, in charge of the Franklin D. Roosevelt Papers at Hyde Park, and Mr. David C. Mearns, head of the Manuscripts Division of the Library of Congress. I am grateful to Mrs. Marie Fischer LaGuardia and Mrs. Miriam Marcantonio for granting interviews which cleared up a number of questions for me. Professor Glyndon Van Deusen of the Albert Beveridge Award Committee of the American Historical Association gave generously of his time to help prepare the manuscript for publication. And my wife, Roslyn Zinn, offered perceptive criticism at every stage. Final responsibility, of course, for any failings in either fact or interpretation is my own. I must add a word of thanks to the students of Spelman College and my friends in the Atlanta University System for making life interesting for me between sessions at the typewriter. Let me say also that I am very grateful to the American Historical Association for sponsoring the publication of this book.

HOWARD ZINN

Atlanta, Georgia
April, 1959

· *Contents* ·

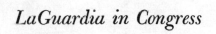

LaGuardia in Congress

1 · The New Congressman

from Manhattan, 1917

WASHINGTON was chilled, gray, and rumbling with talk of war when Fiorello LaGuardia arrived in early 1917 to take up his congressional duties for the first time. The bill to arm merchant ships had just been filibustered to death in the Senate, and Woodrow Wilson was planning his next moves from the seclusion of his White House study. On March 5, opening day for the Sixty-fifth Congress, the new representative from lower Manhattan, short, sturdy, his black hair parted in the middle, wearing a bow tie, walked down the center aisle until he found an empty seat in the front of the House chamber and sat down. There were a few murmurs and grunts, stares from several colleagues, and whispers in the press gallery. The freshman congressman had violated House protocol by taking a seat up front. This was the beginning of LaGuardia's long career as a political upstart. But, more than mere obstreperousness, it was the foretaste of a new kind of ingredient in American national politics.

LaGuardia was the first Italian-American in Congress, an advance agent of the urban immigrant masses who would gather slowly in the Twenties and then shake national politics violently in the era of Franklin Roosevelt. He brought to Washington a fresh progressivism, just as the old was disintegrating. Wilsonian liberalism had swallowed up many of the big-city reformers. More important, the war split the movement badly, for the unity of progressives had always been based on domestic issues, and now pacifists and interventionists rushed off in opposite directions. LaGuardia, listening to the Speaker pound the gavel for order in March, 1917, was very much alone in the crowded chamber. As a first-termer, he was not expected to speak, but he could not possibly hold his tongue. He would speak in Congress this first day, and not until sixteen years later would he stop. The facts of his life, the momentum of his thinking, called for this.

Fiorello LaGuardia was born on December 11, 1882, in an unpretentious flat in Greenwich Village.[1] His parents had crossed over from Italy four years earlier. Achilles LaGuardia, his father, was a gifted musician from Foggia, an Episcopalian by religion,[2] who came to America as an arranger for the famous soprano Adelina Patti, and stayed to join the American army as a bandmaster. Fiorello would be taunted in the Hitler era with the accusation that he was a Jew, and the statement was half-true. His mother was a Jewish girl from Trieste, who was eventually buried in a Jewish cemetery in Rumania.[3] During World War II a Nazi magazine printed LaGuardia's photo, and the caption read: "Fiorello LaGuardia, Warmonger and Eternal Jew." [4]

Fiorello spent his youth in army camps in Arizona, where Achilles LaGuardia was stationed, and, when the Spanish-American War broke out, followed his father to Florida. In the sweltering city of Tampa thousands of American soldiers, held

---

[1] The address was 9 Varick Place, mentioned in a letter from LaGuardia to Bruce Chapman, Feb. 18, 1944, LaGuardia Papers, Municipal Archives, New York City. Jacob Riis, *How the Other Half Lives* (New York, 1890), describes New York in those days. The Italian community in the Village and its beginnings is treated by Caroline F. Ware, *Greenwich Village 1920–1930* (Boston, 1935), 152.

[2] Achilles' father fought with Garibaldi against the Pope's troops and became a Protestant. Fiorello himself never knew too much about his father's background, as he reveals in a letter to LaGuardia-Bueno (who wondered, because of his name, if he was related to Fiorello), May 26, 1943, LaG. Papers.

[3] Her maiden name was Irene Coen Lazzatti, and she was descended from Jewish refugees who had fled to Italy during the Spanish Inquisition. She met Achilles LaGuardia in Trieste. Information on the marriage is given in a report in a Budapest Hungarian-Jewish weekly, Nov. 18, 1933, of an interview with Herman Gluck, a Budapest bank clerk who married Gemma LaGuardia, Fiorello's sister (*ibid.*).

[4] Fiorello's sister Gemma was briefly imprisoned by the Nazis during the war and questioned about her brother. She emerged safely from this experience.

over en route to Cuba, were stricken with food poisoning, victims of the "embalmed beef" sold to the Quartermaster Corps by contractors.[5] Achilles LaGuardia was one of the victims, and he never recovered from his illness. Several years later he died.[6] For Fiorello, this was an embittering experience. All his life he would blame "profiteers" for killing his father in the prime of life.

During Achilles' last years of life the family returned to Europe to live with relatives, and LaGuardia helped support his mother and sisters by taking a job (in 1901) with the American consulate in Budapest. From 1903 to 1906 he served as United States Consul at Fiume, acting as lone representative of his country in a tiny office which was also his bedroom. Then, tired of the frustrating routine of a harassed petty administrator, he returned to the States. The linguistic skill he had acquired in Europe helped him get a job with the United States Immigration Service at Ellis Island,[7] and he worked there four years while attending the evening session at New York University Law School.

Even before he left Europe, LaGuardia had decided to enter

[5] Fifty-seven officers in the entire Quartermaster Department were called upon, within a month after hostilities began, to equip an army of 275,000 men (Walter Millis, *The Martial Spirit* [Cambridge, 1931], 214.). General Nelson A. Miles popularized the term, and a member of the Chicago Health Department, writing to him, said the term was appropriate because he had made laboratory examinations and found that such beef was preserved with boric acid, nitrate of potash, and artificial coloring matter (*Report of the Commission to Investigate the Conduct of the War Department in the War with Spain* [Sen. Doc. no. 221, 56:1; Washington, 1900], VIII, 420). In May, 1898, Armour and Company sold to the army 500,000 pounds of beef which had been sent to Liverpool a year earlier and had been returned. When two months later the army inspector tested the Armour meat, which had been stamped and approved by an inspector of the Bureau of Animal Industry, he found 751 cases containing rotten meat. In the first 60 cases he opened, he found 14 tins already burst, "the effervescent putrid contents of which were distributed all over the cases" (*ibid.*, 406, 424).

[6] A total of 5,462 deaths were reported by the army up to the end of 1898, with only 379 of these the result of combat (Millis, *op. cit.*, 367).

[7] The Commissioner at Ellis Island, recommending LaGuardia in early 1910 for a promotion and a raise from $1,200 to $1,380 a year, said of him: "Mr. La-Guardia is energetic, intelligent and familiar with a number of foreign languages. Against him there may be said that he is inclined to be peppery; that with some of the Board members he is inclined to be argumentative, but he has been spoken to about this and it is not a defect of the first order" (Personnel Folder of Fiorello LaGuardia, Federal Records Center, St. Louis, Mo.).

politics. The exact source of that decision lies buried somewhere in that still-mysterious no man's land of the human brain where conscious and unconscious meet. All we know is that LaGuardia was sick of being the instrument by which far-off legislators played with the lives of unfortunate immigrants. He had retailed political power for enough years—now he wanted to touch with his own hands the machinery that produced it. As soon as he returned to the States, he began reading the *Congressional Record*. In 1910 he passed the bar examinations, left Ellis Island, and began his law practice in a tiny corner of the office of William C. Bennett, a Republican politician. But how could he concentrate on torts and equity when New York City was racked with labor conflict, and the Bull Moose movement was beginning to roar across the American political landscape?

LaGuardia became a Republican rank-and-file worker in the 25th Assembly District in Greenwich Village, where he lived. He had gravitated toward the Republican party as a result of an early-acquired distaste for Tammany Hall (perhaps due to the influence of Pulitzer's *World*,[8] which he read regularly as a boy in Arizona), as well as of his admiration of La Follette, Norris, Theodore Roosevelt, and others who dared challenge traditional Republicanism. During the furious 1912 campaign he served as precinct captain for Theodore Roosevelt and the Progressive party.[9]

It seems natural that Fiorello LaGuardia, out of the composite of his early experiences—son of an enlisted man in the army, minor official in Fiume, observer of pathos on Ellis Island, impe-

[8] The editorial columns of the *World* represented certain ideas which parallel, to a striking degree, those of the later LaGuardia. The *World* was anti-politician generally and anti-Tammany specifically. It refused to be bound to party program on all occasions. It was sympathetic to labor when labor was not what it considered "radical." It was loudly hostile to "special privilege" and it was strongly nationalistic in supporting wars which could be justified on humanitarian grounds. See editorial on Tammany, Nov. 1, 1896, prolabor story on coal strike, Feb. 6, 1898, and editorials for the issue of Feb. 13, 1898. See also William Reynolds, "Joseph Pulitzer" (Ph.D. dissertation, Columbia University, 1950), 338. LaGuardia later recalled about his Arizona days: "When I got home with the *Sunday World* I would carefully read every word of the *World*'s fight against the corrupt Tammany machine in New York" (*The Making of an Insurgent: An Autobiography, 1882–1919* [New York, 1948], 30.

[9] Lowell Limpus and Burr Leyson, *This Man LaGuardia* (New York, 1938), 30.

cunious lawyer using borrowed law books and second-hand furniture—should develop sympathies for the workingman and
organized labor. In December of 1912, when workers in the men's
clothing industry in New York City began walking out of the
shops in protest against their working conditions, LaGuardia was
approached by the union for help. The employers were pitting
Italians against Jews, and LaGuardia was asked to explain the
strike to Italian garment workers. In the course of the ten-week
strike, 120,000 workers left their jobs, rioting took place in several sectors of the city, and injunctions were used to prevent
picketing. LaGuardia spent his days in court and his evenings at
union headquarters, walked the picket lines, and built friendships
among Italian and Jewish garment workers.[10]

It was a combination of aggressiveness and accident that led to
LaGuardia's first race for political office, as Republican nominee
for Congress from the Fourteenth Congressional District. In the
late summer of 1914 he was in the clubhouse of the 25th Assembly
District in the Village when the Republican leaders were preparing petitions for the coming primaries. Someone shouted,
"Who is the candidate for Congress?" The district leader came
out of his back-room office and called out, "Who wants to run for
Congress?" LaGuardia said, "I do," and the leader replied, "O.K.
Put LaGuardia down." When he gave his full name to the man
listing the slate, the man declared, "Oh hell, let's get someone
whose name we can spell!" But the confounding name of Fiorello
LaGuardia ended up on the petitions.[11]

[10] The strike is covered in dispatches in the New York *Times,* Jan. 3, 4, 5,
7, 14, and 23, 1913. At this time, New York and Baltimore dissidents from
the United Garment Workers of America were operating as an autonomous
body within the union, but preparing to form their own group (Matthew
Josephson, *Sidney Hillman* [New York, 1952], 90). The Amalgamated Clothing Workers of America was organized at a convention in Nashville, Tennessee, in mid-1913, several months after the end of the strike. Sidney Hillman was elected president, and when he came to New York in 1914 he and
LaGuardia came to know one another well. Their friendship continued
throughout LaGuardia's congressional career. In 1916, LaGuardia spoke at
mass meetings arranged by Hillman to fight off an I.W.W. invasion of the
clothing workers in New York. In 1923, LaGuardia was on the first board of
directors of labor's first bank, set up by Hillman for the Amalgamated. In the
early years of the depression of the 1930's, Hillman and LaGuardia worked
together on welfare legislation (*ibid.,* 145, 247, 350).

[11] *Making of an Insurgent,* 103.

The lack of competition for the Republican nomination in the Fourteenth District was understandable. Never in the history of the district had a Republican congressman been elected; it was one of the bastions of Tammany Hall, a "sure district" for the Tammany boss, Charles F. Murphy. Any party worker willing to gamble time and money against overwhelming odds could secure the Republican nomination and enjoy a few months of dubious glory.

LaGuardia took his nomination seriously, but he soon learned that this was not expected of him. The first meeting of Republican campaigners in the district was held in September of 1914, and it was announced that all the leading candidates would speak. LaGuardia arrived early and waited patiently while one candidate after another spoke. Every time the chairman said, "And now we will hear from a young and promising candidate . . . ," LaGuardia arose, but it was always someone else being called upon. The meeting ended without his being asked to speak. When the same thing happened at a number of subsequent meetings, it became clear to LaGuardia that he was on his own.

The Democratic incumbent in the district was Michael Farley, saloonkeeper, president of the National Liquor Dealers' Association, and Tammany regular. Aside from distributing the usual handbills and posters in the area, Farley did not bother to campaign. He sat by calmly while LaGuardia stormed at him from every street corner. LaGuardia claimed later that he said nothing disparaging about Farley. "I merely pointed out that he was not a good Congressman, and wasn't even a good bartender." [12]

LaGuardia bought a second-hand Ford to take him around the district. He and the young secretary of the Republican Club, Harry Andrews, covered the Ford with signs and went from corner to corner every night, often taking advantage of a crowd that had gathered to hear other campaign speakers. As the other truck departed, they would pull up and harangue the crowd. The district included part of the lower East Side, with its thousands of immigrant families, and LaGuardia rang doorbells, speaking to these people in Yiddish or in Italian. It was his own private campaign, for to the regular Republican organization his candidacy was simply something for the record.

[12] *Ibid.*, 105.

No Republican had campaigned this way in the district before. Furthermore, this was a new type of Republican, an Italian, the son of immigrants, who could speak his neighbors' tongue and, even more important, talk about the things which were meaningful to them—the price of bread, the garbage in the streets, the firetraps in which their children attended classes and in which they slept. As a result, while LaGuardia was not elected in 1914, he won the largest number of votes ever secured by a Republican candidate in that district.[13]

His fine showing attracted attention. Impressed by the vote-getting ability of the dynamic young lawyer, Republican party leaders in Manhattan began to consider how useful this might be in future campaigns. In the fall of 1914 the Republican family sat down to feast at the patronage table, with Governor-elect Charles S. Whitman doing the carving. After the choice parts had been dished out, there were a few morsels left, and in January, 1915, LaGuardia was appointed a Deputy Attorney-General of the state of New York. His mother and sister were in Italy living with relatives, and he set up a bachelor apartment at 39 Charles Street in the Village.[14]

As Deputy Attorney-General during 1915 and most of 1916, LaGuardia's distaste for the regular party politicians was intensified. His attempt to rid New York's West Side of unhealthful fumes which came across the Hudson from Jersey factories was squelched, he believed, by the influence of corporate wealth on the Republican leaders in Albany. Another attempt to act against large oyster companies on Long Island, which were violating the Conservation Law by taking young scallops, was similarly thwarted by an amendment to the law, rushed through the Republican legislature just before the court decision. When LaGuardia moved against several large packing houses for violating the Weights and Measures Law, he had his first encounter with Jimmy Walker, attorney for the packers, and was bested when the Tammany-appointed judge dismissed the case. LaGuardia wrote later: "Politics, politics, politics! I found very little difference in their philosophy among members of either big party. I was to find the

[13] Farley received 7,336 votes, LaGuardia 5,331, and Progressive party candidate Golden 1,511 (New York *Times,* Nov. 5, 1914).
[14] Limpus and Leyson, *op. cit.,* 32.

same kind of thing going on after I went to Congress. But I just could not be a regular." [15]

The 1916 congressional campaign found LaGuardia anxious to make good on the promise he had shown in his first race, but the Republican organization of New York County, headed by Samuel Koenig, was not prepared to nominate him.[16] The nomination was more desirable this year, for a presidential election was taking place, and a successful candidate for President might conceivably sweep along with him the local candidates. LaGuardia was shocked and hurt to find he was not slated for a place on the ticket, but he did not intend to accept the rejection silently. As he remembered later,

I arranged to see Fred Tanner, who was state chairman. . . . He told me that the candidate they had in mind was Hamilton Fish. I think something was said about a big contribution to the district or to the party. . . . He told me I had made a good run in 1914, that I had no chance of winning and should not take two defeats, and that my day would come. I then told Fred that I felt I was entitled to the nomination and would file a petition. . . . Fred kind of warmed up . . . and said that he would try to help me. We had our petitions already printed. Someone suggested—I can't remember who—that the printer's bill would be paid, and I told him to go to hell. At any rate, opposition vanished, and I entered the Republican primaries unopposed.[17]

This was the initial tryout of a technique that would later become standard operating procedure for LaGuardia—using the threat of an independent candidacy to secure the party nomination. He entered the Progressive party primary also, won easily, and now set out to campaign.

His opponent, Michael Farley, Tammany's fixture in the district, was a perfect target. LaGuardia termed him "the sitting congressman." Farley was rarely seen in the district, and his record

[15] *Making of an Insurgent,* 114.

[16] Koenig's distaste for unorthodox political behavior was shown in his support of Taft in 1912. Koenig candidly acknowledged that he stuck with Taft in spite of the desires of the rank and file. "It was difficult to keep the party in line," he said. "Frankly, the enrolled voters wanted Roosevelt, but it was the pressure that we put on the leaders and the party workers that carried the day for Taft" (interview with Samuel Koenig, in Oral History Project, Columbia University, 1950).

[17] LaGuardia to Harry Andrews, May 6, 1947, LaG. Papers.

in Washington was conspicuously devoid of achievement. He
had been silent, safe, and a veritable giant of inaction. He did
not bother to speak in the area during the campaign; other stump
speakers were imported to urge his re-election.

LaGuardia, on the other hand, whirled through the district at
top speed in the months before election, from the brash night-
club-studded alleys of Greenwich Village to the squeezed-together
tenements of the East Side. He recalled later: "I covered every
corner in that district, I think. We would start early in the evening, on the West Side, keep going east, and it was not unusual
for the last street meeting to end way past one o'clock in the morning. Then to Stuyvesant Hall or some coffee house on the East
Side for another hour or two of campaigning." [18]

This time it was not a one-man campaign. At his side, managing the campaign, was the clever young lawyer Harry Andrews.
Popular local leaders in the Republican party, like Louis Espresso
of the Village, had supported LaGuardia's nomination and now
threw their energies into his campaign. And a young stenographer,
Marie Fischer, who first met LaGuardia when they were both
attached to the State Attorney-General's office, took up secretarial
duties in the vacant store which served as headquarters.[19]

Tammany, with the customary machine-made Democratic majority in the district, remained confident. It could count on some
Republican district leaders, who regularly played ball with Tammany, to turn over a sizable number of votes. There was always,
in addition, that last refuge of electoral desperation, the count,
for paper ballots were still being used, and there were several
accredited methods of adjusting the actual vote to what Tammany
soberly considered a more accurate representation of political
reality. Ballots for the opposition could be destroyed, or they
could be marked in such a way as to render them invalid. Mathematical error was also possible, since election-board members
were not expected to be Einsteins or Newtons.

LaGuardia had some advantages, however. The multilingual
nature of the district was made to order for his special abilities.
The Irish, the Jews, the Italians, the Poles and Hungarians, all
had their special grievances, to which LaGuardia paid close attention. "I knew," he commented later, "more about the history

[18] *Making of an Insurgent*, 123.   [19] Limpus and Leyson, *op. cit.*, 36.

of Ireland than Mike Farley did. . . . In my talks on the East
Side I dismembered the Hapsburg Empire and liberated all the
subjugated countries under that dynasty almost every night." [20]
Furthermore, the presidential candidate of the Republican party
in 1916 was Charles Evans Hughes, and the prosperous section
of the Fourteenth Congressional District, around Washington
Square, could be expected to vote Republican down the line.

For the election itself LaGuardia made careful plans. Watch-
ers were stationed at every polling place and instructed to remain
on duty until the ballot boxes were sealed. Before the polls opened
on election morning, he and a few aides visited several flophouses
in the district. Tammany customarily came to these places with
refreshments and herded the inhabitants to the polls to vote
Democrat. This time LaGuardia made sure the Republican
emissaries arrived first, distributed coffee and doughnuts, and
escorted their charges to the polls before the Tammany men
realized what was happening. LaGuardia stood watch himself
at the water-front polling places on the West Side, where the Democrats usually won five to one. He supervised the count at one
place, noted that he had beaten Farley by a few votes, and made
sure the ballots were packed and sent to the official counting
spot.

By four the next morning the final count was tabulated, and
history had been made in the Fourteenth Congressional District.
Tammany stood defeated. Fiorello LaGuardia, Republican and
Progressive, had drawn 7,272 votes against Farley's 6,915, winning by 357 votes. The tally was so close that for two days the
press reported that Farley was victorious, and not until the Friday
after election was LaGuardia's triumph established.[21]

The victory was surprising to his contemporaries, but understandable to later observers. Eric Goldman has summed up the
reasons for LaGuardia's election.

He did it by shrewd politicking, by providing the street-corner crowds
with clowning that was not excelled in Maurice Schwartz's famous
Yiddish theater around the corner, by speaking Yiddish to the Jews
and Italian to the Italians, and by talking to all his audiences a reformism that was directly related to their ambitions and their fears.[22]

[20] *Making of an Insurgent*, 124.   [21] New York *World*, Nov. 8, 1916.
[22] *Rendezvous with Destiny* (New York, 1952), 259.

The reaction of the Republican party to this unexpected turn of events in the Fourteenth added a reinforcing layer to La-Guardia's thickening insurgency. On the East Side, where progressivism, socialism, and pacifism mingled with less-sophisticated and more fundamental concerns like the price of bread and the safety of fire escapes, LaGuardia was joyfully received by Republican party workers. On the West Side, however, where the crooked streets of Greenwich Village adjoined the swank homes on University Place and Fifth Avenue, there was distinct coldness and even dismay. This was LaGuardia's home district, but, he reported, "I never saw such gloom anywhere. The hangers-on at the club hardly nodded to me." Through the thin partition enclosing the rear office, LaGuardia heard someone phoning the Democratic district leader, saying: "No, Joe, we didn't double-cross you; we didn't do anything for this fellow. You just can't control him." [23]

Nationally, the 1916 election took place against the background of impending war, the clash of labor struggle, and the demise of the Progressive party. Wilson narrowly defeated Hughes, but the Republican party made enough gains in the House of Representatives to end up with almost half the seats.[24] With such a close division between the major parties, a handful of independents (Meyer London, a Socialist, had been elected to Congress from New York; Louisiana and Minnesota had each elected a Progressive; and Montana had elected Jeannette Rankin, first woman in Congress) would command special influence in the Sixty-fifth Congress. Fiorello LaGuardia, nominally a Republican, at heart a Progressive, could be considered part of this group.

LaGuardia had four months to prepare for his congressional debut, and he spent his time familiarizing himself further with his district, its people, and its problems. To an extent his actions from now on as congressman would be influenced by the nature of the Fourteenth Congressional District. This is not to suggest that it was the socioeconomic character of this area which was the decisive fact in forming LaGuardia's outlook on the important policy questions of the day. LaGuardia's philosophy was by this time fairly well crystallized and mature. However, it is reasonable

[23] *Making of an Insurgent*, 127.   [24] New York *World*, Nov. 8, 1916.

to observe that the type of district he represented was such as to strengthen that philosophy.

The Fourteenth Congressional District ran east-west across Manhattan, from the East River to the Hudson River, in a band twelve blocks wide, from Fourteenth Street down to Third Street.[25] The eastern sector of the district was one great slum, consisting of row upon row of six- and seven-story walk-up tenements, criss-crossed by fire escapes, enmeshed by clothes lines, and surrounded by mounds of rubbish. Here lived Jews, Italians, Poles, Ukrainians, Russians, Czechs, Rumanians, and a dozen other national groups, part of the great exodus from southern and eastern Europe which had come to American shores in the preceding twenty-five years. This neighborhood was one of the strongholds of socialist thought, led by a few immigrant intellectuals and reinforced by the sons and daughters of recent immigrants. It was not surprising that class consciousness, pacifism, and internationalism should take hold in a setting such as this, where men and women could sit on the stoops in the stifling summer heat and ponder both the European militarism they had escaped and the sweatshops to which they had come.

In the midst of these tenements in the eastern sector was a small rectangle of green called Tompkins Square, where a few trees, a rough grassy lawn, and wooden benches provided an escape from the sweating asphalt. Here the inhabitants of the East Side could breathe in not only fresh air but political theory, and small knots of impassioned debaters were a common sight at Tompkins Square. It was the historic site of huge open-air meetings called by labor groups and radical organizations. During the great railroad strikes of 1877, 100,000 people had demonstrated in the Square against government violence, and young Samuel Gompers had watched in anger as police used their clubs on the demonstrators.[26]

On the other side of Broadway was the western half of the Fourteenth Congressional District. Around Washington Square Park were the ornate private houses and apartment-hotels of the

[25] Carl Wittke, *We Who Built America* (New York, 1939), describes the lower East Side in this period.

[26] Samuel Yellen, *American Labor Struggles* (New York, 1936), tells of the part played by Tompkins Square Park in the 1877 strikes.

wealthy, with uniformed doormen looking out on clean, broad
avenues like University Place, Fifth Avenue, and Waverly Place.
But between Sixth Avenue and the Hudson River the regular
rectangular pattern gave way to a bewildering patchwork of
narrow streets and alleys, running in all directions and at all
angles. This was Greenwich Village, not yet possessed of those
romantic attributes which would make it, after the war, "The
Village." It was at this time a melange of broken-down houses
and dank little stores, rarely visited by the sun, where newly
arrived Italians and native Irishmen scrambled fiercely for jobs
on the water front or in the factories farther downtown.

When the House of Representatives convened on March 5,
1917, its first job was to organize, and LaGuardia found himself
receiving an inordinate amount of attention from members of
both major parties. With a Speaker about to be elected, regular
Democrats and Republicans were equally matched in voting
strength, each certain of 215 members. Five congressmen were
considered independents, including LaGuardia, who had run
on both Republican and Progressive tickets. He decided to vote
with the Republicans on their choice for Speaker, but Democrat
Champ Clark won by a narrow margin. Almost immediately La-
Guardia attached himself to the Progressives on Capitol Hill.
He had always admired their fight to liberalize the House rules
and break down the dictatorship of the Speaker, and he began
to confer often with George Norris, William E. Borah, and Hiram
Johnson, all of them in the Senate now.[27]

On March 12, 1917, as the Navy Department was preparing
to arm American merchant vessels plying the Atlantic, a German
submarine sank the unarmed S.S. "Algonquin" without warning.
Four days later the sinkings of the "City of Memphis," the "Illinois," and the "Vigilancia" were announced. That same day
Prince Michael of Russia, after holding the throne for twenty-
four hours as the last Tsar, abdicated to a provisional government. And on March 21, 1917, Woodrow Wilson summoned
Congress to convene in special session on the second of April.

Waiting for the session to open, LaGuardia rushed back to

[27] Interview with Marie Fischer LaGuardia, in Oral History Project, Columbia University.

New York to participate in a series of patriotic meetings held on the lower East Side, sponsored by the New York *Evening World*. The issues had not yet come to the forefront which would label LaGuardia an insurgent and make his presence distasteful to the leaders of the Republican party. In early 1917 he was seen by many Republican leaders as a congressman who because of his background could form a link between the immigrant masses of his district and the political leaders of the party. And his speeches on the East Side fulfilled his sponsors' expectations. He told his audience: "The district I represent has never been found wanting in loyalty. It is still truly and sincerely American. These are days when we must renew our love for the land and the flag that flies over us." The speeches were interspersed between the songs "The Story of Old Glory," "Dixie," and "Uncle Sam." [28] It was a time for the public display of patriotism, and LaGuardia went along.

American progressivism before World War I, while it had a strong antiwar wing led by La Follette and Norris, was to a great extent dominated by bellicose nationalists of the Teddy Roosevelt and Albert Beveridge variety.[29] LaGuardia at this time could be said to share both the radical domestic views of the La Follettes and the aggressive foreign policy ideas of the Roosevelts. But while Roosevelt and others could justify American entrance into the war on grounds which smacked of jingoism, LaGuardia insisted that if the United States was to take warlike actions, it must account for them in terms of a higher morality, in terms of democracy and freedom.[30] The war, he felt, would mean liberation for those millions of people in Central Europe still under the domination of the Hapsburgs.

[28] New York *Evening World,* March 22, 1917.

[29] William E. Leuchtenburg, "Progressivism and Imperialism," *Mississippi Valley Hist. Rev.,* XXXIX (Dec., 1952).

[30] The antiwar *Staats-Zeitung* in New York claimed in an article written just before the House vote on the war resolution that LaGuardia, despite his personal feelings, was forced to go along with the prowar majority for fear of jeopardizing his own position as a new and insecure congressman. However, LaGuardia's own utterances do not bear this out, and his wife, Marie Fischer LaGuardia, in an interview with this writer in the summer of 1956 disagreed with the *Staats-Zeitung*'s statement, saying that LaGuardia "was always very patriotic."

On the eve of Wilson's war message, LaGuardia was calling for American participation in the European conflict. In a speech to one thousand Italian-Americans at the Labor Temple in lower Manhattan, he made it clear that he considered the Allied cause to be just and pointed to the Russian Revolution as one of the democratic fruits of the struggle: "We've got to fight hard; we've got to take a man's part in this war. If the European war, with all its bloodshed, does nothing else but bring liberty to Russia, it has accomplished much good." [31]

In the meantime, LaGuardia, almost as soon as the Sixty-fifth Congress convened, had introduced his first bill. He had refused to observe the unwritten rule that freshmen were to remain silent while their seniors spoke. LaGuardia's bill asked imprisonment in time of peace and a death penalty during war for anyone selling inferior food, clothing, ammunition, or arms to the army or navy. His father's death from spoiled beef still rankled him, and he pursued the bill tirelessly. Newspaper comment was favorable:

Congress may or may not pass the bill which provides a penalty of death for any one who should sell inferior or fraudulent supplies to the army or navy in time of war. But there is undoubtedly a strong public sentiment behind the measure introduced by Representative LaGuardia of New York. . . . The country has not forgotten the paper-soled shoes that were sold to the army in the war between the states. It remembers vividly the rotten beef that was disposed of to our soldiers in the Spanish war.[32]

The bill was referred to the Judiciary Committee, and there it died. LaGuardia was to find out again and again that a party irregular could not expect strong support for his legislative proposals.

LaGuardia's declaration that the United States should take a "man's part" in the European troubles did not wait long for fulfillment. President Woodrow Wilson appeared before an extraordinary joint session of Congress on April 2, 1917, and called for

---

[31] Undated clipping from New York *World*, LaG. Papers. Early in the session LaGuardia proposed a message of greeting by Congress to the Convention of Workers' Delegates in Petrograd, but no action was taken (*Revista delle Colonie,* March, 1917).

[32] New York *Evening Mail*, April 3, 1917.

a declaration of war. In a setting of high tension, the House of Representatives began its debate. Lobbyists of all kinds poured into Washington. The corridors of the House Office Building were jammed, and telegrams and letters flooded the offices. Sessions were long and were held before packed galleries. At three in the morning on April 6, 1917, the roll call began, and when it was over the House had voted 373–50 for war. Two days earlier the Senate had acted, and now the nation prepared to take up arms.

2 * Fighting the War, in Congress and at the Front

THERE is a tendency, after brass bands and exhortations have marshaled public opinion, to assume a far greater enthusiasm for war than actually existed at the moment of decision, and World War I was no exception.[1] Certainly among LaGuardia's constituents, antiwar feeling was strong in the spring of 1917. Socialists in his district were vehemently opposed to American entrance into the war, despite the refusal of a number of top Socialist leaders to support the antiwar resolution adopted by their party at its St. Louis convention.[2] In addition, the German-American newspapers expressed a cautious but unmistakable uneasiness about the action Congress had taken. The New York *Staats-Zeitung* said:

[1] Congressional opposition to the war resolution probably would have been stronger if it were known that the sending of American troops abroad would follow. Thomas A. Bailey has said that at the time "there was no clear idea of raising a huge army" and that it "is probably true that if the ballot had been a secret one, and if it had been known that America was to send a conscript army overseas, the vote would have been closer" (*A Diplomatic History of the American People* [New York, 1950], 644). LaGuardia was of this view also and said later: "It was my belief at the time, and I have talked it over with a great many of my colleagues since, that at least sixty to sixty-five per cent of the members who voted for war did so in the belief and firm conviction that we would never have to send a single soldier to Europe" (*Making of an Insurgent,* 140).

[2] Ray Ginger, *The Bending Cross* (New Brunswick, 1949), 341–343, discusses the varying Socialist reactions to the war.

Denunciation of men like La Follette, Norris, Gronna, and the rest ill
serves the cause of democracy. . . . Let every American secure a copy
of the congressional record of the Senate proceedings of the fourth
of April and read for himself the debate previous to our entrance into
the world war. Let him put aside this document in his library and
when the war has run its course and peace again has composed this
shattered world, study the proceedings of this day in the light of experience.[3]

LaGuardia was aware of the sentiment in his district, yet proceeded to support war measures which he believed necessary.
First of these was the draft. With Allied missions in Washington
besieging the White House and Marshal Joffre pleading for
troops, Wilson and the War Department became convinced that
the United States should take the step which might prove decisive for victory. A conference was called of leading members of
the Senate and House Military Affairs Committees, at which
President Wilson presented the case for an expeditionary force
to go to France as soon as possible and asked for a draft law.

LaGuardia had already taken the initiative in his district.
Shortly after the nation declared war, he sent postcards to all
his constituents, on which he asked them to record their feelings
on the draft. His accompanying letter read: "This country is at
war and needs every available man. Shall we have a volunteer
army? Or an army composed of all citizens of military age? I think
conscription is needed and I am trying to educate the people up
to it. It is up to you to respond; don't blame me if you don't like
the way I vote." [4] When the draft bill passed the House by an
overwhelming vote on April 28, LaGuardia was among those
who voted for it.

As the war fever grew in the nation, dissident groups—socialists, pacifists, German-language organizations—continued to insist that entrance into the war was a mistake. Public officials and
important pressure groups began to call for the suppression of
these antiwar views. "National unity" for the successful prosecution of the war became the cry, and Congress was quick to respond. In May of 1917 it began to debate a bill purportedly designed to curb espionage, but with provisions sweeping enough
to cause grave concern to defenders of free speech.

[3] April, 1917.   [4] New York *Times,* April 17, 1917.

LaGuardia opposed the Espionage bill from the first, hitting especially hard at Section Four, which gave the President broad powers to suppress the publication of any information relative to "national defense." He told the House: "Let me assume that a division or a camp were improperly fed, and that owing to that the whole division was disabled and for that reason could not be mobilized. The newspapers and everyone else would be estopped from bringing out those acts because it would reveal the actual condition of that camp or regiment." [5]

When it was proposed to limit each congressman to five minutes in the debate on the Espionage bill, LaGuardia protested vigorously:

This is not a question that can or should be discussed in five minutes. No member of this House should be limited in his opposition to this un-American and vicious legislation. . . . This bill is the most important measure that has come before this House during this and many previous sessions. It is a revolutionary measure. It shocks me as much as if a bill were proposed to change the color and formation of that flag we so dearly love. Gentlemen, if you pass this bill and if it is enacted into law, you change all that our flag ever stood and stands for.[6]

Other congressmen challenged his statement that Section Four of the bill could be used to indict editors who criticized War Department inefficiency, and LaGuardia offered to draw up an actual indictment to prove his contention. "You will find," he declared, "that if you pass this law various U.S. district attorneys will have very resourceful imaginations." He actually did draw up a sample indictment and produced it on the floor of the House. On May 3, 1917, he presented to the House petitions containing 600,000 signatures, gathered by the Hearst newspapers in opposition to the Espionage bill.[7]

President Wilson insisted, in a letter of April 25, 1917, to Arthur Brisbane, that he would not use the broad powers given him under the bill, whereupon LaGuardia commented wryly: "The law admittedly makes the president a despot, but with the comforting assurance that the despot about to be created has the

---

[5] *Congress. Rec.*, 65:1, May 2, 1917, 1700.
[6] *Ibid.*   [7] *Ibid.*, May 3, 1917, 1773.

present expectation to be a very lenient, benevolent despot. . . .
The American people do not want tolerance; they demand the
continuance of their constitutional rights." [8]

The powerful attack by LaGuardia and other progressives,[9]
together with the pressure put on by the press itself,[10] led to the
elimination of the clause on press censorship. However, the other
provisions of the bill continued to withstand the onslaughts of
those concerned for civil liberties. The main organs of public
opinion grew steadily more excited about spies and traitors, who
under the stimulus of war-heated imaginations were said to have
appeared suddenly in the highest echelons of government. A headline in the New York *World,* written at the height of debate on
the war resolution, read: "GERMAN SPY TRAIL KNOWN TO
LEAD TO STATE DEPARTMENT." [11] On June 15, 1917,
the Espionage Act became law, and the worst fears of its opponents were soon realized. Ultimately, over two thousand persons
were prosecuted under the Act, and over eight hundred jailed,
not one of these for actual espionage.[12] Zechariah Chafee has said
of the Espionage Act:

Those who gave their lives for freedom would be the last to thank us
for throwing aside so lightly the great traditions of our race. . . . In
our efforts to silence those who advocated peace without victory we
prevented at the very start that vigorous thrashing out of fundamentals
which might today have saved us from a victory without peace.[13]

Another civil liberties issue arose when Congress passed several
laws restricting the activities of aliens. LaGuardia sharply criticized
the Trading with the Enemy Act because it gave the President
broad powers to include whole groups of aliens under the term
"enemy" without regard for individual rights. His amendments,

---

[8] *Ibid.*   [9] New York *Times,* May 3, 1917.

[10] On April 25 a convention of the American Newspaper Publishers Association at the Waldorf-Astoria Hotel in New York asserted: "The proposed
legislation strikes at the fundamental rights of the people, not only assailing
their freedom of speech but also seeking to deprive them of the means of
forming intelligent opinion" (*Congress. Rec.,* 65:1, April 26, 1917, 1167).

[11] April 4, 1917.

[12] Zechariah Chafee, *Free Speech in the United States* (Cambridge, 1941),
discusses the Act and its consequences.

[13] *Ibid.,* 107.

however, were not included when the bill was passed by Congress, and there followed a hysterical move toward deportation of "dangerous" aliens, which would culminate after the war in the Palmer raids. The antialien feeling was strongly resented by Frederic C. Howe, Commissioner of Immigration on Ellis Island, who described its results:

I became a jailer instead of a commissioner of immigration; a jailer not of convicted offenders but of suspected persons who had been arrested and railroaded to Ellis Island as the most available dumping-ground under the successive waves of hysteria which swept the country. . . . I refused to believe that we were a hysterical people; that civil liberties should be thrown to the winds. But in this struggle there was no one to lean on; there was no support from Washington, no interest on the part of the press. The whole country was swept by emotional excesses that followed one another with confusing swiftness from 1916 to 1920.[14]

Always quick to bridle at intimations that the foreign-born were less patriotic than native Americans, LaGuardia clashed with Chief Examiner Cowley of the New York Naturalization Bureau. Cowley had pointed to the attempts made by a number of Italians in America to evade military service in Italy by declaring their intention of becoming American citizens. LaGuardia resented the singling out of Italians and demanded a retraction.[15] He finally succeeded in getting Cowley to declare that he had not intended to question the patriotism of Italians, but was criticizing all slackers.

Another aspect of the general antiforeign feeling engendered by the war was the belief in many quarters that nationals of countries fighting on the side of Germany were to be considered disloyal. LaGuardia attacked this idea, speaking up, for instance, on behalf of Hungarians in the United States and insisting on their right to communicate with their families in Europe.[16]

At the same time LaGuardia sternly reminded minority groups that the war demanded their complete allegiance. In the midst

---

[14] *Confessions of a Reformer* (New York, 1925), 267.

[15] *Il Giornale Italiano,* April 26, 1917.

[16] *Amerikai Magyar Nepszava,* July 23, 1917. LaGuardia said: "Perhaps the Hungarian people after all will play a great part in the speedy termination of this conflict and for the great cause of democracy."

of the hurried congressional activity which followed the declaration of war, he flew to New York to tell a meeting of a thousand Italian-Americans at the Labor Temple: "I want to drive it home and impress it upon you, if I can, that we are in the midst of the most cruel war in the history of the world . . . and those who prefer Italy to America should return to Italy. I know there are some of you in my district who won't sacrifice themselves for any country—and if I thought I owed my election to that sort, I would resign." [17]

The bill to lend three billion dollars to our war allies drew his strong support. While his colleagues in the House were discussing the merits of the bill in relation to the prospect of repayment, LaGuardia dismissed the question of repayment in the following terms:

I don't share the belief of some of my colleagues who have expressed their complete confidence in the future restitution of these three billions to be loaned to foreign governments. . . . Let us understand that clearly now and not be surprised later. . . . Even so, if this brings about a happy termination of the war, and a permanent peace for our own country, it will have been a good investment.[18]

Although he insisted on all-out support of the war, LaGuardia maintained a constant vigil in those first months following the war declaration to safeguard the living standards of the lower classes. In Congress and out, he denounced profiteering, demanded governmental controls over crucial segments of the economy, and urged that taxation be based upon ability to pay.

In May, 1917, the House began discussion of a revenue bill to meet the huge costs of war. At the time, married persons earning under $4,000 a year and single persons earning less than $3,000 a year were exempt from income taxes.[19] When the House Ways and Means Committee reported a bill taxing all single men earning over $1,000 and married men over $2,000, LaGuardia took the floor in opposition. Deriding the "confetti-throwing" and "flower-showering" with which the House had greeted the bill, he pointed to the effect it would have on the ordinary working people of the nation:

[17] Limpus and Leyson, *op. cit.*, 42–43.   [18] *Ibid.*, 45.
[19] George Soule, *Prosperity Decade* (New York, 1947), 48.

Now you say this bill is equitable. You say that you want to tax every man, and you start taxing a man with an income of a thousand dollars. Without any tax being imposed on his income, the man earning a thousand dollars is paying a greater proportion in taxes than the man who is earning $5000 a year. You tax his coffee, you tax his tea, you tax his soap, you tax his light, you tax his heat, you tax his insurance, you tax his amusements, and you tax his beer and his soda, and even the chewing gum for his children. . . . Income should not be taxed as low as $1000. . . . It is true that we must raise $1,800,000,000, but I believe that can be done in a scientific, equitable, and just manner.[20]

LaGuardia proposed a series of amendments to the revenue bill. He urged the exemption from taxation of single men earning under $1,500, married men earning under $2,000.[21] Other progressives joined him, including Representative Lenroot of Wisconsin, who assailed the idea of taxing the necessities of the poor while leaving the wealth of the upper classes undisturbed.[22] However, all attempts to lift the exemption figure were defeated by Congress.

Postal rates were increased to bring more revenue, and LaGuardia attacked this as discriminating against the poor. He asked instead for a tax on bank checks.[23] Congress did not adopt this suggestion, but it did accept his amendment levying a 10 per cent tax on permanent boxes and season tickets to operas and other amusements. This was his way of making up for the fact that purchasers of the cheaper seats paid admission taxes.

LaGuardia's concern for the underprivileged manifested itself most sharply in the debates over food control by the government. At this time wholesale food prices were 50 per cent higher than they had been in 1913.[24] By August they would be 80 per cent higher. Welfare agencies in various parts of the country took note of the effect of food prices on the living standards of the poor. "Prices of materials, food supplies and labor had not only soared to unimaginable heights, but were almost unobtainable," New York City relief authorities reported.[25] Mounting

[20] *Congress. Rec.*, 65:1, May 14, 1917, 2298.
[21] New York *Times*, May 18, 1917.   [22] *Ibid.*
[23] *Congress. Rec.*, 65:1, May 14, 1917, 2298.   [24] Soule, *op. cit.*, 28.
[25] *Annual Report of the Department of Public Charities of the City of New York for 1917* (New York, 1918), 7.

hardship for hundreds of thousands of people in the city had to be handled by 267 welfare employees.[26]

While prices rose, wages barely kept pace, and corporate profits boomed. Real wages by the end of 1917 had risen 4 per cent over 1914 levels, but 1914 had been a depression year.[27] In the meantime profits were climbing to new peaks. "The more strategically-placed business corporations were the greatest gainers from the war in current money income." [28]

This situation angered LaGuardia. The war was not being fought to make the rich richer, he kept repeating. When Congress debated the Lever Act to establish wartime government controls over the production and distribution of food, the voluble congressman from New York did not think it went far enough. He proposed a constitutional amendment which would make these controls apply in peacetime too.[29] LaGuardia told the House:

Gentlemen, in plain, cold words, the American people are not getting enough to eat. . . . Everyone knows that there is plenty of available food in the country; it is an open secret that the warehouses and cold-storage places are bulging with food. . . . Yet, in the land able to appropriate billions of dollars without a murmur, where billions of bonds can be subscribed for in a few days, where everyone seems to be employed at this time, in its greatest city, we have had food riots. I gave considerable and personal investigation to the food riots which took place in New York City a few months ago, and gentlemen, I give you my personal assurance that the cause of that disturbance, the action of those unhappy women, was nothing else than empty stomachs. Wage earners themselves, most of them, others with husbands working, and yet unable to provide for the proper nourishment of their families. Is that not cause for reflection? . . . It does not take a professor of political economy to know that with what food there is available prices are out of all proportion to the ordinary rule of supply and demand; that somebody is taking advantage of the situation, amassing great fortunes at the expense of the health and happiness of the American people.[30]

26 *Ibid.*
27 Paul Douglas, *Real Wages in the United States* (Boston, 1930), 391.
28 Soule, *op. cit.,* 78.
29 New York *Journal of Commerce,* June 22, 1917.
30 *Congress. Rec.,* 65:1, June 21, 1917, 4014.

Reports from individuals and welfare groups in his district substantiated the stories of hardship in the midst of plenty. The Charity Organization of New York, replying to LaGuardia's telegram asking about prices, said: "Since January, potatoes have increased 75% in price. . . . Bread has increased 50%. . . . Milk has increased 10% and meats from 14% to 20%. . . . In many instances families are cutting down their supply of milk and are resorting to other economies which are certain to be injurious to health." [31] The New York Association for Improving the Condition of the Poor reported that prices had risen 13 per cent in six months without proportionate wage increases for low-income families.[32] One constituent wrote LaGuardia: "If you can do anything for us on this food question in your capacity as a Congressman, in present or future legislation, for heaven's name do so, it is really appalling how the common necessities have gone upward in price and it is the poor sinners like me and my family . . . who are suffering. . . . There seems to be no reason why things should be so high in this glorious land of plenty." [33]

With such pleas in his hands, LaGuardia explained to the House why he thought food control should be a permanent rather than just a wartime measure. "After the war, if we are not careful, the speculators will soon be back to the old game. As long as I live I do not wish to witness another food riot. I have this day introduced a constitutional amendment giving power to the National Government at all times to regulate and control the production, conservation, and distribution of food supplies." [34] Despite his demand for continued government protection against profiteering in food, the constitutional amendment was buried in committee.

LaGuardia however continued to insist that the right to food, shelter, and clothing at reasonable prices was part of that body of liberties for which the war was being fought. While Wilson was making grandiose statements about the political democracy at

---

[31] *Ibid.*   [32] *Ibid.*   [33] *Ibid.*

[34] *Ibid.* In view of LaGuardia's consistency on this issue, Eric Goldman's description of his fight for the constitutional amendment on food control as a performance that "skirted the edge of demagoguery" (*op. cit.,* 259) seems unduly harsh.

stake in the war, LaGuardia maintained that the justification for the war must come in the present as well as in the future and in terms of economic as well as political democracy. It was the failure of the war to produce these deep-going economic changes which many years later brought his deep disillusionment with it and which may, indeed, have played an important part in the failure to keep the peace.[35]

In the summer of 1917 newspapers were taking caustic note of the lethargy with which legislators were volunteering for war service. "SOLONS OF NATION CAN'T SEEM TO HEAR THE BUGLE CALLING," said a headline in the New York *World*.[36] LaGuardia, however, had already begun to fulfill the pledge made to his constituents when he voted for the draft. He had learned to fly on Long Island shortly after the war began in Europe, when he foresaw the possibility of American involvement, and in July, 1917, taking temporary leave from Congress, he joined the Aviation Section of the Army Signal Corps. A month later he was on his way to Europe, commissioned as a lieutenant and headed for Italy, where his knowledge of the language was expected to be useful.

With Italian armies still reeling from the disastrous defeat at Caporetto, LaGuardia in the fall of 1917 led the first detachment of American flyers to the front lines at Padua, Verona, and Aquila. Flying day and night, they bombed airfields, munition dumps, and freight centers behind the enemy lines. LaGuardia flew as copilot and bombardier. Between missions, he made speeches to huge gatherings in Rome, Turin, Naples, and Florence, putting the common war objectives into the stirring phrases of Wilsonian idealism.[37] "LaGuardia is more popular here than if he were an

---

[35] Richard Hofstadter, *The American Political Tradition* (New York, 1948), 276–277, stresses Wilson's failure to plant the economic roots of a lasting peace and quotes an interesting letter to Wilson from George L. Record making that point. The letter is reproduced in James Kerney, *The Political Education of Woodrow Wilson* (New York, 1926), 438–446.

[36] July 31, 1917.

[37] New York *American*, Dec. 12, 1917. See also Florence C. Speranza, ed., *The Diary of Gino Speranza* (New York, 1941), II, 111; New York *Herald*, Feb. 4, 1918; and New York *Evening Post*, Feb. 18, 1918.

Italian deputy," the Italian Commissioner of Aeronautics declared. "I love him like a brother!" [38]

In October of 1918, with the Armistice imminent, LaGuardia
returned to the States, a major now, bemedaled and with an intense desire to be re-elected to Congress in November. During
his absence at the front the strong socialist and pacifist groups
on the East Side had reacted coldly to his war spirit. Why wasn't
he representing his constituents' interests in Washington, where
he belonged, instead of seeking military glory in Italy, they asked?
They organized a petition campaign to unseat him, and LaGuardia
retorted with a characteristic flourish: "If any signers of the petition will take my seat in a Caproni biplane, I shall be glad to re-
sume my upholstered seat in the House." [39] The movement
faded, and his New York colleagues in the House adopted a resolution urging his renomination and re-election. [40]

Normally, the Democratic party would have been expected to
oppose LaGuardia with vigor, remembering fondly its long reign
in the Fourteenth District and noting the narrow margin of La-
Guardia's victory in 1916. However, in the summer of 1918 the
United States was not in a normal condition. The fires of war
enthusiasm which had been stoked up so industriously for a year
were burning brightly. Patriotism almost crowded oxygen and
nitrogen out of the atmosphere. With the Hun too far away for
home-front patriots to attack, righteous anger could be con-
veniently directed at domestic isolationists, pacifists, socialists,
and radicals of all kinds who refused to march in step with the
martial band. In this time of war crisis, it was felt, nothing would
be more disastrous than Socialist victories at the polls, and in
certain districts of New York antiwar sentiment was strong enough
to make such victories a distinct possibility.

To this danger Tammany Hall responded with a majestic
gesture. It would collaborate, it announced, with the Republican
party, to nominate fusion candidates in those districts where

[38] New York *Times,* June 30, 1918.

[39] New York *Tribune,* Feb. 5, 1918. The Philadelphia *Record* mused: "Congressman LaGuardia, absent to fight for his country, is absent little more than
some Congressmen during the baseball season. Why raise a fuss over him?"
(Jan. 17, 1918).

[40] New York *Tribune,* July 14, 1918.

Socialist strength abounded. Members of Tammany's executive committee applauded vigorously as their chief, Charles F. Murphy, exhorted them: "Sink all partisanship. Name only one hundred percent Americans to Congress. Elect them to help win the war and a victorious peace. America First!" The Tammany leader's instructions combined magnanimity and patriotism to an impressive degree:

I care not whether the nominees for Congress in this county are Republicans or Democrats, so long as they are Americans and will back the President in the prosecution of the war. I want you district leaders to consult with the Republican district leaders and see if you cannot agree to unite upon a single Congressional candidate in each of the twelve districts here. Pay particular attention to the doubtful districts where Socialists may prevail. We want only Americans—Americans whose loyalty is unquestioned—in Washington.[41]

The chairman of Tammany's general committee was a young man named Robert F. Wagner. He expressed his strong approval of Murphy's views, and the proposition was unanimously carried.[42]

Tammany leaders moved swiftly to confer with their Republican counterparts. Charles F. Murphy met with Republican county leader Samuel S. Koenig and came to an agreement on coalition candidates in six Manhattan districts, where Tammany would support Republican candidates in three districts and Republicans would back Democrats in the other three. A key aim of this agreement was the removal from the Twelfth District of Socialist Meyer London, who had been elected to Congress in 1914 and was now a special target of the National Security League and similar groups.[43]

One of the districts included in the fusion agreement was the Fourteenth, and it was quickly apparent that on the basis of his war record LaGuardia would be the coalition candidate.[44] Enthusiastic support for his candidacy came from some of the same

[41] New York *Evening Journal,* July 16, 1918.

[42] New York *Times,* July 19, 1918. Much of the impetus for Democratic-Republican unity against Socialist candidates had come from the National Security League, a pressure group formed in 1915, which had urged American entrance into the war and was now concerned with all-out prosecution of the war effort.

[43] *Ibid.*   [44] New York *American,* July 16, 1918.

circles which had regarded him with hostility during the tax legislation debates in early 1917. An editorial in *Financial America*
could hardly restrain its enthusiasm in urging coalition backing
of LaGuardia: "Let Captain LaGuardia be the unanimous choice
of the two older parties as the nominee to Congress from the
Fourteenth New York District. If any opponents contest, then
let them be counted as vassals of the Kaiser, and turn their supporters over for internment or the chain gang. Viva LaGuardia!" [45]

The Socialist party was unperturbed. As its candidate it chose
Scott Nearing, a thirty-five-year-old former professor of economics,
who had been dismissed first from the University of Pennsylvania
and then from the University of Toledo because of his socialist
views. Nearing was the author of several books, and his antiwar
pamphlet entitled "The Great Madness" had resulted in an indictment being drawn against him under the Espionage Act.[46]

Nearing began his campaign while LaGuardia was still in
Italy. Addressing 1,500 people at Webster Hall on Eleventh
Street, a favorite radical meeting place, he urged that "the producing classes of the United States take over the machinery of
production and declare their independence of big business, just
as our ancestors in 1776 took over the machinery of politics and
declared their independence of royalty." He denounced the passage of the Espionage Act and cited the actions of the administration in suppressing critics of the war. Included in his platform
was the demand for recognition of the new regime in Russia.[47]

LaGuardia was not present to reply to Nearing, but the press
took up the fight for him, bearing down heavily on his opponent's
antiwar views, caustically comparing Nearing's pacifism with La-
Guardia's military record. A feature article in the New York *Tribune* said pointedly:

Major LaGuardia, recently decorated and promoted for gallantry in
action, went to Italy in command of the first Yankee battle squadron
and has been in the thick of the Piave fighting for months. Scott
Nearing, his Socialist opponent, was indicted last March for violation
of the espionage act, and faces trial for persistent interference with
America's prosecution of the war.[48]

[45] New York *Financial America,* July 20, 1918.
[46] New York *Evening Post,* Oct. 12, 1918.
[47] New York *Times,* Sept. 17, 1918.   [48] Oct. 23, 1918.

An editorial in the New York *World* was even more blunt about Nearing:

So far as known, there is no record of his volunteering to serve his country either as a soldier, sailor or aviator, although in flights of fancy he has probably exceeded the altitude record of Major La-Guardia over the Alps. But while Major LaGuardia was making a record fighting for democracy, Professor Nearing was establishing a record at home fighting democracy. He has been successful enough to be indicted for sedition, and if he should escape conviction the fact remains that he is within the age of the present draft. The foregoing should be sufficient information for Major LaGuardia and for the voters in the Fourteenth Congressional District.[49]

Newspapermen were on hand to question LaGuardia as he arrived from Italy on October 28, 1918, "a handsome figure in his army khaki, with the silver wings gleaming above the three medals on his breast, and two gold service stripes on his left arm." [50] After telling the reporters that he felt in fine shape and that he was glad to be alive, LaGuardia asked who his opponent was. When informed that it was Scott Nearing, he said he had never heard of him and added, "If he is a young man, I shall ask him what regiment he comes from." [51] The newspapermen were delighted.

LaGuardia reacted soberly to the news that his opponent was under indictment for violating the Espionage Act. He had not forgotten his own strong opposition to that law. "The question of patriotism must not be introduced into this campaign," he told reporters. "Scott Nearing must have a fighting chance. I did not know that he was under indictment, but remember this —under the laws of this country a man is innocent until he is proven guilty." [52]

LaGuardia then proceeded to violate his own admonition to keep patriotism out of the campaign. The evening after his arrival from Europe he spoke to a crowd of Republican supporters at the Lenox Assembly Rooms on Second Street—a crowd which interrupted Governor Whitman's speech to cheer LaGuardia for fifteen tumultuous minutes as he strode into the ballroom re-

[49] Oct. 30, 1918.   [50] Limpus and Leyson, *op. cit.*, 75.
[51] New York *Times*, Oct. 29, 1918.
[52] New York *American*, Oct. 29, 1918.

splendent in his uniform and medals. After the governor had resumed and had finished his remarks, LaGuardia spoke briefly, saying he considered it his "patriotic duty" to oppose the candidacy of a Socialist.[53]

Moving from that meeting to others the same evening, LaGuardia went even further in his attack on Nearing's war record. "Scott Nearing is a man without a country unless he stands for what the American flag stands for," he told one audience.[54] At an open-air meeting on Second Avenue and Tenth Street he compared Nearing unfavorably to those European Socialists who supported the war. "Scott Nearing isn't a Socialist, the kind of Socialist that Albert Thomas or Turati are. He is a silk stocking university professor who condescends to come here and attempt to foist Bolshevism on America." Farther down the street, in the Womens Republican Club, he continued his tirade: "I went into this war because I wanted to stop all wars. I think my remedy is better than that of the yellow dog Socialists." [55]

With the hour growing late, two thousand people gathered at Stuyvesant Place and Second Avenue to hear the bemedaled candidate ask stridently: "If Scott Nearing wants to try out his beautiful theories, why doesn't he go to Russia?" [56] Altogether, it was a strange performance for a foe of the Espionage Act, for a man who would be denounced throughout his congressional career as a radical and a socialist. It is understandable only in the light of war fever and a hunger for office at a time when LaGuardia could not yet stand firmly on his own political feet.

LaGuardia's tirades against the Socialists were one indication of the disintegration in 1918 of the Progressive movement. The coming of the war was like a bomb dropping in its ranks. While Roosevelt and Beveridge rode proudly on their martial steeds, La Follette and Norris maintained stubbornly their antiwar position. Even as LaGuardia attacked Nearing, Amos Pinchot, long a Progressive stalwart, expressed a contrary view:

The main issue before the country is whether we shall have a just and lasting peace, or a temporary one framed in the interest of inter-

[53] New York *Tribune,* Oct. 30, 1918.
[54] New York *Globe,* Oct. 30, 1918.
[55] New York *Evening World,* Oct. 30, 1918.
[56] New York *American,* Oct. 30, 1918.

national profiteers. If we get the former, the war will have been won in a way worth winning; if we get the latter, we will have lost, irrespective of the military outcome, and the whole war's sacrifice will have been in vain. . . . I shall support the Socialist ticket because I believe the Socialist candidates stand behind Mr. Wilson's programme for a just peace that will give the world a chance to develop democracy, free from the blighting threat of militarism and war.[57]

And on the same day that Pinchot made this statement, LaGuardia was telling an audience: "You know, one must be color blind to call an American Socialist a red. They're not red; they're yellow." [58]

With election day approaching, LaGuardia accepted a challenge by Nearing to debate the issues publicly from the same platform. Before an aroused crowd, which filled Cooper Union with cheers, boos, and shouts, the opposing candidates stated their cases. A newspaperman noted the contrast between them:

Their appearance reminded one of a modern equivalent to some old Roman gladiatorial contest. On the one side was the stock broadswordsman, swarthy, muscular, and slow of movement. On the other, the light agile manipulator. . . . Nearing in appearance is the typical man of letters. Blonde, and slender, he looks almost boyish. LaGuardia wins attention by the blunt, honest characteristics of the typical political haranguer. While Nearing's gestures are airy and graceful, LaGuardia's convey simply the impression of strength and fighting energy.[59]

Nearing defended his antiwar stand and presented the Socialist program. Many supporters of the Socialist party were in the audience and applauded him heartily. LaGuardia did not attack socialism, but took the more clever tactic of pointing to the socialists throughout the world who had supported the war. He did not deprecate pacifism, but insisted that the battle against the Kaiser was one designed to establish permanent peace. "I am personally opposed," he declared, "to militarism, imperialism, and all manner of oppression. I am against war, and because I am against war I went to war to fight against war." [60] Although there were a few tense moments in the course of the debate, as

[57] New York *Globe,* Nov. 1, 1918.
[58] *Ibid.*   [59] New York *American,* Nov. 2, 1918.
[60] New York *Evening Telegram,* Nov. 2, 1918.

the crowd reacted angrily first to statements by Nearing and then to those of LaGuardia, the evening ended on an amicable note with both candidates shaking hands and the crowd cheering. It had been a debate, many in the audience recognized, between two men with very much the same objectives but with different approaches.

The voters went to the polls a few days before the Armistice was signed in Europe, with military victory in the air and the patriotic ardor of newspaper editorials and campaign speeches in their ears. Throughout the nation the Democrats fell before a Republican advance which captured a clear majority in the House of Representatives.[61] The Democratic-Republican coalition in New York succeeded in its main objective—defeating the Socialists. Hillquit and Meyer London were defeated, and the coalition candidates won in every district. LaGuardia drew 14,208 votes to Nearing's 6,168, and the New York *Times* reported with satisfaction that "LaGuardia subdued without difficulty the eminent friend of academic freedom and of other kinds of freedom verging on sedition, Scott Nearing." [62]

There were a few unhappy election results for the conservative forces in the nation. Socialist Victor Berger, indicted under the Espionage Act and unseated by the House, had been re-elected in Wisconsin's Fifth District. In Nebraska, George Norris, denounced throughout the nation's press for opposing American entrance into the war, was returned to his seat in the Senate, "in the rejoicing arms of the solid pro-German vote," the New York *Times* said.[63] But LaGuardia, a hero of the crusade against the Germans, rejoiced too. For the war was over, and whatever bombs had failed to bring in the way of a better world could now be won, perhaps, with the special artillery of national politics. He prepared to take his seat in the postwar Congress.

[61] LaGuardia later said that not Wilson's plea for the Democrats but accumulated war grievances were responsible for the Republican victory (*Making of an Insurgent*, 202).

[62] Nov. 7, 1918.   [63] *Ibid.*

3 · The Issues of Peace, 1919

WITH the Armistice, the ranks of the prewar progressives in Congress began to close again. Robert La Follette, George Norris, Fiorello LaGuardia, James Frear, and others would now find themselves voting the same way, speaking the same language in relation to the issues of postwar America. With the magnitude of the Republican congressional victory (Republicans now held 239 seats in Congress to 190 for the Democrats) the Progressives could not be said to hold the balance of power, but they resumed their battles with the old militancy. LaGuardia now left the comfort of the uniform and the war and joined the unpopular little band which began hammering against the stone wall of postwar reaction. Together they protested against profiteering, denounced special privilege, and defended the exercise of free speech, with LaGuardia using the House floor as his personal proving ground.

Resuming his interrupted term in the lame-duck Sixty-fifth Congress, LaGuardia promptly introduced a resolution for the repeal of the Espionage Act at a time when prosecutions of radicals under the Act were multiplying every day. He defended his resolution before the conservative Midtown Republican Club of Manhattan by arguing that the Espionage Act was only serving to cover up the inefficiency of the administration. If it had been justified in wartime, he asserted, it certainly was not necessary in the postwar period, adding: "I suppose what I have said is indictable under the Espionage Law." [1]

[1] New York *Times*, Feb. 9, 1919.

The temper of the House in 1918 reflected the antiradical feeling of the nation, and LaGuardia had to come to the defense of Congressman James Frear of Wisconsin, one of his closest associates in the progressive bloc. Frear had been charged with "disloyalty" by the National Security League,[2] and although the League had recently backed LaGuardia's candidacy in the Fourteenth District, he did not hesitate to criticize its attack on Frear. Accordingly, he supported a resolution to investigate the League, saying that "if its motives are really patriotic, if they had no other interest but that of securing a Congress which would act according to the facts, they should welcome this investigation. We will arrive at a sad time if a member of Congress may be called disloyal because he happens to vote the other way."[3]

Minority groups, withstanding attacks in various parts of the postwar world, found a champion in LaGuardia. With the Peace Conference under way in Paris, he won the plaudits of Jews everywhere by introducing a resolution instructing the American delegates to the conference to protest against the anti-Semitic outbreaks reported in newly created Poland and other parts of Europe.[4] The resolution was read in New York to a mass meeting at Madison Square Garden, which cheered it enthusiastically.[5] The result was that the State Department received assurance from a number of countries that they would not persecute Jews.

LaGuardia's sympathies extended beyond those minority groups —like the Jews and Italians—who were predominant in his district. Equal rights for the Negro also concerned him and, since there were few Negroes in his district, opponents could not easily ascribe this to vote seeking.[6] His actions on behalf of the Negro in the Sixty-sixth Congress angered exponents of racial supremacy. When a bill to charter the American Legion was on the House floor, LaGuardia proposed an amendment to open the Legion to all who served in the war without discrimination. Southern congressmen insisted that this be left to local posts, but LaGuardia

---

[2] *Congress. Rec.*, 65:3, Dec. 10, 1918, 262.   [3] *Ibid.*
[4] *Ibid.*, 66:1, May 21, 1919, 102.   [5] Limpus and Leyson, *op. cit.*, 95.
[6] However, it could be argued that LaGuardia as a Republican did not have to face the same intraparty conflicts on the race question that liberal Democrats encountered. In his favor it could be said that he did not dodge intraparty conflicts with Republicans on other issues.

retorted: "The Negro soldiers fought alongside us, did they not?" [7]

He took a similar position during debate on a bonus bill proposed by Congressman Edward Pou of North Carolina, and the following exchange took place:

MR. LAGUARDIA: Would the gentleman be willing to so amend his bill that every soldier who rendered service to his country should not be deprived of a vote regardless of his color?
MR. POU: I do not think that needs any answer.
MR. LAGUARDIA: I think it does.[8]

No answer was forthcoming, but LaGuardia had shown clearly that his belief in equal rights for minorities was not limited to those national groups in the Fourteenth District upon whose votes he depended for election.

The summer of 1919 saw a bitter floor fight over passage of the Volstead Act to enforce the Eighteenth Amendment. LaGuardia entered the fray immediately, launching what for him would be a long personal crusade against prohibition. He clashed repeatedly with Congressman Volstead and delivered a long speech calling for the bill's defeat, saying, in what were to be prophetic words:

I disagree with some who say that if this law is enforced, we shall have trouble because of its enforcement! I maintain that this law will be almost impossible of enforcement. And if this law fails to be enforced —as it certainly will be, as it is drawn—it will create contempt and disregard for law all over the country.

He denied that he was an advocate of overindulgence in drinking:

Now, I do not say that excessive drinking of whiskey is good. I don't know anything about that. As I told you, none of my ancestors had that failing. I have traced them way back, and the only one I could find who drank to excess was a certain Nero—and he got the habit from his mother, who was born on the Rhine. (Laughter and applause.)

Drinking, LaGuardia felt, was a deep-rooted problem which could not be solved by police legislation:

[7] *Congress. Rec.,* 66:1, Aug. 20, 1919, 4071.   [8] *Ibid.,* 5544.

Temperance or Prohibition is a matter of education and not of legislation. The Womens Christian Temperance Union has been doing good work for many years along educational lines. . . . By proper education, by proper training—if you really have the interest and welfare of this country at heart—you can train the people so that the next generation will not use alcohol, and will not require any law of this sort.[9]

An issue that was even closer to LaGuardia's heart, however, though less-publicized than prohibition, was the economic welfare of low-income groups. He carried on in Congress a ceaseless battle against profiteering, pointing always to the fact that large numbers of the population were not benefiting from the prosperity which the war had brought to corporate interests.

Business groups had done well during the war. The profits of the United States Steel Corporation, which had averaged $76,-000,000 a year from 1912–1914, reached $478,000,000 in 1917. The twenty-four leading copper companies netted, after taxes, 24 per cent profit on their invested capital in 1917, double their profit percentage of 1913. The four leading meat packers, who had averaged $19,000,000 in profits during 1912–1914, made $68,000,000 in 1917. Furthermore, even these figures did not represent adequately the extent of wartime profiteering, because costs were padded, salaries were huge, and large bonuses to executives were frequent.[10]

The wartime excess profits tax did succeed in lowering the seven billion dollars in net earnings of all corporations in 1916 to four and a half billion dollars in 1918, but this was still higher than the very prosperous year of 1913. By the end of the war there were 42,000 millionaires in the nation. Most of the wartime gains were resting, however, not in the bank accounts of individuals but in the huge undistributed surpluses of corporations. It was this accumulation that would enable the continued distribution of dividends and interest in almost undiminished volume for the next two and three years, while wage earners and farmers would complain about decreased income.[11]

Aware of these facts, LaGuardia was determined to do something about what he considered to be an inequitable situation.

---

[9] *Congress. Rec.*, 66:1, July 12, 1919.
[10] Soule, *op. cit.*, 78–79.   [11] *Ibid.*

He charged the administration with disposing of surplus copper in such a manner as to augment the wealth of the great copper companies. When a bill came up to appropriate one million dollars to pay the salaries of the Bureau of Surplus Supplies, LaGuardia took the floor. He attacked the $25,000 annual salary of the bureau's chief and noted the resale to the copper companies, at huge losses for the government, of surplus copper. This same copper had been originally sold to the government at a profit, by the same companies. Continuance of such a policy, LaGuardia declared, would "cinch the copper monopoly." [12]

The same bureau chief had to withstand one of LaGuardia's tirades on the question of the disposal of surplus canned beef and bacon:

Now let us see what this $25,000 beauty says about meat and foodstuffs. We asked him what he was going to do with it. He said he thought he might find a market in Rumania or Bosnia or Herzegovina or some other country like that. The gentleman does not know that those countries never use canned beef. They use very little, if any, meat. That you could not find a can opener in all of Rumania. And yet we are paying this gentleman $25,000 a year and his assistants $10,000 a year each for expert advice. . . . It surprises me he did not offer this bacon to some Jewish synagogue.

What should be done with the surplus meat? LaGuardia's answer was prompt:

If he will put that stuff on the market in New York City or Philadelphia or Boston he will find the bellies of the hungry people are in a receptive mood and they will be able to digest army bacon. It may interfere with the profits of the packers but I am not interested in that.[13]

LaGuardia missed no opportunity to bring to the attention of the House the fact that millions of low-income families were having a difficult time obtaining the necessities of life with the high prices of the postwar period. His speeches were dotted with references to "the high cost of living" and the "hungry people of the cities." [14]

He was dubious about some of the efforts being made by some

---

[12] *Congress. Rec.,* 66:1, June 9, 1919, 876.
[13] *Ibid.*   [14] *Ibid.,* Aug. 22, 1919, 4196.

representatives of the farming states, like Iowa's Gilbert N. Haugen, to improve the condition of the farmer. He felt that the city worker was being neglected and that much farm legislation was designed to help the well-to-do farmers. In debate on an Agricultural Appropriation bill in the summer of 1919 he said:

I would like to know just how many champions of the farmer really ever come in contact with the farmer. I'm afraid a good many of those farmers whose interests you have in heart reside in my city and the only part of his hand you will find calloused will be the forefinger and the thumb of the right hand from cutting coupons. The real farmer, the real producer, gets very little, if any benefit out of this appropriation.[15]

Discussing an amendment made by Haugen to the Wartime Food Control bill, in which Haugen had criticized not only profiteering but also "high wages," LaGuardia expressed his resentment at the reference to "high wages" and called for genuine enforcement of the antihoarding provisions of the Lever Act as the most effective means of curbing profiteering.

Mr. Chairman, I want to digress for a minute from the talkfest and say a word relative to the high cost of living. I just want to call the attention of the Committee to the fact that the hungry people of the cities should have something to say about this bill. . . . The stomachs of the families of the country are full and the stomachs of the residents of the cities are empty. Now if your Department of Justice means business, let them get after these hoarders.[16]

LaGuardia and his fellow progressives in Congress, calling in 1919 for economic measures to aid the underprivileged and to curb profiteering, were hopelessly outnumbered. In the Senate, William E. Borah of Idaho was at this time denouncing the profiteers and then writing to a constituent: "It is like hammering at the pillars of Gibraltar with a tack hammer to get after these fellows here in Washington."[17]

Foreign policy occupied a good deal of the public spotlight in 1919, and no single issue engendered as much controversy as the

[15] *Ibid.*, June 3, 1919, 584.   [16] *Ibid.*, Aug. 22, 1919, 4196.

[17] Borah to B. F. Flint, Feb. 4, 1919, Borah Papers, Library of Congress, Washington, D.C.

League of Nations. In the spring, when the League was still only a provision of the still-to-be-signed Versailles Treaty, and the great battle for its ratification was several months away, LaGuardia discussed it in the House. It was not on the agenda, but he used the familiar parliamentary trick of moving to strike out the last word of a motion then being debated in order to get the floor. He spoke with even more than his usual fervor:

Mr. Speaker, . . . If you will consult the two million American men who fought overseas, you will find no difference of opinion among them. They are all absolutely for an arrangement—I do not care what you call it, a League of Nations or anything else—which will make impossible another world war. (Applause.) We told our boys before they went across that we were fighting for an ideal. . . . Now we have a right to demand that out of all this gigantic struggle and for the millions of lives sacrificed we shall come to an understanding among the nations that a sudden declaration of war will be impossible.[18]

In this speech he also made a statement which was to prove tragically incorrect when the Japanese began their undeclared war on China in 1931. "Provide the machinery that will delay a declaration of war," he told the House, "or that will retard the commencement of hostilities, and war will be impossible."[19]

While LaGuardia believed strongly in the idea of international organization for peace as represented in the League of Nations, he was sharply critical of specific provisions in the peace settlement,[20] particularly the question of Fiume. A crisis had been precipitated at the Peace Conference by Italy's demand for Fiume, which went even beyond the secret provisions of the Treaty of London. Despite the withdrawal of Italy's delegates, Wilson won out in his insistence that Fiume should not be given to the Italians. When the Senate Committee on Foreign Relations met to discuss the provisions of the treaty, Fiorello LaGuardia was one of the chief spokesmen for the Italian position.[21]

---

[18] *Congress. Rec.,* 66:1, March 3, 1919, 4948.   [19] *Ibid.*

[20] Many Americans, because they objected to certain features of the treaty, were carelessly labeled "isolationists." This point is discussed by William A. Williams, "The Legend of Isolationism in the Twenties," *Science and Society,* XVIII (Winter, 1954).

[21] U.S. Senate Committee on Foreign Relations, *Hearings on Treaty of Peace with Germany,* 66:1 (Washington, 1919), 1109–1112.

LaGuardia appeared before the Senate committee shortly after the Jugo-Slav Republican Alliance of the United States had testified strongly in favor of allowing Fiume to remain a Yugoslav port. He challenged their arguments (that Fiume was a vitally needed exit to the sea for the new nation), insisting that "the people of Fiume are Italian in spirit, blood, language, and in every way." One of the stumbling blocks to a clean-cut solution of the problem was the fact that Susak, an important suburb of Fiume, was largely Croatian, but LaGuardia blithely swept over this point, saying that "the spirit of Fiume, including Susak, would be Italian." [22]

LaGuardia's wartime speeches in Italy were now rendered hypocritical by Wilson's action, he said. In order to keep up the morale of the Italian people at a critical juncture in the war, he had "embraced everything that really was Italian in the Adriatic and told them that that took it in. . . . I want my word made good. I feel somewhat embarrassed." [23] LaGuardia told the committee that when he left Colonel House in Paris on May 9 he had the distinct impression there would be a settlement satisfactory to Italy. [24]

He reminded the committee about Point Nine in Wilson's Fourteen Points, which promised a revamping of Italy's frontiers along "clearly recognizable lines of nationality" but did not mention Point Eleven, which promised the new Serb state "free and secure access to the sea." There was little doubt that LaGuardia in espousing Italy's cause was voicing the feelings of most Italian-Americans, who angrily compared Italy's huge war casualties with her small gains at the peace table. However, his position had the clear markings of a petty, carping nationalism rather than the judicious world view for which LaGuardia would argue in later years. [25]

[22] *Ibid.*   [23] *Ibid.*, also New York *Times,* Sept. 6, 1919.

[24] Relations between Wilson and House were becoming strained on this issue, with Wilson angry because he felt House was acting in many instances behind his back (Thomas A. Bailey, *Woodrow Wilson and the Lost Peace* [New York, 1944], 260).

[25] Most American students of the Fiume crisis see the Italian demand for Fiume, as does James T. Shotwell, as an example of the policy of *sacro egoismo,* or consecrated selfishness (*At the Paris Peace Conference* [New York, 1937], 293). LaGuardia's emotionally charged position seems especially ill

LaGuardia's sharp denunciation of administration policy abroad somewhat assuaged the antagonism of Republican party leaders who had been dismayed by his broadsides against big business. His criticism of Wilson's Fiume policy and in addition his charges of incompetency directed against American Ambassador Francis in Russia,[26] were only the beginning. He reserved his strongest artillery for the government's policy in Mexico.

The Carranza government in Mexico had incurred American displeasure during the war by its friendliness to Imperial Germany and by its pressure campaign against American oil companies. The resulting strained relations reached the breaking point in July, 1918, when the Mexican government enacted a law heavily taxing American petroleum companies. With the oil interests, backed by Secretary of the Navy Daniels, demanding intervention, a White House conference weighed the idea of using force against Mexico. Only the strong insistence of President Wilson and Bernard Baruch that this would be as immoral as Germany's invasion of Belgium prevented armed intervention. This created an issue for the new Republican-dominated Congress of 1919, which charged the State Department with a weak and vacillating policy toward Mexico.[27]

LaGuardia played a strange role as the imbroglio continued, taking a stand which coincided in many respects with the position of the American oil companies, guardians of the "special privilege" he had attacked so often. The administration was still undecided, with Wilson's policy one of nonintervention while the army prepared to take action against the Carranza regime.[28] At

conceived in view of the fact that Italy's powerful demand for Fiume may simply have been a bargaining maneuver, as one historian suggests (René Albrecht-Carrié, *Italy at the Paris Peace Conference* [New York, 1938], 200). Ray Stannard Baker says that Italian acquisition of Fiume would perhaps have led to war with Yugoslavia (*Woodrow Wilson and World Settlement* [New York, 1922], II, 203–204). Thomas A. Bailey points out that Fiume was just a third-rate port and "an islet of Italians in a great Slavonian sea" (*Woodrow Wilson,* 258–262).

[26] *Congress. Rec.,* 66:1, Jan. 22, 1919, 1881. He said the American Embassy had lost contact with the Russian people.

[27] Howard F. Cline, *The United States and Mexico* (Cambridge, 1953), 184–192, discusses U.S.–Mexican relations in this period.

[28] The New York *Times,* June 22, 1919, reported: "Plans for throwing a new punitive expedition into Mexico, should the situation take a turn justifying such action, have been worked out by the General Staff."

this point, LaGuardia spoke on the House floor in a direct assault on administration policy in Mexico, which he charged had been "one series of inconsistencies." [29]

Pointing to the "disorder, chaos, revolution and disease" prevalent in Mexico under the Carranza regime, he said that "Carranza should be told in plain terms that he cannot be tolerated a moment longer." The United States should go into Mexico "with beans in one hand, and, if necessary, hand grenades in the other, and put an end to the present situation." [30] LaGuardia asked the State Department to call a conference of the anti-Carranza factions in order to set up a more stable government. "I am informed that Díaz, Palaez, Angeles, and Villa can be gotten together, that they are ready to name as Provisional President . . . any man acceptable to the United States." [31]

The anti-Carranza faction led by Felix Díaz came in for special praise by LaGuardia, who pointed out that this group controlled over 250,000 square miles in southern Mexico. "The Felix Díaz faction represents the intellectual faction of Mexico, who for years ruled Mexico, and its forces are made up of the educated people of Mexico and the better element," he said.[32] This was strange language for LaGuardia.[33] That the Díaz faction was actually the counterpart of those wealthy and conservative forces whom La-Guardia had been opposing in the United States was revealed clearly in a proclamation issued by Díaz, which was in LaGuardia's possession. This proclamation charged:

The wealthy class has been driven from their homes and their goods have been confiscated to be consumed in the orgies of the Carrancista government. . . . The majority of the people belonging to the leading classes on account of their culture, education or social position, has been driven out of the country. . . . The Carrancista Revolutionary leaders come from the lowest social extraction.[34]

[29] *Congress. Rec.,* 66:1, July 10, 1919, 2416.

[30] New York *American,* July 11, 1919.

[31] *Congress. Rec.,* 66:1, July 10, 1919, 2416.   [32] *Ibid.*

[33] A striking contrast with LaGuardia's position was the stand taken at this time by the conservative leader of the American Federation of Labor, Samuel Gompers, who deplored the "jingo spirit" driving the United States toward war with Mexico at the instance of "the special interests" (New York *Times,* July 11, 1919).

[34] "Proclamation," Oct. 1, 1918, from "General Headquarters, Vera Cruz" by "General in Chief Felix Díaz," LaG. Papers.

The same LaGuardia who had introduced a constitutional amendment to nationalize food production and distribution in the United States now took a dim view of the land-distribution scheme of the Carranza government. "Mexico is surely the last place in the world that experiments of this kind could be attempted. . . . The Mexican question is a problem of life and death of a nation; it cannot be treated lightly or made an experimental station of ideals and fancy theories." [35]

LaGuardia's stand on Mexico brought him new favor with the important people in the Republican party. He received a letter of congratulations for his speech on Mexico from Nicholas Murray Butler,[36] who wrote from California:

I have duly received, out here on the Pacific Coast where I am spending the summer under ideal conditions, your able and convincing speech on conditions in Mexico delivered in the House on July 10th. I congratulate you heartily upon it. The Administration's dealing with Mexico has been from the beginning both feeble and futile, and the world is reaping the harvest in loss of life, destruction of property, and widespread misery and disorder. I hope that your speech will help to force action of a different sort.[37]

On the same day that LaGuardia made his House speech, the army announced tha: military planes would patrol the Mexican border from dawn to dusk daily.[38] A week later LaGuardia intro-

---

[35] *Congress. Rec.*, 66:1, July 10, 1919, 2417. It perhaps should be noted that at this time there was no clear-cut Progressive voice in Congress on foreign policy issues. Progressives were always most divided on matters beyond the shore line, and in the Sixty-sixth Congress this seemed particularly true. One student of Progressive politics in this period says that in this Congress "the overshadowing issue of foreign policy was not subject to a single Progressive interpretation" (James H. Shideler, "The Neo-Progressives: Reform Politics in the United States 1920–1925" [Ph.D. dissertation, University of California at Berkeley, 1945], 7).

[36] Butler was proud of his prominence in the national circles of the Republican party. He drew attention in his autobiography, to the fact that he had known seven presidents of the United States "more or less intimately," that he had attended fourteen Republican National conventions, and that Theodore Roosevelt "urged high public office upon me again and again" (Nicholas Murray Butler, *Across the Busy Years* [New York, 1939], I, 11–12, 207).

[37] July 29, 1919, Butler Papers, Columbia University.

[38] New York *American,* July 11, 1919.

duced a resolution to create a commission of congressmen and senators to confer with Mexican leaders to "re-establish order and stability in Mexico." [39] Representative Hudspeth of Texas thereupon asked: "Did anyone ever arrange a conference among a coyote, a rattlesnake, and a hyena?" [40] At the end of July, LaGuardia issued a statement to the press pointing to letters sent him by the captain of police at El Paso, which told of firing into that city from the Mexican side. LaGuardia assumed that the Carrancistas must have done it and demanded that the administration withdraw recognition from the Carranza government.[41]

Turning briefly from the Mexican situation, LaGuardia became concerned with developments in Costa Rica and launched an attack on administration policy there, declaring that "corrupt American oil interests," encouraged by the Wilson government, were despoiling that country.[42] In 1917, he charged, "American oil interests overthrew the Constitutional government because they could not obtain their desired ends, and have proceeded with Tinoco [Federico Tinoco, who became dictator of Costa Rica and ruled there from 1917 to 1919] . . . to loot and despoil the country." [43]

Thus, LaGuardia was attacking the oil interests in Costa Rica while allying himself with their position in Mexico. Both of his policies had one feature in common: they involved criticism of the Wilson administration. True, LaGuardia had shown on numerous occasions his willingness to defy his own party and to side with the Democrats when he thought they were right. However, with his eye at this time on Republican support for the presidency of the Board of Aldermen in New York and then perhaps for the mayoralty, it is likely that he was tempted to play the antiadministration game which the Republicans were directing. There were several times in LaGuardia's political career when

[39] New York *Evening Sun,* July 19, 1919.

[40] New York *Times,* July 18, 1919.

[41] Press release, July 31, 1919, LaG. Papers.

[42] Typed copy LaGuardia speech, *ibid.*

[43] LaGuardia had in his possession information charging that Tinoco's sister was the mistress of the general manager of one of the large American interests in Costa Rica. He also had biographical data, verging on the lurid, on most of the principals in the Costa Rica affair (pamphlet, author unknown, "A Brief Who's Who in the Costa Rican Conspiracy," LaG. Papers).

the graph of his political honesty was suddenly broken by a jagged streak of opportunism, and this was one of those instances.

Alongside this element of political expediency, however, must be reckoned that strong tinge of moralistic interventionism which made LaGuardia support American entrance into World War I. He was willing to concur with the idea of intervention in Mexican affairs because he could convince himself that it would result in economic and social progress for that country. Indicative of this was his statement on the House floor, on the tenth of July, urging economic rehabilitation for Mexico after a new government had been set up by popular election: "Let us send in our Public Health Service to wipe out disease and pestilence, let engineers go and work out a system of irrigation for that country, . . . let the Red Cross . . . bring succor to those dying natives, and help Mexico establish a real system of education." [44]

LaGuardia stood at this time somewhere between the Borah-Norris anti-imperialist wing of the Progressive movement and the jingoist group to which Roosevelt and Beveridge had given voice. He epitomized the concept of a unilateral intervention, justified on moral grounds, which has been such a significant feature of American belief.[45]

By the autumn of 1919 the rash of crises in foreign policy seemed to have faded. The Costa Rica issue disappeared with the fall of the Tinoco government that year, and the Mexican troubles, after reaching a climax in November, began to quiet down.[46] With Woodrow Wilson a helpless invalid and the League issue under fierce debate in the Senate, LaGuardia was in New York, campaigning for the presidency of the Board of Aldermen.

He had taken time out of his activity in Washington during the Sixty-sixth Congress to make one of the most important moves of his life. In January the newspapers announced his engagement to Miss Thea Almerigotti of Manhattan, a pretty young woman with whom he had become acquainted during the garment strike of 1913.[47] At the time of their meeting she was a dress designer for

[44] *Congress. Rec.,* 66:1, July 10, 1919, 2416–2417.

[45] Arthur K. Weinberg, *Manifest Destiny* (Baltimore, 1935), gives an excellent elaboration of this aspect of American intellectual history.

[46] Cline, *op. cit.,* 192.   [47] Limpus and Leyson, *op. cit.,* 29.

a Fifth Avenue firm, recently arrived from Trieste, her birth-place. LaGuardia had pursued her with as much speed and ardor as he put into his political campaigns but with less immediate success, and he went off to war uncertain about Thea's feelings toward him.

Albert Spalding, the famous violinist, who was in LaGuardia's squadron during the war, recalls that when they were overseas LaGuardia showed him Thea's photo, saying that this was the girl he wanted to marry after the war. Spalding remembers that "she was frail and delicate-looking, as fair as an Illyrian spring." [48] It was not until 1919 that she consented to marry LaGuardia, and on March 9, 1919, they were wed in a quiet ceremony at the Cathedral College on Madison Avenue, a Catholic priest officiating (the bride was Catholic). The honeymoon was brief, and a few days later LaGuardia was back in action on the political front.

[48] Albert Spalding, *Rise to Follow* (New York, 1943), 237.

4 · *Bitter Interlude, 1920-1922*

AS LaGuardia stormed from one congressional battle to the next, he was observed with considerable interest by the Republican leaders in New York City. The presidency of the Board of Aldermen was open because Al Smith, holder of that position, had been elected Governor. Like the mayoralty, this post had usually been a Tammany plum, but Samuel Koenig and other Republican leaders were enthralled now with the idea that it might be within reach. The immigrant population of New York, whom they had not been able to woo away from the Democratic party, seemed to react enthusiastically to at least one Republican candidate—Fiorello LaGuardia. His speeches in Congress for lower-class interests attracted attention far beyond his own district. The Jewish and Italian population of New York found in him a constant champion, battling antialien legislation, denouncing anti-Semitism, defending the immigrant against congressional xenophobes. In addition, he was a war hero—and it was less than a year after the Armistice.

In the summer of 1919 LaGuardia learned that the Republican leaders had picked him to make the race in November for president of the Board of Aldermen.[1] He wrote to Nicholas Murray Butler that he was "quite unhappy" at the assignment but would accept it "as a Party proposition." [2] However, he was not completely distressed by the turn of events. Although he enjoyed his

[1] New York *Times,* July 24, 1919.   [2] Aug. 11, 1919, Butler Papers.

work in Congress, he had been conscious for some time of his increasing popularity in New York City and had begun to think vaguely about becoming mayor some day. A city-wide electoral victory in the aldermanic campaign would make him second only to the mayor himself in the New York municipal hierarchy.[3]

The race was close, but LaGuardia, campaigning on firetraps, food prices, and the five-cent fare and gaining the endorsement of the Citizens Union [4] as well as much of the press,[5] defeated Tammany candidate Robert L. Moran by 2,500 votes.[6] The Republican party rejoiced, and LaGuardia resigned from Congress December 31, 1919, the day before he was to take up his aldermanic duties.

Two years as president of the Board of Aldermen,[7] aside from sharpening LaGuardia's appetite for the mayoralty, were filled with LaGuardian hubbub. As usual, his Republican label meant little to him. While clashing bitterly with Comptroller Charles Craig,[8] a Tammany man (who at one meeting asked the mayor to hit LaGuardia on the head with his gavel to quiet him), he developed a warm friendship with Democratic Mayor John Hylan. The Republican organization grew more and more suspicious of him. He had appeared first as a slightly erratic but powerful magnet for picking up Italian and Jewish votes and dropping them into the Republican yard. But he was becoming a political nuisance.[9] He

---

[3] This view of his motives is held by the one person in the best position to know, his secretary at the time and his wife in later years, Marie Fischer LaGuardia (interview with Mrs. LaGuardia, Aug., 1956).

[4] New York *Times,* Oct. 26, 1919.   [5] New York *Times,* Nov. 3, 1919.

[6] LaGuardia received 145,108 votes, Moran 142,501 votes, and Socialist candidate James Oneal 45,112 votes (New York *Times,* Nov. 26, 1919).

[7] New York City's Board of Aldermen did not at this time enjoy a particularly good reputation. It had been created by the 1901 charter as a replacement for the bicameral Municipal Assembly and possessed a notoriously undistinguished record of achievement. Lack of financial power hampered it, for one thing. LaGuardia found himself part of a minority of 26 Republicans and 4 Socialists, which could be easily outvoted by the 37 Democratic members (Frederick Shaw, *The History of the New York City Legislature* [New York, 1954], 15, 27).

[8] They hurled the epithet "liar" at one another frequently. At one time LaGuardia almost came to blows with Craig's secretary. Craig began to refer to his antagonist as "Blackguardia" and charged that LaGuardia and Mayor Hylan were conspiring to make his job unpleasant.

[9] He lashed out at the profits of the telephone company (New York *Times,*

denounced the Republican legislature for ejecting five duly-elected Socialist members, raged at Republican Governor Nathan Miller for not restoring the five-cent fare, and went up to Albany to tell a cheering crowd of tenants demanding rent relief that he had come to the capital "not to praise the landlord, but to bury him." [10]

The party had long experience in meting out punishment to rebellious offspring. When LaGuardia showed up one night to speak to members of the Junior Republican League, no one spoke to him or offered him a seat, and soon the chairs were removed and it was announced that the meeting was off.[11] The party organization rebuffed LaGuardia's bid for support in the mayoralty primary, and he had to run on his own against the regular party candidate and with the loss of former supporters like the New York *Times,* which now referred to him as "picturesque, amusing, and impossible." [12] Primary day had the old-time New York flavor. A Queens Democrat was shot through the right temple. A foe of the reigning Tammany machine was blackjacked, beaten, and shot.[13] Against this blood-splashed backdrop, LaGuardia's loss to the regular Republican candidate was a minor event.

Political blows were now joined by personal ones. LaGuardia's delicately lovely young wife Thea had given birth to a little girl in November, 1920, and for a time the couple was rapturously happy. They shared the delights of their home life with a small circle of friends: the sculptors Attilio Piccirilli and Onorio Ruotolo, LaGuardia's wartime companion, the violinist Albert Spalding, and attorney Paul Windels of New York. Occasionally Enrico Caruso joined their group; no one dreamed that this was the last year of his life. But in the spring of 1921, when he was in the midst of furious political struggles and no antagonist could shake him, LaGuardia was staggered by tragedy at home. His

---

Feb. 7, 1920), questioned the $50,000 annual salary of August Belmont, president of the Interborough Rapid Transit Lines (New York *Times,* Feb. 26, 1920), helped shoe workers of the city in a strike (S. Seidel to LaGuardia, May 11, 1920, LaG. Papers), and denounced "weak-kneed, spineless, saffron-yellow" state assemblymen who supported Governor Nathan Miller (New York *Times,* Jan. 28, 1921).

[10] New York *Times,* March 24, 1920.

[11] Brooklyn *Eagle,* April 14, 1921.

[12] Aug. 6, 1921.   [13] New York *Times,* Sept. 14, 1921.

daughter Fioretta was stricken with spinal meningitis and a month later was dead. The blows did not stop falling. His wife's health had been poor since the baby was born. She was taken to a hospital, then to a sanitarium in upstate New York. The doctors diagnosed her condition—tuberculosis. She insisted on coming home to be with her husband, and LaGuardia stayed at her bedside day and night. He left her once, to honor the memory of his friend Caruso in a ceremony at the Metropolitan Opera House, but returned to take up the vigil. Two days later Thea died.

With a few weeks remaining to his term as president of the Board of Aldermen, LaGuardia sailed to Havana for a ten-day rest, accompanied by his good friend Piccirilli. When he returned, his sorrow was buried deep inside him, his voice was as powerful as ever, and an inner engine, strengthened perhaps by his torment, drove him once again at top speed.

As his aldermanic term ended in December, 1921, LaGuardia issued a farewell statement: "New York is the richest city in the world. But until every child is fed and every home has air and light and every man and woman a chance for happiness, it is not the city it ought to be." This was seized upon by a staff writer for the New York *Evening Mail,* who interviewed LaGuardia and asked: "Could you take the million dollars which is the daily budget of New York City and go shopping with it so that the people could have those things?" LaGuardia's reply was flooded with the emotion he had been suppressing in these last few weeks of grief. It also represented a forecast of the approach that would mark his activities for the next decade:

Could I! Could I! Say—first I would tear out about five square miles of filthy tenements, so that fewer would be infected with tuberculosis like that beautiful girl of mine, my wife, who died—and my baby. . . . Then I would establish "lungs" in crowded neighborhoods—a breathing park here, another there, based on the density of population. . . . Milk stations next. One wherever needed, where pure, cheap milk can be bought for babies and mothers learn how to take care of them. After that the schools! I would keep every child in school, to the eighth grade at least, well-fed and in health. Then we could provide widows pensions and support enough schools for every child in New York on what we saved from reformatories and penal institutions. . . .
I would remove censorship from movie films. Why, say, what do you suppose the men behind this censorship law care how long a kiss lasts

or whether the villain uses a gun or an axe? What they do care about is that the motion picture is the most marvelous educator in the world today. And if films are shown that will teach people the truth about government, about war, about civics, about prisons and factories and tenements and every phase of life that touches their rights and their happiness, there will be trouble. . . . I would provide more music and beauty for the people, more parks and more light and air and all the things the framers of the constitution meant . . . when they put in that phrase "life, liberty, and the pursuit of happiness." [14]

This outburst was looked upon by many as the last retort of a politician whose career was finished. The Westchester *Globe* inscribed LaGuardia's political epitaph on its editorial page: "The prestige of a LaGuardia in office has gone and will not return. A political party, in the march onward, has little use for the man who denounces the party which gave him office, when he goes out of that office. . . . The Republican Party will live on, while individuals drop out of sight." [15]

The editorial, however, did not convince LaGuardia, who began now slowly picking up and piecing together the remains of his political career. Turning from municipal politics, he began to eye once again the national scene.

[14] New York *Evening Mail,* Dec., 1921.
[15] Limpus and Leyson, *op. cit.,* 128.

5 · Return to Congress
in the Age of "Prosperity"

THE riotous New Year celebrations that ushered in 1922 could barely be heard above the general din, for it was an era identified in terms of sound—the "Roaring Twenties," the "Jazz Age." The noise was, all agreed, simply the joyful gurgle of prosperity.[1] Employment was to reach an all-time high in the twenties, with the number of jobless persons declining from 4,270,000 in 1921 to 2,055,000 in 1927. Wages too reached record heights as the real earnings index of workers rose between 1919 and 1928 from 105 to 132. The number of prosperous farmers increased throughout the twenties, so that by 1929 approximately 25,000 farms had gross annual incomes over $20,000.[2]

When Professor Thomas Nixon Carver of Harvard University wrote in 1925 of an "economic revolution" diffusing wealth

[1] Part of it, however, was undoubtedly the sound of violence, which seems to scar every age of high living. F. Scott Fitzgerald wrote: "A classmate killed his wife and himself on Long Island, another tumbled 'accidentally' from a skyscraper in New York. One was killed in a speakeasy in Chicago; another was beaten to death in a speakeasy in New York and crawled home to the Princeton Club to die; still another had his skull crushed by a maniac's axe in an insane asylum where he was confined. These are not catastrophes that I went out of my way to look for—these were my friends; moreover, these things happened not during the depression but during the boom" ("Echoes of the Jazz Age," Scribners, XC [Nov., 1931], 459–465).

[2] Recent Social Trends: Report of the President's Research Committee on Social Trends (New York, 1933), II, 820; Fred A. Shannon, America's Economic Growth (New York, 1940), 701.

throughout society,[3] he could point to the widespread purchases of automobiles, radios, and refrigerators. There was more spending money and more leisure time to go with it; these could be used to buy the daring new bathing suits, to watch Dempsey fight Tunney, to dance the Charleston, and to drink illegal whiskey. Those who had no money and little time could read, in simple prose and pictures, the New York *Daily News* and *True Story Magazine* and note, with mingled disapproval and envy, the evil effects of prosperity on others.

Prosperity was real for substantial numbers of Americans. Those who made more than $2,000 a year, 40 per cent of all families, could buy a fair share, either in cash or on the installment plan, of the exciting new gadgets and machines crowding the show windows in every city and town. For the 305,000 people who received 15 per cent of the total national income, there were more expensive autos, as well as jewels, furs, and endless amusements. Because spending is by its very nature a conspicuous activity, and because frolic is more newsworthy than a ten-hour day in a textile mill, the general aura of the twenties—prosperity and well-being —was that given to it by its most economically active members.

Amid the general self-congratulation, however, amid the smug speeches of the business leaders and the triumphant clatter of ticker-tape machines, millions of Americans worked all day in mines, factories, and on patches of rented or mortgaged land. In the evening they read the newspaper or listened to the not-yet-paid-for radio and looked forward to Saturday night, when they might hold their mouths under the national faucet for a few drops of the wild revelry that everyone spoke about. For the fact was that a large section of the American population was living sparely and precariously and, though not jobless and impoverished (as many would be a decade later), were shut out of the high, wild, and prosperous living that marked the upper half of the population.

After a detailed study of economic conditions in the twenties, George Soule concludes that, while production and profits rocketed in bursts of happy speculation, "the American people did not all enjoy the ride." [4] There are two implications in this statement which bear upon any general estimate of the prosperity of

[3] *The Present Economic Revolution in the United States* (Boston, 1925).
[4] Soule, *op. cit.*, 5.

that period. One is the fact that even the wage earner who improved his economic position in the twenties did not advance as much as the dividend-holder and business executive. Another is that many sections of the population were bypassed in the general prosperity and lived at the edge, or over the edge, of poverty.[5]

The remarkable increase of productivity in the twenties enabled wage gains to be outdistanced by the burgeoning of corporate profits. In the period 1919–1928, productivity grew 40 per cent, compared to a 26 per cent rise in real earnings,[6] so that "business did not fully share its productive gains with wage earners and consumers by a combination of wage increases and price reduction." This led to a "tremendous growth of profits for the more fortunately situated sectors of business and for the big corporations that dominated them."[7] In the period 1922–1929, while real wages per capita in manufacturing advanced at a rate of 1.4 per cent a year, common stockholders gained 16.4 per cent a year.[8]

The general rise in real wages concealed the fact that this rise was unequally distributed among the nation's wage earners, with skilled members of the craft unions accounting for much of the total increase, while unorganized, unskilled workers in the mass production industries were having a difficult time supplying their families with necessities.[9] The recurring strikes of coal miners and

[5] Lewis Mumford commented on the twenties: "Capitalism, with respect to the working mass of humanity, has been like a beggar that flaunts a hand covered with jewels, one or two of them genuine, whilst it shivers in rags and grabs at a crust of bread" (*Technics and Civilization* [New York, 1934], 397–398). Oswald Garrison Villard said: "Nobody was interested in the fact that, in the midst of unheard-of luxury and unprecedented fortune, vast numbers of Americans were not only living at or below the subsistence level but were steadily sinking in the economic scale" (*Fighting Years* [New York, 1939], 498).

[6] Paul H. Douglas, *Real Wages in the United States 1890–1926* (Boston, 1930), 391.

[7] Soule, *op. cit.*, 222, 283.

[8] Frederick C. Mills, *Economic Tendencies in the United States* (New York, 1932), 555. In the same period the general index of real wages advanced 2.1 per cent a year, indicating that the larger wage fund was being spread over a greater working population (*ibid.*).

[9] Foster Rhea Dulles makes this point, talking of "glaring inequalities in the way these material and social gains were distributed among the workers" (*Labor in America* [New York, 1949], 244). The traditional generalizing about

textile workers in the twenties told of some of the hardships of people in those industries.

There has been general acceptance of the fact that at least one sector of the economy—agriculture—was "sick" in the twenties. Particularly in the South and some areas of the West, farmers were in distress. However, below-subsistence conditions were not confined to rural areas or to the south. On the lower West Side of New York, for instance:

The mass of factory, white-collar workers, skilled trades and small businesses received wages of $20 to $35 per week with little variation from 1921 through 1930. . . . It was never easy to maintain a family on the wage of the general run of inhabitants of this locality, and those heads of families whose earnings were not supplemented were able to provide little more than the bare necessities, if that. Home work by mothers, though usually bringing in three dollars to five dollars a week, often meant the difference between being able to make ends meet or not.[10]

The classic sociological study of the twenties, that of Muncie, Indiana, in the Lynds' *Middletown*, shows graphically that ordinary working people did not share the prosperity of the time and went about their mundane lives day to day never free from "the long arm of the job." In Middletown, whose 30,000 people lived much like people in the hundreds of other industrial towns scattered across the nation, there were two clearly defined groups: "the Working Class and the Business Class."

The Lynds reported: "As one prowls Middletown streets about six o'clock of a winter morning one notes two kinds of home: the dark ones where the people still sleep, and the ones with a light in the kitchen where the adults of the household may be seen moving about, starting the business of the day." [11] A speaker

---

"corporations" and "labor" often serves to conceal the marked variations within each group. Just as laboring people fared differently in the twenties, businessmen did too. There was a tendency for profits to become concentrated among the top echelons of the corporate structure. While in 1922–1923 two-thirds of a selected group of corporations earned at least a 20 per cent net return on investment, by 1928 only one-fifth of those corporations did so (Ralph C. Epstein, *Industrial Profits in the United States* [New York, 1934], 239).

[10] Ware, *op. cit.*, 72–73.

[11] Robert S. Lynd and Helen M. Lynd, *Middletown: A Study in American Culture* (New York, 1929), 23, 53.

urging parents to help children by making of breakfast a "lei-
surely family reunion" did not realize that for two-thirds of the
city's families "the father gets up in the dark in winter, eats hastily
in the kitchen in the gray dawn, and is at work from an hour to
two and a quarter hours before his children have to be at school."
The United States Bureau of Labor minimum budget for a family
of five in 1924 was $1,920, but in Muncie about 85 per cent of
the married workers made less than that.[12]

For the nation as a whole, unemployment affected only a small
percentage of the labor force, roughly two to three million annually throughout the decade, but the fact that a worker might
be unemployed for a month or two during the year meant that
many more than two or three million were temporarily unemployed, and loss of earnings for even a short period could bring
hardship to a family. As the twenties progressed, there was a slight
but noticeable worsening of the unemployment picture, and one
economic study of the period points out that even before 1929
unemployment was growing.[13]

However, these evidences of the limited nature of postwar
prosperity were buried beneath the signs of lavish living and
conspicuous enjoyment which were everywhere in the twenties
and which, though not shared by all segments of the population,
effectively crowded out of the public eye any signs of distress.[14] It
was a picture that has been almost universal in modern-day
America, where a single line of marbled skyscrapers and luxury
apartment dwellings is enough to block from view the layers-in-
depth of tenements and slums.

When some people looked behind the façade to catch a glimpse
of suffering, their voices were either shouted down or ignored. As
Merle Curti has observed:

[12] *Ibid.*, 85.

[13] Mills, *op. cit.*, 481. Through the twenties, Louis D. Brandeis had been
making suggestions to Paul Kellogg of the *Survey Graphic* on writing up the
unemployment situation. On March 11, 1928, he wrote to Kellogg: "Now
that unemployment has been forced upon public attention would it not be
possible for the *Survey* to take up vigorously and persistently the musts of
Regularity in Employment?" (Alpheus T. Mason, *Brandeis—A Free Man's
Life* [New York, 1946], 587).

[14] F. Scott Fitzgerald wrote about this period: "It was borrowed time, . . .
the whole upper tenth of a nation living with the insouciance of grand ducs
and the casualness of chorus girls" (*op. cit.*).

It was, in fact, only the upper ten percent of the population that enjoyed a marked increase in real income. But the protests which such facts normally have evoked could not make themselves widely or effectively felt. This was in part the result of the grand strategy of the major political parties. In part it was the result of the fact that almost all the chief avenues to mass opinion were now controlled by large-scale publishing industries.[15]

Not all voices were stilled. There were some, too eloquent, too powerful, or simply too insistent to be ignored: Sinclair Lewis, Theodore Dreiser, John Dos Passos, H. L. Mencken, Oswald Garrison Villard, Lewis Mumford. They spoke to their generation with kindliness or with cynicism, with anger or with irony. They probed into the vitals of the social structure, sometimes crudely, sometimes delicately, but in any case deriding the cult of material wealth and the deification of orthodoxy.

While Dreiser and Lewis and Mencken were slashing at the curtain of prosperity ballyhoo with literary scalpels, a more direct onslaught was begun by their political counterparts, the progressives of the twenties. In the Senate the small but formidable progressive group included: Thomas J. Walsh and Burton K. Wheeler of Montana, Bob La Follette and Irvine Lenroot of Wisconsin, Hiram Johnson of California, William E. Borah of Idaho, Smith W. Brookhart of Iowa, and George Norris of Nebraska. In the House there were James Frear, Victor Berger, and others from Wisconsin, along with Thomas D. Schall and William Kvale of Minnesota. And now, in 1922, after a three-year absence, Fiorello LaGuardia prepared to join their ranks in Congress, thinking to represent with his shrill voice the smothered outcry of the city tenement dwellers against the elite of wealth and power who ruled the new Gilded Age.

The 1920 campaign had seen progressivism reach its low point as a national force.[16] Several small, determined groups attempted to hold ranks, with the Committee of Forty-eight [17] joining the newly

---

[15] *The Growth of American Thought* (New York, 1943), 692–693.

[16] Wesley Marvin Bagby, "Progressivism's Debacle: The Election of 1920" (Ph.D. dissertation, Columbia University, 1954); also Herbert Croly, "The Eclipse of Progressivism," *New Republic*, XXIV (Oct. 27), 210–216, 1920.

[17] The Committee of Forty-eight arose in mid-1919 as "a melange of intellectual liberals, perennial reformers, and some of the left-wing of the old Progressive Party" (Shideler, *op. cit.*, 16). It included men like J. A. H. Hopkins, Arthur Garfield Hayes, John Haynes Holmes, and Will Durant.

formed Farmer-Labor party to nominate Parley Christensen and Max Hayes on a ticket emphasizing public ownership of the basic industries and anti-imperialism. However, the big guns of progressivism were either silent or supported the major-party candidates. La Follette condemned both Democrats and Republicans, but found the Farmer-Labor group too radical for his taste.[18] Harold Ickes, a newcomer to the progressive Republicans, supported the Democratic standard-bearer Cox, calling Harding a "platitudinous jellyfish." [19] With foreign policy playing an important part in the campaign, progressive unity was especially difficult to maintain. Thus, Hiram Johnson and Borah, despite their dislike for his domestic program, declared for Harding because of his anti-League views.

LaGuardia's own support of Harding reflected the divisive role of nationalism in 1920. Democrats, he believed, had failed Italian-Americans on the Fiume question and made a mockery of Wilson's cry of self-determination. In September, 1920, an Italian-American Republican League was formed, with LaGuardia as national chairman, and the League set out to campaign for Harding on the issue of Wilson's "betrayal" of Fiume. A convention of the League, attended by delegates from twenty-three states, cheered messages from Harding, Coolidge, and Henry Cabot Lodge.[20] LaGuardia's stand, while satisfying his outrage over the Fiume question, also cemented, in an election year, his always shaky relationship with the Republican party.

In March, 1922, after a number of discussions with friends in the Italian community of New York, LaGuardia led in the formation of the League of Italian-American Republican Clubs and began making speeches on some of his favorite topics. He denounced the public utility interests for profiting excessively on the sale of electricity to the people of New York City.[21] When it was proposed that New York build some kind of memorial for the war dead and an army colonel proposed "an arch of stone in a conspicuous place," LaGuardia countered with a proposal for a "memorial school." This school, he suggested, would have students from all over the world and "would teach the brightest

---

[18] Shideler, *op. cit.*, 44.　　　　[19] Bagby, *op. cit.*, 567–569.
[20] New York *Times,* Sept. 21, 1920. Lodge was conscious, a number of writers have suggested, of the growing Italian vote in Massachusetts.
[21] New York *American,* March 13, 1922.

youths of all nations the futility of warfare." [22] He continued to argue that the lofty ideals of the war had not been fulfilled.

Undoubtedly LaGuardia was conscious at this time of the importance of the Italian vote in New York City. The 1920 census showed that more than a third of New York's population was foreign-born, and of these foreign-born, one-fifth were Italian. It was estimated that over 100,000 Italians in New York were voters.[23] With Italian-American Republican Clubs formed all over the city and even upstate, political leaders in New York City were eyeing LaGuardia with concern. The primary elections for Governor were to take place in August, 1922, and Republican backers of Governor Nathan L. Miller began to get uneasy about LaGuardia's future plans.

This uneasiness gave way to alarm when the Hearst newspapers began mentioning LaGuardia as a possible Republican candidate for Governor. Hearst insisted that his motive was a purely disinterested one; he wanted to see a progressive in office, whether Republican or Democrat.[24] Therefore, he urged the selection of LaGuardia as Republican candidate and John Hylan as Democratic nominee. Some observers of the New York political scene, however, believed that Hearst, despite his own disclaimer, wanted to be Governor and that his support for LaGuardia was a clever stratagem designed to split the Republican ticket.[25]

LaGuardia, in the meantime, warned the newspapers that he might become an independent candidate for governor if Governor Miller were renominated on a "reactionary" platform,[26] and he went ahead to prepare a forty-one-plank progressive platform for presentation to the Republican State Convention. His platform was a well-shaken mixture of Populist-Progressive doctrine. It called for restoration of the direct primary, a child labor law, a minimum wage law for women, a five-cent fare, and old-age insurance. Anticipating the Norris-LaGuardia Act by ten years, the platform called for limitations on injunctions in labor dis-

[22] New York *Daily News,* May 13, 1922.

[23] There were 1,989,216 foreign-born out of a population of 5,620,048, with 388,427 born in Italy, making Italians, next to Jews, the most numerous single foreign group in the city.

[24] New York *Times,* May 24, 1922.

[25] Limpus and Leyson, *op. cit.,* 132.

[26] New York *Times,* May 24, 1922.

putes, and jury trials in contempt cases arising out of such disputes. It pointed to the common problems of farm and city people exploited by monopolies, called for the continuation of emergency rent-relief legislation and declared that incomes under five thousand dollars should not be taxed by the state. The platform denounced the suppression of free speech and press by the legislature and called for repeal of the motion picture censorship law and of the loyalty tests for teachers.[27]

His hat was now definitely in the gubernatorial ring, and the reactions were swift.[28] The newspapers might treat his candidacy as a joke (the *Times* said his platform was "full of noble and Hearstian thoughts"),[29] but Republican leaders in the state could not ignore it. An independent candidate would split Republican votes and throw the election to the Democrats. Adding to Republican fears, perhaps, was LaGuardia's friendly luncheon talk with Herbert C. Pell, Jr., chairman of the New York State Democratic Committee.[30] Lowell Limpus, editor of the New York *Daily News* and a close observer of political events in this period, describes the reaction of the Republican high command to LaGuardia's bid for Governor:

The leaders went into a hasty conference. It was all too apparent that they had written the LaGuardia political obituary somewhat prematurely. They recognized his present strategic position. He could not possibly be elected, but his independent candidacy would undoubtedly defeat Miller and with him the Republican ticket. Something had to be done—and Sam Koenig was delegated to do it.[31]

There was one well-tried and eminently successful method of getting a political nuisance out of the way and Koenig, an old hand at the game, employed it. He offered LaGuardia an enticing alternative—a return to Congress.[32] Tammany was back in control of LaGuardia's old district, the Fourteenth, but in the

[27] Printed copy of platform, LaG. Papers.

[28] The Hearst papers were, as expected, sympathetic (New York *Evening Journal,* Aug. 19, 1922). The *World* preferred Governor Miller as Republican candidate (New York *World,* July 24, 1922).

[29] Aug. 31, 1922.   [30] Pell to LaGuardia, Aug. 17, 1922, LaG. Papers.

[31] Limpus and Leyson, *op. cit.,* 133.

[32] State and municipal benefices have often seemed more stable and lucrative to local political machines than the more uncertain national posts.

Twentieth Congressional District on the upper East Side of Manhattan, an area predominantly Jewish and Italian, Republican Congressman Isaac Siegel was leaving in order to take a judgeship. LaGuardia had always received rousing welcomes in this area. He considered Koenig's offer, received assurances of support from Edward Corsi, a popular leader among Italians in the district, and then agreed to accept the deal.

Knowing how desperately the Republican leadership wanted him to get out of the gubernatorial picture, he laid down one condition. He insisted that he run for Congress on his own platform, reserving the right to repudiate completely the regular Republican platform. Koenig was unhappy, but he agreed. LaGuardia officially accepted the Republican nomination on August 29, 1922, and the *Times* commented: "Some of our keenest lawyers hold that Mr. Koenig could be indicted under an old New York statute for the technical seduction of Mr. Hearst's apprentice." [33]

LaGuardia's campaign for Congress was already well launched. He had been writing a series of articles for Hearst's New York *Evening Journal*,[34] commenting in his own blunt style on all the important issues of the Harding administration. He denounced immigration restriction, supported a veteran's bonus, attacked the Supreme Court for voiding welfare legislation, assailed the use of injunctions by Attorney-General Daugherty to break the 1922 railroad strike, and supported the mine strike of the same year.

In 1922, two thousand manufacturing corporations were realizing net profits of one and three-quarters billion dollars, making almost ten per cent of their capital investment.[35] But it was also a year when millions of people had difficulty securing enough milk and meat for their children, paying the rent, and buying enough coal to face the coming winter. LaGuardia, trying to be heard through the blanket of optimism woven by the followers of Emile Coué, kept pointing out these facts.[36]

[33] Aug. 31, 1922. The Brooklyn *Daily Eagle* commented (Aug. 30, 1922), "From now till November, we suppose LaGuardia will make no more attacks on Governor Miller."

[34] Copies of articles in LaG. Papers. See particularly those of Aug. 17, Aug. 25, Aug. 29, Sept. 25, July 31, Sept. 6, and Aug. 4, 1922.

[35] Mills, *op. cit.*, 486.

[36] "The American people," LaGuardia wrote in the *Evening Journal* on

From the start of his congressional campaign he made it clear that he was running not on a Republican, but on a Progressive platform. He pointed to the advanced political reforms in Oregon (initiative, referendum, recall),[37] noted New York's backwardness ("New York this year goes back to the convention system. Shame!"),[38] encouraged insurgency in Republican ranks,[39] and hailed La Follette's renomination in Wisconsin, saying: "He was always known as a radical; yet, three-fourths of every reform and every forward-looking piece of legislation ever advocated by him have been written into the laws of this country." [40]

LaGuardia told the *World:* "I stand for the Republicanism of Abraham Lincoln; and let me tell you that the average Republican leader east of the Mississippi doesn't know anything more about Abraham Lincoln than Henry Ford knows about the Talmud. I am a Progressive." [41]

Running against LaGuardia in the Twentieth Congressional District were the designee of the regular Democratic machine, Henry Frank, and the Socialist candidate, William Karlin. Early in the campaign LaGuardia said there would be no mudslinging. He had met his opponents, he said, and found them "fine gentlemen." Throughout the campaign, Karlin and LaGuardia fought hard but amicably. "Mr. Karlin," LaGuardia told the *World,* "is a conservative running on a radical ticket. I am a radical running on a conservative ticket." [42] Karlin insisted that a Republican, despite his own personal platform, could not represent labor in Congress, and the two men engaged in a friendly debate on this question before three thousand persons at the New Star Casino, with George Soule acting as chairman.[43]

Aug. 19, 1922, "are having a hard time making both ends meet. The American breakfast of cereal, ham and eggs, potatoes, rolls and coffee has entirely disappeared from the breakfast table. Every daily paper contains recipes and advice on how to get along with less food owing to the high cost of necessities. . . . It is the proper function of government to prevent monopolies and profiteering in food." In an article on Sept. 14, 1922, he urged that the price of coal be kept down.

37 New York *Evening Journal,* Sept. 22, 1922.
38 New York *Evening Journal,* Sept. 26, 1922.
39 LaGuardia to J. P. Murphy, Aug., 1922, LaG. Papers.
40 New York *Evening Journal,* Sept. 11, 1922.   41 Oct. 1, 1922.
42 *Ibid.*   43 *Harlem Home News,* Oct. 25, 1922.

Relations with the Democratic candidate Frank, however, reached a point of bitter enmity by the time the campaign ended. Frank was becoming concerned, as election day drew near, over the amount of support his opponent was building. Not only Republican Hiram Johnson, but Democrat Mayor Hylan had spoken out for LaGuardia.[44] He seemed to have the Italian vote in his pocket, and a number of prohibition and civil liberties groups had expressed their support.[45] The New York *American* and the New York *Evening Mail* were backing him, while the *World,* the *Times,* and other newspapers were giving him much favorable publicity.

Frank's campaign strategists decided, as a last-ditch effort, to appeal to the heavy Jewish vote in the district.[46] Their first move, on the Jewish holiday Rosh Hashanah, was to mail greetings cards to every Jewish voter in the district. The card, signed only "The Jewish Committee," read:

The most important office in this country for Judaism is the Congressman. Our flesh and blood are united with our own on the other side of the ocean. Only through our Congressman can we go to their rescue.

There are three candidates, who are seeking your vote: one is Karlin, the atheist, the second is the Italian LaGuardia, who is a pronounced anti-Semite and Jew-hater.

Be careful how you vote.

Our candidate is Henry Frank, who is a Jew with a Jewish heart, and who does good for us. Therefore it is up to you and your friends to vote for our friend and beloved one, Henry Frank, for Congressman.[47]

LaGuardia was furious. He now accelerated his activities in a way that left his campaign workers breathless. His secretary, still the dependable Marie Fischer, took down in shorthand a letter which he dictated, in Yiddish, to be printed in Yiddish and distributed throughout the district. It was an open letter to Frank, and ended with:

[44] New York *Times,* Oct. 23, 1922; Limpus, *op. cit.,* 138.
[45] LaGuardia to "The Anti-Fanatic League of Women," Sept. 2, 1922, LaG. Papers.
[46] New York *Mail,* Oct. 21, 1922.
[47] Limpus and Leyson, *op. cit.,* 141–142.

Very well, then. On the issue which you have raised, I hereby challenge you to publicly and openly debate the issues of the campaign, THE DEBATE TO BE CONDUCTED BY YOU AND ME ENTIRELY IN THE YIDDISH LANGUAGE—the subject of the debate to be, "Who Is Best Qualified to Represent All the People of the Twentieth Congressional District. . . .[48]

LaGuardia knew that Frank could not speak Yiddish, and he now sat back calmly, pretending to be waiting for the acceptance he knew would not come. Then he set out on a speaking tour of the Jewish areas in the district, making three speeches in Yiddish and winning the plaudits of his Jewish listeners as he denounced Frank for refusing to accept his challenge.[49]

Frank belatedly explained his failure to appear, in an open letter, saying: "A challenge from you, with your well-known anti-Semitic tendencies, to debate in Yiddish, is an insult and an affront to the Jewish electives [sic] in our community." LaGuardia retorted: "My Democratic opponent is making a racial appeal. He is asking the voters of this district for their votes on the ground that he is a Jew. . . . After all, is he looking for a job as a *schamas* [the Yiddish term for caretaker of a synagogue] or does he want to be elected Congressman?" [50]

The election results kept both candidates nervous until the last tallies were in. They showed that LaGuardia had beaten Frank by 245 votes, with 8,466 to his opponent's 8,221. Karlin ran third with 4,393 votes.[51] It was another of LaGuardia's amazing hair-breadth victories, and though Frank contested the count, the courts ruled that the vote must stand.[52]

In that election, Al Smith was returned to the Governor's mansion in Albany, and the Democrats made sharp gains throughout the nation, leaving such an even balance of power in both House and Senate that the New York *Times* predicted: "In the next Senate the balance of power will be held by the progressive-radical group led by Senator La Follette. . . . The more than seven million majority given to President Harding has been wiped out. The demonstration of disapproval for the Administration was

[48] *Ibid.*, 143–144.   [49] New York *Mail*, Oct. 21, 1922.
[50] Limpus and Leyson, *op. cit.*, 145.
[51] New York *Times*, Nov. 9, 1922.   [52] *Ibid.*, Nov. 15, 1922.

unmistakable." [53] Joining the old senatorial progressive bloc of La Follette, Norris, Borah, and Johnson, were the newly elected Smith Brookhart of Iowa, Henrik Shipstead of Minnesota, and Burton K. Wheeler of Montana. In the House, Socialist Meyer London was gone, but Victor Berger, also a Socialist, who had been twice expelled by the House, was elected in Wisconsin. It seemed that Fiorello LaGuardia, ready once again to do battle in Congress, would not be alone.

[53] *Ibid.,* Nov. 9, 1922. Shideler, *op. cit.,* 112, says the election showed a "drift towards a nebulous progressivism."

6 · *LaGuardia, La Follette, and Progressivism, 1922-1924*

THOSE who saw the United States in the 1920's as a place of well-being and contentment may well have been perplexed by the staccato bursts of progressive activity in the early twenties, which culminated in the almost religious fervor of the La Follette movement of 1924. To Fiorello LaGuardia, however, walking the streets of his new district and observing the day-to-day living of his constituents, rebelliousness seemed a natural reaction.

The Twentieth Congressional District had been created in 1911 by the redistricting operation of a Republican legislature.[1] It encompassed an area known as East Harlem on the upper East Side of New York, extending from Fifth Avenue to the East River and from 99th to 120th Streets. Except for a fringe of plush apartment houses and hotels along Madison and Fifth Avenues near Central Park, it was an overwhelmingly working-class district.

Ethnically the area's composition reflected that peculiar process by which immigrants, landing on the lower tip of Manhattan, worked their way north decade by decade, from the lower end of the island to the uptown areas, bypassing the well-to-do mid-town residential sections. Some Jews had moved into East Harlem from their original first-arrival habitats on the lower East Side, and even more Italians did the same, making the easy transition

[1] Peter Kenneth Ewald, "Congressional Apportionment and New York State" (Ph.D. dissertation, New York University, 1954), 168.

from Mulberry and Cherry Streets to a new "Little Italy," east
of Second Avenue between 110th and 120th Streets.[2] Greenwich
Village Italians also moved uptown into this area,[3] detouring east-
ward to bypass the Negro ghetto of Harlem. As yet, Negroes remained on the West Side, leaving East Harlem almost all white.
The only trace of color was the small community of Puerto
Ricans, mingling easily with Catholic neighbors from Italy.[4]

In many respects LaGuardia's new district resembled his old
Fourteenth District, although it was more uniformly poor than
the crazy-quilt Greenwich Village section. Houses in the Village
were usually one- or two-story dwellings, set on narrow, crooked
streets, interspersed sometimes with ornate apartment houses,
small hotels, or night clubs. In East Harlem, on the other hand,
block after block of straight-rowed, almost military-ordered five-
and six-story dirty-faced tenements looked out over wider streets,
where the garbage had more room to scatter than on the streets
downtown.

That the postwar prosperity had bypassed most of the residents
of East Harlem was easily apparent to anyone who walked down
these streets, and even more obvious to anyone who stepped into
the dark hallways, walked up the rickety stairs, and entered the
small, littered rooms were children, parents, and often grand-
parents gathered around the coal stove on winter days. Luxuries
were being produced in mass quantities for a larger part of the
population than ever before, but there were still millions who
knew nothing of them. One of these unnoticed citizens, Charles
Tese, who lived on East 115th Street in the Twentieth Congressional District, wrote to LaGuardia during the 1922 campaign:

I am a citizen of the United States and have been in the army. Since
I got back from France I have not had a good job. Just little bits.
What did we soldiers get out of being patriotic, nothing. Not even our
old jobs back. I'm so disgusted now, that I don't feel like voting for

[2] *Ibid.*, 209.   [3] Ware, *op. cit.*
[4] Interview with Miriam Marcantonio, July, 1956. Mrs. Marcantonio,
widow of Congressman Vito Marcantonio, who represented the same district after 1934, recalls that in the early 1920's the Italians were predominant
in the district, with practically no Negroes. Marie Fischer LaGuardia, in an
interview with the author in July, 1956, gives a similar ethnic picture of
the area in the twenties.

anybody. Who feels like thinking of votes when they have not got a dollar in their pockets? [5]

With this kind of constituency behind him and with the satisfaction of having won the election on his own platform in defiance of both Democratic and Republican machines, LaGuardia set out confidently to align himself with the progressives. Shortly after the election of 1922 LaGuardia received a letter from Basil Manly, director of the People's Legislative Service.[6] This organization was one of the small pockets of resistance which kept the progressive movement alive after the demise of the Bull Moose party. Manly asked LaGuardia to attend a progressive conference in Washington on December 1. The Progressives, Manly predicted, would hold the balance of power in the next Congress. "With proper organization and assistance they can not only block reactionary measures, but can initiate a program of fundamental constructive legislation. It is the opportunity of a lifetime." [7] Marie Fischer, at her post in LaGuardia's office, affirmed the New York congressman's interest, and asked that the Service keep in touch with him.[8]

This December meeting was to include many of the members of the Conference for Progressive Political Action, which had been set up in February, 1922, at a meeting called by the fifteen railroad brotherhoods, attended by representatives of the Non-Partisan League, the Socialist party, and the Committee of Forty-eight. The aim of the C.P.P.A. was, it insisted, not the formation of a new party, but the achievement of unity around a program of progressive action.

The meeting opened in Washington on December 1, 1922, with twenty-four congressmen present, and heard speeches by Senators

[5] Tese to LaGuardia, undated, LaG. Papers.

[6] The People's Legislative Service was born of a meeting in Washington in Dec., 1920, attended by representatives from the Farmer-Labor party, the Non-Partisan League, the Farmers' National Council, and other groups and was designed to provide research and information for Progressives in and out of Congress. Basil Manly had been a director of research and investigation of the United States Commission on Industrial Relations and had served as joint chairman of the National War Labor Board (Shideler, *op. cit.*, 52–53).

[7] Manly to LaGuardia, undated, LaG. Papers.

[8] LaGuardia to Manly, Nov. 22, 1922, *ibid.*

Borah and Norris. LaGuardia arrived in time for the afternoon session and voted for the resolution offered by Bob La Follette, which said that the purpose of the meeting was to "drive special privilege out of control of government and restore it to the people." [9] On the second day LaGuardia and the other congressmen met at a City Club dinner with over two hundred non-congressional delegates, including Edward Keating, editor of the magazine *Labor,* Benjamin C. Marsh, director of the Farmers' National Council, George L. Record of Jersey City, Frederic C. Howe of New York City, Andrew Furuseth, Samuel Gompers, Mrs. Edward P. Costigan, Amos Pinchot, Roger Baldwin, and Herbert Croly.[10] La Follette acted as chairman, and the guests heard Norris, Wheeler, Gompers, and Samuel Untermyer speak.[11]

LaGuardia left Washington with even more than his usual enthusiasm. If ever he had felt that he was not alone in his fight and that the outlook for progressive reform was bright, this was the time. His speech a week later at the Institutional Synagogue on 116th Street was entitled "The Awakening of the Progressive Spirit in this Country." He told his audience:

The awakening of the Progressive spirit throughout the country means nothing else than the arousing of a united protest against conditions which have become intolerable. There is nothing about this movement that is complicated or difficult of being explained. Exploitation, the result of favored legislation; poverty, the result of the greed of monopolies; dissatisfaction, the result of privileged government—have resulted in the alliance between the farmers, industrial producers, the believers in democracy and the true lovers of America. That is all there is to it.[12]

He noted the disparity between the nation's wealth and the economic condition of many of its people:

When, in the land of plenty, richest in the world in natural resources, with less density of population than any other country, pro-

---

[9] Belle and Fola La Follette, *Robert M. LaFollette* (New York, 1953), II, 1067.

[10] *Ibid.;* also, mimeographed report on conference by Basil Manly in LaG. Papers.

[11] Untermyer soon began corresponding with LaGuardia on the proposed reform of bankruptcy laws.

[12] Mimeographed copy in LaG. Papers; also, New York *Times,* Dec. 11, 1922.

ducing enough food not only to feed itself, but a quarter of the world, there is a large part of its population working and producing and yet not having proper and sufficient nourishment, not having proper and cheerful living accommodations, then there is something wrong with its government, which must be righted and corrected without delay.

The Progressive group in the next Congress has not only the desire to do good, but the absolute power to do it.

While LaGuardia was making this speech, the second Conference for Progressive Political Action, attended by five hundred delegates from every state in the Union, was meeting in Cleveland to draft a program for progressive legislation and incidentally to criticize the frustration of reform by Supreme Court decisions. Their views were brought to Congress by James Frear of Wisconsin, who in January, 1923, speaking in the House, outlined the views of the nation's progressives and denounced judicial review. "That the poor man does not have equal opportunity in litigating as the rich man is a fact of which we are ashamed," Frear said. He proposed a constitutional amendment giving Congress the power to determine how many members of the Court could declare laws unconstitutional and permitting a review of court decisions by a two-thirds vote of both houses.[13] LaGuardia read Frear's speech and was delighted. In a letter to Frear he called it a "masterpiece" and suggested another conference of progressives in the spring, saying he was making the same suggestion to La Follette in another letter.[14]

In preparation for what they knew would be a bitter battle over the House rules at the opening of the Sixty-eighth Congress, Frear and LaGuardia began an exchange of correspondence with Hamilton Fish, Jr., who had been elected to Congress from one of the "silk-stocking" districts of New York, but who claimed still to be progressive (Fish had been a Bull Mooser in 1912) and had solicited LaGuardia's support in the campaign on that ground. Their aim was to get Fish to introduce at the Republican caucus a liberalized set of House rules. LaGuardia confided to Frear: "I think it would be a splendid idea if the initiative came from the 'conservative East.' "[15] Frear replied: "I hope Fish will act

---

[13] *Congress. Rec.,* 67:4, Jan. 27, 1923.   [14] Feb. 21, 1923, LaG. Papers.
[15] LaGuardia to Frear, Feb. 3, 1923, *ibid.*

in the matter. . . . Concessions of course are required among Progressives and I assume that the influences that surround Fish are such that he cannot always act independently but I hope he will come through." [16] As an inducement LaGuardia began dangling before Fish's eyes the prospect of a nomination for Governor in 1924.[17]

More and more, LaGuardia's own stature in the progressive movement began to be recognized. A dinner in his honor was held at the Hotel Pennsylvania, with seven hundred people attending and listening to speeches by James Frear, Smith Brookhart, and James Weldon Johnson. Frear once again hit at the Supreme Court, saying: "Congress and the country stand, hat in hand, waiting to find when a law is not a law according to five judges." [18] The speakers predicted that LaGuardia's term in Congress would see the enactment of much progressive legislation.[19]

As LaGuardia waited through the spring and summer months of 1923 for Congress to convene, he did not remain idle. His activities in those months certainly did not bear out the picture of over-all national prosperity. Complaint after complaint came to him in early 1923 of the prohibitive price of meat. After a meeting with community leaders, a meat strike was planned. The strike began in East Harlem, soon spread throughout the city, and resulted in the reduction of the price of meat by five to ten cents per pound.[20] Interviewed by the *Harlemite* shortly after the meat strike, LaGuardia told the reporter:

Call me a radical, if you will, call me anything, but when there are people right in my own district who are working day and night and can't earn enough for their families to eat, something is wrong. Such conditions should not exist and they are the conditions I am determined to change.[21]

He promised that in Congress he would fight for increased tax rates on high incomes. His interest in legislation of national scope,

[16] Frear to LaGuardia, Feb. 6, 1923, *ibid.*
[17] Limpus and Leyson, *op. cit.,* 156.
[18] Printed copy of speech, LaG. Papers.
[19] New York *Times,* March 11, 1923.
[20] Limpus and Leyson, *op. cit.,* 151.
[21] *Harlemite,* April 28, 1923, in LaG. Papers.

he said, came from his recognition of the fact that no one community in the nation was independent of the others, that all
basically faced the same problems. Demonstrating his refusal to
take a parochial view of the needs of his own district, he was off
to Buffalo in June, after a conference with Sidney Hillman, to
help the Amalgamated Clothing Workers in a strike for union
recognition and the abolition of the black list.[22]

The tenement dwellers of his district faced a constant struggle
with high rents and intolerable living conditions, and LaGuardia
led a group of tenants to hearings at City Hall held by the State
Housing Commission. The tenants' aim was to convince the
commission (which had been set up by Governor Al Smith) that
a serious housing crisis existed, requiring prompt governmental
action. At the hearings two Catholic priests, Father Silipigni and
Father Silvestri, told of families of eight and nine, living in their
parishes in two-room flats, some in cellars and coal bins. This
testimony, LaGuardia angrily told the commission,

stands out in glaring contrast to the learned college professors, scientific experts, figure-jugglers and truth-distorters who attempted to
confuse the issues and make the Commission believe that there is no
shortage in housing. You cannot feed babies on statistics, nor house
families in blue prints, nor better conditions on theories. The time
has come when housing must be regulated as a public utility.[23]

The Housing Commission recommended repassage of the emergency rent law, although no measures were taken to tear down
the tenements and build new homes.

The months before the opening of Congress were crowded with
meetings of progressives, sharing ideas, making plans for what
they knew would be a titanic effort—the attempt to scale the lofty,
crag-filled mountain of postwar conservatism. During March and
April a "group for liberal discussion," at it was termed by Amos
Pinchot, began holding meetings, attended by LaGuardia, Pinchot, George L. Record, Oswald Garrison Villard, and others.[24]
In May, LaGuardia received a letter from La Follette asking him

22 New York *Call,* June 14, 1923.
23 Undated press release, LaG. Papers.
24 Amos Pinchot Papers, Library of Congress, Washington, D.C.

to participate in a conference of progressives to be held in Chicago
at the end of the month, and La Follette scribbled a notation:
"This is of very great importance, don't miss it." [25] LaGuardia
replied that he would come.

Accompanying LaGuardia to the Chicago conference, to the
consternation of both Republican and Democratic machines in
New York, was Mayor John Hylan.[26] The Brooklyn *Eagle* took
wide-eyed note of LaGuardia's daring: "The boy that stood on
the burning deck had not a fuller measure of isolation than
Fiorello LaGuardia . . . standing with Progressive Republicans
of the La Follette school, remaining on fine terms with Mayor
Hylan, and more or less defiant of the party organization." The
Republican state and county committees were biting their tongues
in frustration. "But," the *Eagle* observed, "nobody is anxious to
chill LaGuardia because in a pinch he's a great help in getting
the Italian-American vote on Election Day." [27]

The grass-roots support for LaGuardia in New York brought
him invitations to speak at local Republican clubs, and he wasted
no opportunity to strike hard at the Republican high command.
When the Republican State Committee decided there would be
no state convention and no platform in 1923, LaGuardia appeared
before a meeting of precinct captains in Brooklyn and said that
economic conditions demanded a new approach to politics by
Republicans: "There was a time," he said, "not twenty years ago,
when people didn't worry much about the platform, because the
cost of living was cheaper then and rents were reasonable. Food
was good and cheap and our children were properly nourished." [28]
Times were different now, however, LaGuardia insisted.

Today you must talk of wages, meat, clothing, transportation and all
those things which so directly affect the daily lives of the public. You
don't have to be a professor of political economy to know that something is wrong. Take the case of a housewife whose husband works

[25] May 5, 1923, LaG. Papers.   [26] New York *World,* May 25, 1923.
[27] July 9, 1923.
[28] There are two elements of interest in this statement. One is LaGuardia's
contrast of the earlier Progressive period and the 1920's in terms of "prosperity," which reveals a different view from that of most historians, who see
both periods as times of general prosperity. The second point is the element of romanticism in LaGuardia's backward look at what he believed to
have been a better time.

hard every day. He is not shiftless and yet, when she counts up what he makes and what her needs are, she finds that she cannot make ends meet. Naturally she knows that there is something wrong. But if you state such facts to some people you are called an agitator and a radical.[29]

Congressman John M. Nelson of Wisconsin was now acting as the unofficial spokesman for the progressive group in the House, and Nelson called a meeting of eighteen congressmen who conferred for three days on their strategy for the Sixty-eighth Congress. LaGuardia was the one easterner who participated in the talks, and he later gave the newspapers a statement which highlights the relationship of reform movements to economic conditions and reflects the belief that the upsurge of progressivism in 1923–1924 was not a freak development, but an accurate register of the degree to which the "prosperity" of the twenties was a hollow and partial one. LaGuardia said: "The Progressive movement is not the result of the ambitions of any one man, nor is it a movement artificially created. The Progressive movement is simply the inevitable result of economic and political conditions throughout the country."[30]

In the same interview LaGuardia nailed another popular assumption, that progressivism was a western phenomenon because its leadership in Congress came largely from the West.[31] He said:

Nothing more misleading can be said of the Progressive group than that it simply represents the Western states or the farmers in particular. Through these Western representatives thousands upon thousands of Eastern Americans voiced their protest in the last Congress. The trouble with the Eastern delegations is often that they have not that close contact with the people that some of our Western colleagues have and thereby do not reflect the ideas and ideals of the great mass of working people of the East.[32]

[29] Brooklyn *Times,* June 28, 1923. [30] New York *Times,* Nov. 29, 1923.

[31] Some students of the Progressive movement have, perhaps, oversimplified it in sectional terms, judging its nature by the regional background of the movement's leaders, without considering the extent to which the Progressive program reflected the needs of urban groups east and west. The traditional sectional approach is only valid if movements are to be assessed on the basis of their articulated leadership without considering the unvoiced aspirations of the followers.

[32] New York *Times,* Nov. 29, 1923.

LaGuardia pointed to the common needs of people of both sections:

To say that farm legislation is detrimental to the consumers of the East is incorrect. . . . It is the artificially created sectionalism which has made possible the isolation of the producer, the distant relation with the consumer, and the existence of monopolies and wasteful middlemen, as well as greedy bankers who have thrived and prospered while consumers and producers have suffered.[33]

When the Sixty-eighth Congress prepared to convene in December, 1923, Warren Harding had been dead four months, and Calvin Coolidge sat in the White House. A few weeks before the congressional session began, LaGuardia attended (on the invitation of Michigan Congressman Roy O. Woodruff) another meeting of progressives in Washington.[34] There, a legislative program was drafted, calling for the following: farm relief, the child labor amendment, aid for veterans, lower railroad rates, government control over the necessities of life to prevent profiteering, limits on the power of injunction, the curbing of legislative action by the judiciary, a presidential primary, the conscription of wealth in wartime, the abolition of profit on war materials, the end of tax exemption for securities, the restoration of excess profits taxes, and freedom for the Philippines.[35] House progressives then held a separate caucus and told the press: "The Old Guard will soon wake up, rub their eyes, and learn that we are living in a new day." [36]

Their program would not have a chance, the progressives knew, so long as the existing House rules remained standing. For one thing, 95 per cent of all business in the House was done as a Committee of the Whole, where no record votes were taken. Even more important was the fact that any reform legislation could easily be bottled up by the seven men who formed a majority of the House Rules Committee. Therefore, the progressive bloc, acting upon carefully laid plans, kept the House in an uproar for the first two days of its session by blocking the election of a Speaker. "How long will they dare stick to their little game?"

[33] *Ibid.*   [34] *Ibid.*
[35] Press release, Dec. 13, 1923, LaG. Papers.
[36] New York *Times*, Dec. 2, 1923.

the *Times* asked anxiously.[37] With Democrats and Republicans closely divided, the election could be held up by the casting of seventeen votes, on ballot after ballot, for progressive Henry Allen Cooper of Wisconsin.

In desperation, Republican Majority Leader Nicholas Longworth agreed to meet privately with LaGuardia, Woodruff, and John M. Nelson. He knew that they were not concerned with the speakership, but wanted to force a change in the House rules. In return for the election of Frederick H. Gillett of Iowa as Speaker, Longworth agreed that during the nexty thirty days, while operating under the old rules, amendments to these rules would be considered, with reasonable discussion and record votes on these amendments. However, the progressive recalcitrants did not go unpunished, and the Republican caucus studiously kept them off the important House committees. LaGuardia, who had been quietly planning with Nelson and Frear for a post on the Judiciary Committee,[38] was left out in the cold.

During the ensuing debate over the rules, the progressive bloc fought hard, with the assistance of Texas Congressman Tom Connally, for a provision enabling one hundred congressmen to get a bill discharged from committee by petition. LaGuardia clashed sharply on this issue with his fellow New York Republican, Hamilton Fish, Jr., on whom he and Frear had lavished such gentle care during the summer in the hope that Fish would aid them in the liberalization of the rules. Fish carried the ball for the Republican stalwarts, opposing the discharge petition idea as "minority rule." [39] Fish was joined by Congressman Walter F. Lineberger of California, who told the House:

I am not for the radicalization of the rules of this House. . . . I recognize further that a small number in this House calling themselves progressives—and God save the word—are not progressives at all but radicals, and we should not mince words but call a spade a spade.[40]

The progressives did succeed in making some minor changes in the House rules, but the awesome power of the Rules Committee remained unaltered.

[37] *Ibid.*, Dec. 4, 1923.
[38] Letters from Nelson, April 18 and Dec. 11, 1923, LaG. Papers.
[39] *Congress. Rec.*, 68:1, Jan. 16, 1924, 1055.   [40] *Ibid.*, 1063–1064.

As the session continued,[41] the fact that LaGuardia was a Republican in name only became more and more evident. Soon the designation itself was dropped, with the congressman from the Twentieth District referring, in a letter to constituents, to his membership in the "Progressive Group of the House." [42] The Women's National Republican Club sent LaGuardia a wire censuring him for siding with La Follette.[43] New York Republican leader Samuel Berger spoke to a meeting of Republican women at the Hotel Marie Antoinette in New York City and urged LaGuardia's defeat in the 1924 elections, charging: "He is no Republican at all. He is no more a Republican than the representatives of Soviet Russia are republicans." [44] Rubbing salt on the Republican wounds, LaGuardia commented sentimentally upon news of the death of Tammany boss Charles F. Murphy, saying, "He was a great leader, because he kept his hand on the pulse of the people—the kind of leader we need so much these days.[45]

As if to underscore his break with the regular Republican organization, LaGuardia even dared to push forcefully against one of the mighty pillars of the Republican temple, Nicholas Murray Butler. When told that Butler had spoken out against prohibition, LaGuardia was not impressed. "Dr. Butler," he said, "has weakened every movement with which he has been affiliated. He does not speak for the Republican Party, at least not for my faction." [46] In response to reports that he and other insurgents would be read out of the party, LaGuardia told a mass meeting of constituents in his district, "No one is going to read any one out of any party." [47]

In February, 1924, a third Conference for Progressive Political

[41] See the chapters following for an account of LaGuardia's battles on the various issues of the Sixty-eighth Congress.

[42] Feb. 12, 1924, LaG. Papers.   [43] New York *Times,* Feb. 22, 1924.

[44] *Ibid.,* March 7, 1924.

[45] *Ibid.,* April 25, 1924. M. R. Werner, *Tammany Hall* (New York, 1928), 557, says, on the other hand: "It was Murphy's great and lasting contribution to the philosophy of Tammany Hall that he taught the organization that more money can be made by a legal contract than by petty blackmail." He notes that Murphy left an estate of more than two million dollars.

[46] New York *Times,* May 11, 1924.

[47] *Ibid.,* June 16, 1924.

Action issued a call for a national convention, with delegates from farmer, labor, and reform groups, to take place on the Fourth of July weekend. It was a wildly enthusiastic, singing assemblage that gathered in Cleveland to express its dissatisfaction with the two major parties. As Kenneth C. MacKay has described them, "These were all kinds of men, these Progressives of 1924. Populists, Single-taxers, Socialists, writers from the East, farmers from the West, railroad men, Bull Moosers, Greenbackers, politicians, college students, dreamers and opportunists, they were all here." [48]

LaGuardia was there too. He listened to Edwin Markham read a long poem on Lincoln. Then he told the crowd he had come "to let you know there are other streets and other attitudes in New York besides Wall Street. I speak for Avenue A and 116th Street, instead of Broad and Wall." [49] He drew cheers with his declaration, "I would rather be right than regular!" [50]

Endorsing La Follette for President, the convention gave him the right to choose his own running mate (he later picked Burton K. Wheeler of Montana). The new Progressive platform drew from the old Populist and Bull Moose programs, but went even further. Resentment against the reform-blocking decisions of the Supreme Court was reflected in the demand for abolition of judicial review and the popular election of judges. Labor's influence in the movement was shown in the call for a law against injunction and insistence that the right to organize and bargain collectively be placed in the lawbooks. The platform called for changes in the national political structure, with the direct nomination and election of the President and the use of the initiative and referendum for national legislation. Downward tariff revision and other forms of aid to the farmer were included. The wartime split in Progressive ranks was healed somewhat, as 1917 interventionists like LaGuardia joined La Follette and Norris to call for a popular referendum before entering a foreign war. The platform also called for public ownership of the railroads and water power, and more direct government control of the Federal

[48] Kenneth C. MacKay, *The Progressive Movement of 1924* (New York, 1947), 12.

[49] *Ibid.*, 115. MacKay points out that it was only a few days after this speech that the Democrats nominated Davis, whose office was at Broad and Wall.

[50] Belle and Fola La Follette, *op. cit.*, II, 1114.

Reserve System. It was, in all, a program which LaGuardia could enthusiastically endorse.[51]

When the Democratic National Convention took place in late July, supporters of Al Smith and William McAdoo gave way before a compromise candidate, John Davis, a conservative West Virginian who had become a New York corporation lawyer, representing J. P. Morgan and other powerful financiers. The Republicans chose Calvin Coolidge, who in accepting the nomination said, "In the commonplace things of life lies the strength of the nation," leading the *New Republic* to comment, "These are the words of a pigmy at a great task." [52] The choice of Coolidge indicated that the Republicans were even less sensitive than the Democrats to the economic problems of many Americans. "Through the 1920's," Samuel Lubell has noted, "the Republicans generally were either unaware of or indifferent to the aspirations of the climbing urban masses." [53] Even Nicholas Murray Butler was disgusted (though his reasons were different) with the Republican choice, saying:

The Convention of 1924 was the first of three on a rapidly descending scale of competence, intelligence and courage. The addresses at Cleveland . . . and the appallingly long platform . . . made an impression of intellectual sterility which time has done nothing to improve.[54]

The Progressive party set up headquarters in New York to cover the entire Northeast, with LaGuardia and Gilbert Roe (a friend of La Follette) in charge.[55] LaGuardia knew that his Progressive activities would ruin his chances for Republican backing in his congressional race, and he was prepared to risk it. He talked with Samuel Koenig, who offered the support of the party if La-

[51] MacKay, *op. cit.*, 11. The platform reflected the demands of urban organized labor even more than those of the farmer, and thus casts doubt on any idea that the progressive movement of the twenties was predominantly western agrarian.

[52] Claude Fuess, *Calvin Coolidge* (Boston, 1940), 348.

[53] Samuel Lubell, *The Future of American Politics* (New York, 1951), 79.

[54] *Op. cit.*, I, 282.

[55] New York *Times*, July 27, 1924. While the A.F. of L. endorsed La Follette, it could not deliver the labor vote. Intellectual reformers dominated the La Follette camp in New York (Shideler, *op. cit.*, 265–266).

Guardia would back Coolidge for the presidency. LaGuardia's reply was to withdraw formally from the Republican party in a letter to Koenig, saying:

Desirable and comfortable as a party nomination may be, I cannot sacrifice principle for the sake of a party nomination or anything else. . . . The platform of the Republican Party as adopted at Cleveland makes no appeal to the hope of the people whom I represent. . . . You are correct when you say that on many of the important bills that came before the House . . . I did not support the reactionary attitude of the Republican majority. On these issues I am willing to go before the people of my district.[56]

The Republicans designated their former congressman in the Twentieth District, Isaac Siegel, to run against LaGuardia, and Henry Frank was once again the Democratic nominee.

The American Labor party in New York, a mixture of Socialists, single taxers, Farmer-Laborites, and trade unionists, met at the Rand School and ratified the Progressive party ticket, including LaGuardia in the Twentieth District.[57] The Socialist party, despite Morris Hillquit's personal differences with LaGuardia, voted to put him on the Socialist line, with Norman Thomas, Socialist candidate for Governor joining LaGuardia in a common effort to elect Progressives.[58]

LaGuardia set out to campaign for the La Follette ticket and for his own candidacy in the Twentieth District. He enlisted the support of Vito Marcantonio, a young, capable attorney who was now his law clerk. Their acquaintance dated from 1921, when LaGuardia spoke at DeWitt Clinton High School in Manhattan and was impressed with a speech on old-age pensions and social security made that day by Marcantonio, a student.[59]

Worried about the effects of the Progressive campaign on the Coolidge chances for election, a number of 1912 supporters of Theodore Roosevelt, including James R. Garfield, Frank Knox, and Raymond Robins, issued a statement charging that La Follette's candidacy was "based on radicalism." They used T. R.'s

[56] New York *Times*, Aug. 11, 1924.   [57] *Ibid.*, Aug. 12, 1924.

[58] Interview with Norman Thomas, in Oral History Project, Columbia University. Thomas knew LaGuardia only slightly during those years.

[59] Annette Rubinstein, ed., *I Vote My Conscience* (New York, 1956), 314. This is a collection of Marcantonio speeches.

designation of La Follette as "a most sinister enemy of democracy." [60] This charge was repudiated by LaGuardia, George L. Record, Harold Ickes, Amos Pinchot, and Jane Addams, who reaffirmed their support for La Follette. LaGuardia, to indicate that La Follette was simply carrying on the old fight of the Bull Moosers, pointed to strong similarities in the 1912 and 1924 platforms.[61]

The climax of the Progressive campaign was a huge meeting at Madison Square Garden where 14,000 people paid admission (only the Socialists had dared to ask payment at political rallies before this) to jam the seats inside the Garden, and 6,000 gathered in the park outside. Arthur Garfield Hays was chairman, and Norman Thomas drew loud applause by calling the Democratic party "the party of the Espionage Law, the cruel and illegal anti-Red raids, the spy system, the war frauds, child labor in the South, A. Mitchell Palmer, and his anti-labor injunctions." As for the Republican party, it was, he said, "the party of Forbes, Fall and Daugherty, the party of Judge Gary and company-owned towns, the party of big business and big injunctions against labor." La Follette made a long speech (too long, so that many hearers began flocking to the door as the hour grew late) on the usurpation of legislative power by the Supreme Court. LaGuardia spoke briefly, predicting a Progressive victory in New York.[62]

One of the chief handicaps facing the Progressive ticket was the linking of the movement with Bolshevism [63] (in spite of the fact that the Workers party—Communist—had been refused admission to the Progressive conferences and then to the July convention). Name-calling was but a short step from intimidation,

---

[60] Belle and Fola La Follette, *op. cit.*, II, 1121.

[61] New York *Times*, Sept. 16, 1924.   [62] *Ibid.*, Sept. 19, 1924.

[63] An article in the *Saturday Evening Post* said: "Recent surveys of the activities of the Reds in this country show that, however much Senator La Follette may deny his association with men of this type, he seems powerless to prevent their association with him. . . . In any event, his motley collection of Socialists, Reds, committees, blocs, half-baked parties, combined with the dissatisfied Republicans and Democrats, is in a position to work havoc with the chances of President Coolidge and Mr. Davis, with our two-party system, with our economic situation, with our American theory and practice of government, and ultimately, with our Constitution" (quoted by MacKay, *op. cit.*, 166).

legal and extralegal.[64] Another handicap was the coolness of some important members of the Progressive movement. Senators Borah of Idaho and Norris of Nebraska were not as willing to defy the Republican machines in their states as was LaGuardia in New York. Both men concentrated on their own campaigns.[65]

Even LaGuardia was not completely at ease in the Progressive party; his was the kind of personality, and his ideas were the kind of ideas, that did not easily accept compromise, and the unity of any large organization in a vital battle requires compromise. Despite the similarity of the Progressive party platform with his own views, he was disturbed by the smugness of the Progressive leaders, and told Eric Goldman [66] that La Follette, Wheeler, and Borah were not the kind of men who could be self-critical.[67]

In his own district LaGuardia faced the handicap of running on two minor lines, the Socialist and Progressive, with the probability that a victorious major party candidate would sweep the congressional candidate into office with him. He was forced to endure both the attacks leveled against La Follette and the personal diatribes against himself. The Ku Klux Klan entered the campaign, spreading handbills through the district which appealed to "Protestant Americans" to defeat LaGuardia. However, this approach in a Jewish-Italian district may have helped LaGuardia more than it hurt him.

As usual, he ran his campaign at a furious pace. Outside support came from such diverse sources as Hamilton Fish, Jr. (with whom his relations always improved in election years, when Fish

[64] MacKay says: "The amount and extent of intimidation, social, economic and even physical in the 1924 campaign raises the question whether it should not be included with such notorious campaigns in our history as 1828 and 1896. Sometimes the disturbances bordered on physical violence" (*op. cit.,* 170–171).

[65] Norris said he was for La Follette but did not campaign on his behalf; Borah backed Coolidge, saying he had faith in the Vermonter's personal integrity. Both Borah and Norris were pessimistic about the chances for success of any third party. A letter from Norris to one of his constituents, written at another time, expresses his general lack of faith in all political parties (Norris Papers, Library of Congress, Washington, D.C.). Also see Claudius Johnson, *Borah of Idaho* (New York, 1936), 303.

[66] Goldman, *op. cit.,* 315.

[67] LaGuardia's correspondence in this period gives the general impression of his lack of comfort in any organization (LaG. Papers).

needed LaGuardia's aid), and Gene Tunney. Vito Marcantonio organized a corps of "Ghibonnes," [68] young Italian-Americans who swore personal fealty to LaGuardia and kept the district afire with their activity on behalf of "The Major."

Slightly over half of the eligible voters went to the polls on election day, and Coolidge won overwhelmingly with 15,275,-003 votes to 8,385,586 for Davis and 4,826,471 for La Follette. LaGuardia was re-elected with 8,753 votes against 6,080 for Frank and 5,956 for Siegel. Other Progressives were elected too, but the Republican sweep of Congress gave them a majority of four in the Senate and forty-seven in the House, leaving the Progressives holding the balance of power in the senior chamber, but not in the House.[69] LaGuardia promptly asked the House clerk to classify him as a Progressive rather than a Socialist,[70] but his request was ignored.

The Progressives had been decisively beaten. But close to five million voters had registered their dissatisfaction with the major parties, in the face of legal obstacles, the onus of Bolshevism, and the overwhelming opposition of the nation's press. The Progressive campaign had proved that congressmen could be elected on other than the major party designations. Furthermore, the 1924 progressive movement represented the first major alliance of labor-farmer-socialist groups in independent political action. And, perhaps most significant of all, the campaign kept alive among millions of people the spirit and ideology of progressive reform, a spirit which would soon be quieted but not crushed and which would erupt in angry rebellion during the terrible days of depression to form the groundswell of a new and more successful progressive movement.[71]

[68] Lowell Limpus says the closest American translation is "swashbuckler."

[69] The line-up in the House was now 241 Republicans, 188 Democrats, 3 Farmer-Laborites, and 2 Socialists.

[70] New York *Times,* Nov. 20, 1924.

[71] Samuel Eliot Morison and Henry Steele Commager, *The Growth of the American Republic* (New York, 1954), II, 357, say that the 1924 insurgency "may be said to have laid both the philosophic and legislative foundations for the New Deal of the 1930's."

7 * Battling Nativism
in the Coolidge Era

THE Age of Jazz was also an age of racial, national, and religious bigotry. It was the decade of the Scopes trial, the Sacco-Vanzetti case, and the Ku Klux Klan. The drastic curtailment of immigration became a fixed part of American law in this period, and preoccupation with "national origin" moved from the meeting halls of superpatriotic groups into the nation's statute books.

Immigration restriction was an issue which revealed a peculiar weakness in the progressive movement—the failure on the part of many progressives to see the connection between the injustice of monopoly and that of nativism. Men who loudly denounced economic inequality remained silent on the issue of national superiority. The one progressive who consistently and loudly opposèd the new quota laws was the only one who himself came from an urban community of recent immigrants—Fiorello La-Guardia. His actions attempted to move progressivism toward maturity on this question and thus, in a series of quick flashes, illuminated the future, when the New Deal descendants of the progressive movement would woo and win the immigrant masses of the nation's great cities.

LaGuardia was not in Congress when the Immigration Act of 1921 established for the first time a quota system, limiting the annual immigration from any nation to 3 per cent of the number of that country's nationals living in the United States in 1910. His views on the subject, however, were known to all. If anyone had doubts, his sharp attacks on immigration restriction in his New York *Evening Journal* articles in the summer of 1922 laid them to rest. And when his election to Congress in November, 1922, brought him back into national politics, he began immediately with a barrage against nativism that reached its climax during the furious congressional debates over the 1924 Immigration Act.

Before the Sixty-eighth Congress convened in the spring of 1923, nothing could be done legislatively on immigration restriction, so LaGuardia concentrated on the administration of existing law. His years on Ellis Island had shown him the cruelty involved in the rejection of immigrants on technical grounds and in the arbitrary separation of families. Thus, shortly after his election in 1922, when a young Italian girl named Giuseppina Licata, whose entry was barred because she suffered from trachoma, asked a delay in her deportation so that her mother might return with her, the Department of Labor refused her request, and LaGuardia was asked for aid. He swiftly dispatched a telegram to Secretary of Labor James J. Davis in Washington, saying:

We may as well understand each other at once. You and your department cruel, inhuman, narrow-minded, prejudiced. Attitude toward immigrants and unwarranted interpretation law been rebuked all over the country. . . . This attitude must change at once. I will not tolerate any more this hard-hearted treatment of immigrants. I insist upon this stay being granted. Am going to start fight this cruel, inhuman system at once. I am serving in next House and hope we get along but if you want to fight I will give department all it wants and start fight from Washington down.[1]

Davis replied tersely that he was simply obeying the law.

When LaGuardia could not get action from the Department of Labor, he went higher. He did not hesitate to interrupt Warren Harding, vacationing on a houseboat in Florida, to tell him of the plight of three hundred Jewish immigrants awaiting deportation to Ellis Island because the quotas had been filled while they were en route to America. Most of these had debarked from Greece and Turkey and return to those countries might endanger

[1] Nov. 14, 1922, LaG. Papers.

them, LaGuardia said. He urged Harding to delay their deportation until the quota opened again, telegraphing: "I appeal to you for the sake of humanity and charity to do something in these distressing cases affecting hundreds of families. Were it not for extreme nature of situation would not disturb you at this time. I implore you to act in the matter and prevent sorrow, distress and ruin to so many people." [2] Harding complied.

The lame duck Congress in early 1923 began consideration of a new immigration law, designed to restrict even further the flow of immigrants from southern and eastern Europe. LaGuardia wrote to Frank Mondell, Republican majority leader in the House, charging that the Department of Labor, which was backing the bill, was "susceptible to British influence." He asserted:

The proposed law is no doubt the result of an alliance between the bigoted and narrow-minded, nursing religious and racial hatreds, and the British steamship companies. Such a change would immediately throw a large passenger trade to the Northern ports now entirely controlled by the British steamship companies.[3]

The position of the Coolidge administration pleased the restrictionists and irritated LaGuardia. Coolidge had maintained a firm silence on the Klan in his 1924 campaign, while his running mate, Charles G. Dawes, as LaGuardia put it, "praised it with faint damn." The President's first annual message to Congress, emphasizing that "America must be kept American," was looked upon by proponents of immigration restriction as dealing with that question "in a constructive manner." [4]

Almost as soon as the debate over rules ended in the first session of the Sixty-eighth Congress, the House began consideration of a bill sponsored by Congressman Albert Johnson of Washington, chairman of the House Immigration Committee. This bill aimed to move from 1910 to 1890 the base year in which the estimated number of foreign-born people of each nationality determined how many immigrants were admitted from that nation. Since in 1890 there were far less Americans from eastern and

[2] New York *Times*, March 24, 1923; also, copy of wire to Harding, LaG. Papers.

[3] New York *Times*, Feb. 25, 1923.

[4] Roy L. Garis, *Immigration Restriction* (New York, 1928), 169–170.

southern Europe, the effect would be to reduce drastically immigration from Italy, Poland, Russia, and the Balkans. Furthermore, the percentage of each national group to be admitted was reduced in the Johnson Bill from 3 per cent to 2 per cent. From the start LaGuardia took the leadership of those forces opposing the bill, and he was joined by Congressman Adolph Sabath of Illinois, as well as Emanuel Celler and Samuel Dickstein of New York.

Congressman Elton Watkins of Oregon, supporting the Johnson bill, argued that "we have too many aliens in this country and . . . we want more of the American stock," and he was reinforced by Louis C. Cramton of Michigan, who told the House: "Our trouble is that in the city of New York today that foreign population, hugging to their bosoms yet the ideals of the land from which they come while they thrive on the opportunities of this land, is leading in the demand for repudiation of the Constitution." They waved aside LaGuardia's curt question: "Is not this country made up of immigrants no matter what period of history you take?" [5]

National pride and racial consciousness swelled as the debate wore on. Grant M. Hudson of Michigan said: "We are slowly awakening to the consciousness that education and environment do not fundamentally alter racial values." New York's Bertrand Snell added: "It is a fact, not merely an argument, that this country was created, kept united and developed . . . almost entirely by people who came here from the countries of Northern and Western Europe." [6]

LaGuardia told Snell: "I can understand the pride, the pardonable pride in my colleague whose ancestors came here on the *Mayflower,* and I hope that you can understand my pride when I say the distinguished navigator of the race of my ancestors came to this continent two hundred years before yours landed at Plymouth Rock." [7]

Coming to LaGuardia's support on this issue were Congressman Sabath of Illinois [8] and Congressman Dickstein of Manhattan. Dickstein delivered a long and powerful speech on behalf of the immigrant. He concluded by giving the details of an act of hero-

[5] *Congress. Rec.,* 68:1, Feb. 2, 1924, 1896–1902.

[6] *Ibid.,* April 5, 1924, 5641–5643.   [7] *Ibid.,* 5657.   [8] *Ibid.,* 5650–5651.

ism during the war and then recited the names of the eight soldiers who had co-operated in that act: John Bilitzko, Lonnie Moscow, Aloizi Nagowski, Isaac Rabinowitz, Epifanio Affatato, Wasyl Kolonczyk, Daniel Mosckowitz, Antony Sclafoni.[9]

The sentiment back home in New York was unmistakable. During a lull in the House debate, LaGuardia traveled hurriedly to attend a packed meeting at the Brooklyn Jewish Center, protesting against the Johnson bill. The crowd overflowed and extended out into the street. Dickstein, Celler, and LaGuardia spoke, and LaGuardia warned his hearers that if the bill were to come up for a vote the next day it would pass overwhelmingly. He pointed to the consequences of the bill. "The mathematics of the bill disclose the intentional discrimination against the Jews and the Italians. By going back to the figures of the census of 1890, Jewish immigration would be cut from about 80,000 under the present law to less than 4,000. The Italian immigration would be reduced from 45,000 to 3,000." [10]

As the debate continued, the galleries of the House became more crowded and the language more unrestrained. LaGuardia explained his opposition to the bill on the grounds that

it is unscientific, because it doesn't fit with the economic condition of the country, because it is the result of narrowmindedness and bigotry and because it is inspired, prompted and urged by influences . . . who have a fixed obsession on Anglo-Saxon superiority.[11]

His exchange with Congressman J. N. Tincher of Kansas drew from Tincher a classic expression of nativist ideology:

TINCHER: I think this chamber here is a place where we ought to think, act and do real Americanism (Applause). That is what we are elected for and if you thrust open the gates the districts such as we have examples of here will keep increasing until finally when you get up and say "Mr. Speaker" you will have to speak in Italian or some other language. . . .
LaGUARDIA: Will the gentleman yield?
TINCHER: Oh hello, there you are, I knew you would come.
LaGUARDIA: The gentleman doesn't know what he is talking about.
TINCHER: I think the issue is fairly well drawn. On the one side is

9 *Ibid.*, 5654–5657.   10 New York *Times,* March 3, 1924.
11 *Congress. Rec.,* 68:1, April 8, 1924, 5886–5890.

beer, bolshevism, unassimilating settlements and perhaps many flags—
on the other side is constitutional government; one flag, stars and
stripes; a government of, by and for the people; America our country.[12]

On the whole, the western progressives remained silent on the
bill. One notable exception was Congressman Kvale of Minnesota,
who attacked immigration restriction and said: "I will tell you
of the kind of hyphenates you had better worry about. A new
breed that is fast springing up, and they are your native-born,
dollar-a-year, loud-mouthed, flag-waving, 100%, paytriotic, [*sic*]
graft-Americans. These and not your Americans of foreign blood
and language are the menace to America today." [13]

Not only in the House, but in the Senate too, the Progressives
west of the Mississippi did not show the same militancy on immigration restriction that they did on issues of labor or monopoly.
William E. Borah's correspondence during this period is revealing. A constituent wrote to him: "Immigration should be completely stopped for at least one generation until we can assimilate
and Americanize the millions who are in our midst. . . . We no
longer receive the sturdy immigrants from northern Europe and
those who come from southern and eastern Europe will most certainly degrade the American race." Borah's reply was: "With
reference to the question of immigration I am completely in accord with your views." [14] When the Immigration Act of 1924
was passed by the Senate 62–6, not one of the leading progressives voted against it. La Follette, Wheeler, and Lenroot did not
vote. Borah, Brookhart, Johnson, Norris, and Walsh voted for
the bill.[15]

On the eve of the voting in the House, LaGuardia engaged in
a spirited debate with Kentucky's Fred Vinson, who had referred to
him as heading the "Italian bloc" from New York.[16] When La-
Guardia retorted with a reference to the illiteracy of Kentucky's
mountain folk, Vinson's Kentucky colleague defended his Blue
Ridge constituents in stirring language:

They suckle their Americanism and their patriotism from their
mother's breast and hear the story of the sacrifices and the struggles

[12] *Ibid.*, 5918–5920.   [13] *Ibid.*

[14] M. L. Pearson to Borah, Nov. 2, 1922, Borah Papers, Library of Congress, Washington, D.C.

[15] *Congress. Rec.*, 68:1, April 18, 1924, 6649.

[16] *Ibid.*, April 11, 1924, 6117–6118.

that made this republic on their father's knee, and I resent the gentleman's insolent, infamous, contemptible, slander against a great,
honest, industrious, law-abiding, liberty-loving, God-fearing, patriotic
people.[17]

LaGuardia's last-minute amendment to change the quota year
from 1890 to 1920 was quickly voted down.[18] With the strong
backing of the Coolidge administration,[19] the Johnson bill was
passed by the House, 323–71.[20] Voting for it was LaGuardia's
close associate in the progressive bloc, James Frear of Wisconsin.
Representative Kvale, despite his attack on nativism in debate,
bowed to pressure and voted for it also.[21]

The failure of the 1924 law, even in terms of its own aims, was
to become more and more apparent as the years wore on. Although
the new base year of 1890 gave northern and western Europe a
quota about six times that of southern and eastern Europe (the
ratio had been five to four by the 1921 law),[22] the actual number
of immigrants arriving from northern Europe never matched the
quotas, while southern and eastern Europeans stretched their
quotas to the maximum every year. The crash of 1929 and the
subsequent huge unemployment, coming after five years of drastic
immigration restriction, seemed to indicate that unemployment
and economic crises have roots which go far deeper than immigration policy.[23] As for easing the process of assimilation, Oscar
Handlin has noted that "far from ending, restriction intensified
the group consciousness of the immigrant peoples." [24]

[17] *Ibid.,* April 12, 1924, 6253.   [18] *Ibid.,* 6245.

[19] While Congress was debating the measure, Secretary of Labor Davis
passed on to Coolidge a telegram he had received, denouncing Japanese immigration and asking passage of the Johnson Bill. Davis told Coolidge he
approved the sentiments expressed in the telegram and said: "I go a step
further and advocate the enactment of a law for the annual enrollment of
all aliens" (Coolidge Papers, Library of Congress, Washington, D.C.).

[20] *Congress. Rec.,* 68:1, April 12, 1924, 6258.

[21] Opponents of the bill were singled out by nativist groups for defeat in
the 1924 campaign. The *Fellowship Forum,* Oct. 18, 1924, listing such congressmen, said: "Fiorello LaGuardia was one of the most active hyphenates
in the fight against the 1890 census bill. . . . Vote against LaGuardia."

[22] Edward P. Hutchinson, "Immigration Policy Since World War I," *The
Annals,* CCLXII (March, 1949), 15–21.

[23] William S. Bernard, ed., *American Immigration Policy* (New York,
1950), 55–97.

[24] Oscar Handlin, *The Uprooted* (Boston, 1951), 295.

With the quota restrictions in effect and the chances for repeal extremely slim, LaGuardia began concentrating on amendments to alleviate some of the hardships caused by the bill. In December, 1924 he introduced an amendment to allow the families of citizens and applicants for citizenship to enter the country on a nonquota basis.[25] On the other side of the Capitol, newly elected Senator James Wadsworth of New York began working on a similar measure. Support for easing some of the restrictions came from both inside and outside of Congress. Congressman Ogden Mills received a barrage of racist letters because he expressed support for a measure that would reunite immigrant families.[26] The National Conference of Social Work, meeting in 1925, listened sympathetically to criticism of the new immigration law.[27] *Liberty Magazine*'s editor, William Hard, published data supplied by LaGuardia on two tragic cases where immigrants were deported because of a strict and literal interpretation of the law.[28]

However, these were not enough to offset the heavy-laden atmosphere of Anglo-Saxon supremacy that pervaded the nation in the twenties. Groups like the Sons of the American Revolution were active in marshaling opposition to LaGuardia's amendment.[29] The Chicago *Tribune* wrote that LaGuardia was "foreign-minded" and said: "Mr. LaGuardia looks at American affairs through Italian-tinted glasses. . . . Until several more generations have been born in this country, the thoughts and utterances of men and women concerning the country's welfare and international business must be judged in the light of their ancestry."[30]

In early 1927, LaGuardia succeeded in getting the House to extend nonquota status to the children of American citizens who were between eighteen and twenty-one years old, but with only a few days left in its session, the Senate failed to act and the bill died.[31] The following year, despite angry letters from nativist

[25] *Congress. Rec.,* 68:2, Dec. 6, 1924, 247.

[26] Ogden L. Mills Papers, Library of Congress, Washington, D.C.

[27] *Proceedings of the National Conference of Social Work* (Chicago, 1925), 605.

[28] LaGuardia wire to Marie Fischer, March 6, 1926, LaG. Papers.

[29] 1926 pamphlet, LaG. Papers.   [30] Chicago *Tribune,* Jan. 16, 1926.

[31] LaGuardia wire to *Bollettino Della Sera,* March 2, 1927, LaG. Papers.

groups and labor unions,[32] LaGuardia introduced his bill again and was rebuked by Congressman Johnson of Washington, father of the 1924 Act, who said:

I take this opportunity of saying . . . that I have no feeling of hatred toward any alien whatsoever, but I do have great contempt for alien-minded people in the United States who persist in airing their alien views, and I can not agree with them even if they sit in the House of Representatives.[33]

In the spring of 1928, LaGuardia sorrowfully replied to a letter from a Connecticut man that "the present temper of the House is against any modification of the Immigration Laws." [34]

He continued, however, to point out inconsistencies on the part of those who had asked for immigration restriction. The House listened quietly as he denounced the importation of thousands of Mexican laborers, in violation of the alien contract labor law, by "greedy exploiters" who spoke loudly against European immigration.[35] He never lost the opportunity to point, always with scorn, to the stream of titled and penniless exiles from the cast-out royal families of Europe, who came to America to be feted by awe-struck and titleless American millionaires. He even accused these "repudiated, unemployed, and shiftless Dukes and Grand Dukes" of plotting the return of monarchy to America.[36]

The severe restriction of immigration brought about by the 1924 law was still insufficient for many guardians of the "Anglo-Saxon" character of the American people. Many undesirables were already in the country, they asserted, spreading crime, disease, and revolution. Hence, the spring of 1926 saw a rash of alien deportation bills, setting forth certain conditions under which aliens might be deported to the countries of their origin. One was the Manlove bill, giving aliens under forty who had

[32] The Central Craft of Chicago wrote LaGuardia Nov. 21, 1927, that in opposing the Johnson bill he "voted against the best interest of American workmen" (*ibid.*).

[33] *Congress. Rec.,* Jan. 9, 1928, 1252.

[34] LaGuardia to William Renatore, March 24, 1928, LaG. Papers.

[35] *Congress. Rec.,* 68:2, Jan. 27, 1925, 2533.

[36] New York *Times,* Jan. 16, 1925. *Time Magazine* in reporting LaGuardia's accusation (Jan. 26, 1925) referred to him as the "smiling, swarthy, confident little Socialist from New York . . . with a voice twice the size of himself."

been in the United States for five years and had not applied for citizenship one year to do so or be deported.[37] This did not get very far, for the chairman of the House Immigration Committee, Albert Johnson, had his own pet deportation bill, and it was this bill, twenty pages long, which became the object of an intense struggle on the floor of the House.

The Deportation bill of 1926 simply made more drastic the deportation provisions of the 1924 Act. It increased from five to seven years the time after entry during which an alien became deportable for insanity, for "chronic alcoholism," for becoming a public charge, and for "constitutional psychopathic inferiority," with the burden of proof on the alien to show that the condition did not exist at the time he entered the country. It also extended from five to ten years the time in which an alien was deportable for having committed a crime involving imprisonment of one year. "Gentlemen," Johnson told the House, "this is not a vicious bill." [38] But LaGuardia, Victor Berger, Sabath, Dickstein, and others disagreed, Berger pointing out that under this bill persons sent to prison for political reasons were deportable.[39]

In order to speed the Deportation bill's passage, the House, by a two-thirds vote, suspended the rules to forbid any amendments and to limit debate to forty minutes. LaGuardia managed to get the floor to say heatedly: "I venture the statement that a bill coming from the Committee on Agriculture and dealing with livestock would not be considered in this fashion." The deportation provisions, he noted, could be used to intimidate labor, since men sentenced to prison for picketing would be liable for deportation, even if the arrest occurred nine years after entry into the country. Furthermore, people arrested for their unorthodox views would come within the purview of the bill. "In this day of suppression of speech," LaGuardia said, "and with the wave of intolerance that is now sweeping the country, a man might find himself behind the bars for a period of one year and deported for the mere expression of an opinion." To bear out his statement, he pointed to the recent sentencing of a New Yorker to imprisonment for more than a year because he had read the Constitution on the steps of a city hall in New Jersey.[40] But the bill passed.

In the last two years of the Coolidge administration, LaGuardia

[37] *Congress. Rec.,* 69:1, April 6, 1926.   [38] *Ibid.,* June 7, 1926, 10861.
[39] *Ibid.,* 10818.   [40] *Ibid.,* June 7, 1926, 10861–10863.

stood watch against what he considered still another attempt to restrict the freedoms of noncitizens. Congressman Blanton of Texas introduced a bill in 1926 providing for the registration of aliens, and when two years of stubborn opposition by a small House bloc prevented its passage, the Department of Labor moved on its own to require all aliens to carry identification cards. LaGuardia could not get the order revoked and sent a blistering telegram to Secretary of Labor Davis, calling the order "outrageous and indecent" and saying:

This order marking immigrants for life is result of insistence of Ku Klux Klan. I challenge you to disprove this statement stop You would not dare to issue the order yourself and you waited until you were out of city to have an employee do it stop. . . . This double crossing double-dealing must be exposed.[41]

Trying to bring the pressure of the labor movement to bear on Davis, LaGuardia wired William Green, president of the American Federation of Labor, saying that the requirement for registration cards "will submit every worker to inquisition and molestation on alleged ground of determining identity." [42] Green replied several weeks later with a letter saying that the A. F. of L. was opposed to alien registration, but he did not believe that the identity card order embodied the registration principle.[43] LaGuardia, looking about anxiously for support at this point, appealed to his old associate, Edward Keating, editor of *Labor,* writing him:

This whole scheme of bringing about registration after Congress has repeatedly refused to consider it, I charge, is nothing but a scheme of the Manufacturers Association and the open shop champions bent upon getting cheap labor and keeping employees under a constant state of intimidation.[44]

Davis, however, persisted in seeing the plan through, saying it was for the benefit of the immigrant himself and was simply aimed at preventing bootleg immigration.

The 1924 Act had provided that a new quota system, based not upon resident nationals but upon the "national origin" of the entire population, would go into effect in 1927. LaGuardia and other foes of restrictive legislation kept up a barrage of ide-

[41] June 26, 1928, LaG. Papers.   [42] July 12, 1928, *ibid.*
[43] July 12, 1928, *ibid.*   [44] July 13, 1928, *ibid.*

ological warfare against the "national origins" concept. The November, 1928, issue of *Current History* featured an exchange of
opposing views, "The National Origins Quota System," by author
David Orebaugh and LaGuardia. Orebaugh sounded an alarm:

The time to gird our loins for battle is here and now. The crisis is
upon us. . . . If it fails to maintain the barrier of immigration restriction, America will have demonstrated its incapacity further to
resist the inroads of the degeneracy which arises from the mixture
of unassimilable and disharmonic races and which has spelled the
decline and fall of many great nations in the past.

LaGuardia replied by calling the plan "the creation of a narrow
mind, nurtured by a hating heart." The New York *World* also
criticized the new system, saying: "Its scientific value is dubious,
while it is certain to cause confusion, inconvenience and a revival
of racial jealousies and resentments." [45] Even proponents of drastic
restriction found the plan unworkable.[46]

The national origins plan was delayed for two years, but the
pressure for putting it into effect grew irresistible. While small
and unpopular civil liberties groups had to carry the brunt of
the battle against it, wealthy and powerful organizations insisted,
in a barrage of wires and letters to Congress, that it be activated.
Paul V. McNutt, national commander of the American Legion,
wired key members of the Senate and House in early 1929 that
the Legion wanted the national origins plan to go into effect by
July 1, pointing to the unanimous vote of one thousand delegates
to the Legion convention in favor of the plan.[47] In 1929 the national origins quota system was put into operation by President
Hoover. LaGuardia had swum with powerful strokes, but with
increasing futility, against the nativist tidal wave of the twenties.

[45] April 25, 1929.

[46] Secretary of Commerce Herbert Hoover preferred the old 1890 census
quota, according to William Starr Myers and Walter H. Newton, *The
Hoover Administration* (New York, 1936), 376. Cabinet members Hoover,
James Davis, and Frank Kellogg, on a committee designated to work out the
quota allotments, reported to the President that "in our opinion the statistical and historical information available raise grave doubts as to the
whole value of these computations as a basis for the purposes intended"
(*Current History*, XXIX [Nov., 1928], 223–230).

[47] Feb. 19, 1929, LaG. Papers.

8 · The Legacy of the Red Scare

THE anti-radical hysteria engendered by the war did not end with the coming of the Armistice. In the twenties, "patriotic" societies bloomed abundantly all over the American landscape,[1] and the decade saw a wave of textbook-purging, teacher loyalty oaths, Ku Klux Klan activity, and court decisions unfavorable to civil liberties. Referring to the twenties as a whole, Robert K. Murray notes that "insistence upon ideological conformity, suspicion for organized labor, public intolerance toward aliens and a hatred for Soviet Russia" were hang-overs from the postwar Red scare.[2] Climaxing it all was perhaps the most celebrated civil liberties case in American history, a strange mixture of nativism, antiradicalism, murder, perjury, and high drama—the case of Sacco and Vanzetti.

When a list was compiled, in the mid-1920's, of those Americans who had most often been attacked by the "100% Americans," Fiorello LaGuardia occupied a conspicuous place.[3] Aside from his incessant attempts to lift immigration restrictions, LaGuardia ranged himself on the side of every victim of the jingoist, antiradical, and anti-Negro feeling which pervaded the era. He saw through the twin shams of patriotism and prosperity; the roar of

[1] Robert K. Murray, *Red Scare: A Study in National Hysteria* (Minneapolis, 1955), 264.

[2] *Ibid.*

[3] Norman Hapgood, ed., *Professional Patriots* (New York, 1927), 197.

97

the twenties, he knew, was not simply the spontaneous rumble that accompanies well-being, but also, in part, a deliberate attempt to drown out the voices of dissent.

LaGuardia's concern for free speech had been evident ever since his criticism of the Espionage Act during his first months in Congress. As president of the Board of Aldermen he had denounced in powerful language the ousting of socialists by the New York State Assembly and the Lusk Laws. During his 1922 congressional campaign he had, in the New York *Evening Journal*, attacked a film censorship law passed by the legislature. In this statement, LaGuardia revealed an approach to civil liberties which he maintained throughout his time in Congress, what might be called an "economic interpretation" of free speech. That is, LaGuardia saw a crucial link between the right of dissent and the existence of economic inequality. The safeguarding of the first, he felt, was essential to insure the removal of the second. Accordingly, he wrote:

Censorship has always been the handmaid of oppression. Censorship is an agency for the prevention of thought. . . . Censorship in any form has always been found useful to those who have a purpose and interest in thwarting the exchange of thought and the expression of protest against unfair economic conditions.[4]

The real purpose of film censorship, he maintained, was to prevent the production of films which would reveal important economic truths:

Think of a film illustrating to the millions of American people the quantity of food produced in this country, and how it is monopolized by a few and kept in storage so as to keep prices high; how prices are artificially fixed; how much good food is permitted to rot, while many cannot afford the mere necessities of life. Think of a picture giving the history of a lump of coal. Showing how it is mined and transported, what part of it goes to pay for labor and what big majority goes to the coupons cut by persons thousands of miles away who have taken no risks and contributed no thought, no labor, no effort towards its production. Think of a picture showing how public officials are selected by a hand-picked convention controlled by those who profit in the exploitation of the masses.

[4] New York *Evening Journal*, Aug. 3, 1922.

LaGuardia reacted indignantly to the passage by the legislature of loyalty tests for school teachers. "No citizen should be compelled to submit to a test of his political affiliations, his theories of economic questions and his views on necessary government reforms. . . . One school teacher is more valuable to a democracy than three generals or two ministers." [5]

Several years later, when the Sixty-ninth Congress was discussing a school appropriation bill for the District of Columbia, LaGuardia listened to Congressman Blanton of Texas warn his House colleagues: "I want you to know that in the colleges and universities of the United States you had better pay some attention to what is going on before you send your boys there." LaGuardia rose to his feet and replied:

Of course we are to have criticism of government in the study of civics and political history. If anyone who criticizes our form of government is guilty of a serious crime, then Abraham Lincoln was guilty of such a charge. . . . We can not stand still in the science of government. . . . As times change so must your government change. . . . At this time there seems to be a wave of intolerance in thought and everything else. . . . Our children are safe in the schools; they are learning to think; and as they grow up they will be able to look after their government and to make laws to meet changed conditions and to bring about a more equal distribution of happiness and the good things of life. [6]

Despite his concern with maintaining the right of people like himself to criticize the existing economic order, he also defended the right to free speech of those with whom he disagreed. LaGuardia's old foe on the Board of Estimate, Charles Craig, had been sentenced to prison for sixty days by a federal judge for writing a letter criticizing an action by that judge. The decision was appealed to the Supreme Court, and Chief Justice Taft wrote the majority opinion upholding it, with Holmes and Brandeis dissenting. LaGuardia sprang immediately to Craig's defense, saying that he would introduce a bill in the House to prevent the carrying out of Craig's sentence. City officials, he declared, must be free to criticize the courts. [7] Similarly, when a Communist member of the British Parliament, Shapurji Saklatvala, was prevented from entering the United States by Secretary of State

[5] *Ibid.*, Aug. 22, 1922. [6] *Congress. Rec.*, 69:1, March 16, 1926, 5748.
[7] New York *Times*, Nov. 20, 1923.

Kellogg, LaGuardia joined Frank Walsh and Samuel Untermyer in asking for the lifting of the ban. He called Kellogg's decision "a stupid act of a stupid man."[8]

One of the new patriotic societies which sprang up in the United States after the Armistice was the Military Order of the World War. In 1927, LaGuardia and the Order collided head-on over a meeting of the American Civil Liberties Union at Stuyvesant High School in Manhattan, at which LaGuardia was one of the speakers. The American Civil Liberties Union had fought for a year to get permission from the Board of Education to hold a meeting in a public school, and Chairman Harry F. Ward of the Union Theological Seminary noted this when he began the meeting. He then introduced Protestant minister Charles N. Lathrop, who told the audience:

Somehow I feel disturbed when I think of how the people in New York City live. There is one family I visit occasionally, living in four small rooms in a towering tenement, three small children, the father and mother living in those rooms. Always when I go there . . . everything seems in disorder . . . and the father trying to earn enough to support his family. . . . As I look at these homes I think of the homes in the coal mine districts and cannot help but compare them with the palace of the owner of those mines—a veritable Italian villa. . . . I want more clean houses with a reasonable amount of light and fresh air. I want houses that have room enough for a couple who marry and for their children as well as for themselves.[9]

The Military Order of the World War issued a press release on the meeting, quoting Lathrop's speech and then commenting in capital letters: "NOTE THE DOCTRINE OF SOCIALISM IN THE STIRRING UP OF CLASS CONSCIOUSNESS AND A TENDENCY TO BLAME CONDITIONS UPON THE 'SOCIAL ORDER' RATHER THAN UPON THE INDIVIDUAL."[10]

LaGuardia, in his remarks at that A.C.L.U. meeting, criticized the use of judicial review by the Supreme Court in recent decisions. He also made some reference to the fact that conservatives favored the commission form of government, and the Order, calling attention to this, said: "NOTE THE ATTACK ON THE SUPREME

[8] *Ibid.*, Sept. 29, 1925.

[9] Press release of Military Order of the World War, June, 1927, LaG. Papers.

[10] *Ibid.*

COURT, THE CONSTITUTION AND THE APPEAL FOR FREE SPEECH AND
PARTICULARLY THE REFERENCE TO 'THE COMMISSION FORM OF GOV-
ERNMENT' WHICH BORDERS CLOSELY UPON THE SOVIET IDEA OF GOV-
ERNMENT BY COMMITTEES." In a letter to A.C.L.U. official Morris
L. Ernst, LaGuardia, aroused by the distortion of his remarks,
said:

The person who drafted and compiled my remarks with deductions
which he draws is not only an artistic liar, but in good plain military
language, may I be permitted to state, in all candor and calmness, that
he is only an everyday ordinary son-of-a-bitch. I hope I have made
myself sufficiently clear.[11]

Throughout this period, the case of Sacco and Vanzetti was
getting an increasing amount of attention by the nation. The
"skilled shoemaker" Sacco and the "poor fish-peddler" Vanzetti
had been in jail for two years (after their conviction before Judge
Thayer in the Dedham, Massachusetts, courtroom on charges of
armed robbery and murder in 1921) when the Sacco-Vanzetti
Defense Committee contacted LaGuardia. LaGuardia talked to
Attorney Fred H. Moore, who had helped with the trial defense,
and then flew to Boston to interview Vanzetti. He found the behavior of the convicted man disturbing and later said that he
could get no real information from the interview because Vanzetti
just walked back and forth and denounced the "class war" which
had victimized him and his friend.[12] Nevertheless, LaGuardia
was convinced the men had not received a fair trial and agreed
to aid in preparing briefs asking for another trial based on new
evidence.[13] The motions for a new trial were eventually denied

[11] June, 1927, *ibid.;* also, New York *Times,* June 10, 1927.

[12] Ernest Cuneo, *Life With Fiorello* (New York, 1955), 107, says: "I once
asked Fiorello if he had taken any active part in the Sacco Vanzetti case. . . .
He said he had gone to the prison and spoken to both men, but had been
unable to get any direct answers to his questions. He described Sacco grip-
ping the bars of his cell and staring past him, repeating over and over: 'The
world will be cleansed by my blood.' It was obviously an unpleasant subject
for Fiorello, and I never brought it up again."

[13] Among the data LaGuardia helped to present were: the repudiation of
their testimony by two of the witnesses for the prosecution; the additional
testimony of an eyewitness to the crime that Sacco and Vanzetti were not the
bandits; the disclosure that a key prosecution witness, Carlos Goodridge,
was really a fugitive from justice and a twice-convicted criminal at the very

by Judge Thayer, as were four other motions filed in the three years following the conviction.[14] In 1926–1927 a request for a new trial based on the confession of one Celestino Madeiros was rejected first by Judge Thayer and then by the Supreme Court of Massachusetts. In April, 1927, the sentence of death was pronounced on both defendants.

With the execution set for August, the entire nation became alive with excitement and angry controversy. Prominent figures from other countries began a campaign of protest against what they believed to be an act of vengeance directed at two men who were both foreigners and anarchists. In July, Governor Fuller of Massachusetts was besieged with requests for executive clemency, and he appointed a distinguished advisory committee to guide him in his decision.[15] LaGuardia had faith in Governor Fuller's sense of justice, saying, "He is free from bigotry and prejudice and will investigate fairly and fully." [16]

However, abiding by the recommendation of his Committee, Fuller refused to change the verdict. Last-minute requests to assume jurisdiction were turned down by the federal courts, and with only a few days left, the defenders of Sacco and Vanzetti tried frantically to rouse public opinion. The tension became almost unbearable. Police details were set up to guard subway, railroad, and steamship terminals. Special guards were posted around important buildings and the homes of public officials. A uniformed detachment was dispatched to the West 14th Street pier in Manhattan, where Vanzetti's sister was due to arrive from Italy on the "Aquitania." On the eve of the execution, LaGuardia agreed to address a protest rally called by Socialists in the Community

time he testified; photo micrographs allegedly proving that the fatal bullet which killed a guard could not have come from the gun supposed to be Sacco's (press release, June 11, 1923, LaG. Papers).

14 Louis Joughin and Edmund M. Morgan, *The Legacy of Sacco and Vanzetti* (New York, 1948), 3–25.

15 Heywood Broun later commented bitterly in a column which became a journalistic classic: "If this is a lynching, at least the fish peddler and his friend the factory hand may take unction to their souls that they will die at the hands of men in dinner coats or academic gowns."

16 New York *World,* July 8, 1927. Close students of the case say LaGuardia should have known better, having heard Fuller vent strong antagonism toward Victor Berger and other radicals (Joughin and Morgan, *op. cit.,* 299).

Church in Manhattan.[17] The meetings were held, the speeches were heard, and the crowds quietly went home with no outbreaks of violence. On August 23, 1927, a few minutes after midnight, Sacco and Vanzetti were electrocuted.

A funeral procession through Manhattan, bearing the ashes of Sacco and Vanzetti, was planned by members of a memorial committee, but permission was refused by Police Commissioner Warren on grounds of "insufficient information." LaGuardia wrote a letter for two members of the committee to take to the Commissioner. It was couched in the most gentle language he could muster:

This will introduce Mr. Charles Harrison and Mrs. Clarina Michelson, who have been entrusted with the preparation for the funeral procession of the Sacco and Vanzetti ashes. As you perhaps know, Miss Luigia Vanzetti is taking the ashes of her brother back to Italy and she is naturally coming through New York on her way home. I am confident that there will not be the slightest disorder in any manner, shape or form. I believe that I know the temperament of the people somewhat and can assure you that the procession will be carried on with all solemnity and decorum fitting its purpose. A refusal of a permit for this purpose would be misunderstood not only by a great body of people in New York City but all over the world. Trusting you will give this matter your favorable consideration.[18]

The reply was given by Chief Inspector Lahey: "There will be no parade of sympathizers bearing the ashes of Bartolomeo Vanzetti through the streets of New York on Monday or on any other day." [19] The case of Sacco and Vanzetti, it appeared, was closed.

Despite the deep feeling of frustration that accompanied his efforts in the Sacco and Vanzetti case, LaGuardia continued to raise his voice wherever he felt the right of dissent was being impaired. He was invited to a Philadelphia conference of the American Academy of Political and Social Science in late 1928 and led a discussion on "Freedom of Speech in the United States," tying together the procedural right to free speech with the substantive issue of world peace:

[17] New York *Evening Graphic,* Aug. 19, 1927.
[18] New York *Times,* Aug. 27, 1927.
[19] New York *Daily News,* Aug. 27, 1927.

If the future of our Republic depends upon the suppression of free speech, there is no future. The right to criticize public officials is not only wholesome, but necessary in a republic. . . . Haven't I the right to say that war is stupid, that war is unnecessary, that war is brutal? Show me the man that protests against the peace movements and I'll show you one that was not within hundreds of miles of the front. Show me the man that protests against the limitation of armament and I'll show you a war profiteer.[20]

In the summer of 1929, the United States Supreme Court ruled that Rosika Schwimmer could be denied American citizenship because she refused to swear she would bear arms to defend the United States.[21] LaGuardia defended not only her right to express her ideas but also the validity of the ideas themselves. Writing in the New York *Evening Graphic,* he said:

Rosika Schwimmer has been denied the privilege of becoming an American citizen. . . . She may be ridiculed by munition makers, war profiteers, and payroll jingoists, but her name will be known to future generations and inscribed in history's roll of honor when the names of the war profiteers will be carded and indexed along with the criminals of the twentieth century. The Supreme Court of the United States sustained the decision of the Federal judge, holding that Miss Rosika Schwimmer was unworthy of becoming an American citizen because she stated that she would not throw a hand grenade to kill another person and that she would refuse to jab a bayonet through the body of another human being.[22]

He took this occasion to note the irony of the court decision in view of the fact that the United States, only a few months before, had led forty nations of the world in signing the Kellogg-Briand Pact, renouncing war as an instrument of national policy.

A good part of the intolerance of the twenties was directed against Negroes. The Ku Klux Klan, reformed in 1915, became a powerful force after 1920, and by the middle of the decade perhaps four or five million Americans had joined.[23] It declared, at

[20] New York *Times,* Nov. 17, 1928.

[21] *Schwimmer* v. *United States,* 279 U.S. 644 (1929).

[22] From undated copy of column in *Evening Graphic,* June, 1929, LaG. Papers.

[23] Preston Slosson, *The Great Crusade and After, 1914–1928* (New York, 1930), 307–308.

the end of the war, that it stood for "uniting native-born white Christians for concerted action in the preservation of American institutions and the supremacy of the white race." [24] At least seventy Negroes were lynched in a series of frenzied race riots which swept the nation in the latter part of 1919. In 1925 Detroit was stirred by a dramatic murder trial following the killing of a white man during an attack on the home of a Negro doctor who had moved into a white community. The war for democracy, many Negroes pointed out sorrowfully, had brought no end to discrimination, segregation, and violence.[25]

Fiorello LaGuardia reacted as sharply to anti-Negro attitudes as to nativist attacks upon the foreign-born and expressed his sentiments a number of times in the House of Representatives. Congress was debating in the summer of 1926 an appropriation for Howard University in Washington, D.C., a Negro college which had been founded by the Freedmen's Bureau in 1867 and had received federal support ever since then. A number of congressmen from the deep South expressed opposition to the appropriation, with Congressman Lowrey of Mississippi doubting that federal support for Howard had ever been justified and Congressman Almon of Alabama calling the bill "discriminatory." Congressman John J. McSwain of South Carolina questioned the value of academic education for Negroes, saying: "Well, the colored race ought to excel in athletics, we can easily understand that; but we are here and now talking about education of the brain." Others charged that undue political pressure had been brought to bear by Negro constituents upon their congressmen for passage of the bill. This brought LaGuardia into the debate. He retorted that politics certainly was involved and that he was glad of it. He said:

My advice to the colored people is to keep in politics, so that their race will get all of their rights guaranteed to them under the Constitution. A theoretical equality is not sufficient. . . . Instead of criticizing the colored people for bringing pressure to bear, I praise them. They have only learned that from the whites. In this instance political pressure is brought to bear for a lofty, useful and altruistic purpose.[26]

[24] John Hope Franklin, *From Slavery to Freedom* (New York, 1956), 471.
[25] *Ibid.*   [26] *Congress. Rec.,* 69:1, July 1, 1926, 12585.

The anti-Negro feeling of some congressmen was brought into public view again in the spring of 1929, when the newly elected Representative Oscar De Priest of Chicago prepared to take his seat in Congress. A number of congressmen from the South expressed their displeasure at the thought of a Negro occupying an office near them. LaGuardia promptly wired Nicholas Longworth, saying: "I shall be glad to have him next to my office." [27]

Harlem's Negro population remembered this when LaGuardia came to be mentioned as a possible candidate for the 1929 mayoralty race. He was invited to speak at the Beth-El African Methodist Church on 132nd Street and took the occasion to berate Tammany for practicing what he claimed was race prejudice. He also took to task Federal Judge Martineau, a native of Arkansas, who sat in the New York district and who a week before had criticized a Brooklyn jury for acquitting a Negro prisoner. "We will not stand for Jim Crow laws or for Jim Crow judges here," LaGuardia told his predominantly Negro audience. "We don't want any judges or other public men here who do more credit to the spirit of the Ku Klux Klan and the ignorance of the provincial backwoods than to the democracy and equality of opportunity of our land." [28] The meeting responded with what may have been more welcome to LaGuardia than applause—an endorsement of his candidacy for mayor.

[27] New York *Evening Journal,* April 10, 1929.
[28] New York *Times,* July 29, 1929.

9 · *Pointing to a New Foreign Policy*

IF LaGuardia, in the twenties, represented the Progressive link with the New Deal in his urban-immigrant orientation and his rejection of nativism, he was also a harbinger of that "good neighbor" policy in Latin America and of the active concern with European affairs which marked the years of Franklin D. Roosevelt.[1] He opposed economic imperialism in Latin America, whether supported by dollars or bayonets, asked the United States to encourage liberation movements in other parts of the globe (Ireland, in particular), and vigorously urged participation in all international agreements designed to prevent war.

American "isolationism" in the twenties, like the "prosperity" of the twenties, has often been exaggerated, to a great extent because students of the period have concentrated on American rejection of the League and World Court.[2] The fact was that the

[1] Lubell, *op. cit.*, 140–141, talks about the "alliance of leftist economics and isolationism" in the interwar period. With reservations about the validity of the term "isolationism" his observation is true about a number of progressives but does not apply to LaGuardia. This suggests that in foreign policy, as in other areas, the progressive movement was not monolithic, and its component elements should be carefully distinguished from one another.

[2] William A. Williams, "The Legend of Isolationism in the 1920's," *Science and Society*, XVIII (Winter, 1954) has as his thesis the idea that "far from isolation, the foreign relations of the United States from 1920 through 1942 were marked by express and extended involvement with—and intervention in the affairs of—other nations of the world." He claims that

United States emerged from the war as the industrial and financial leader of the world and would therefore, regardless of its participation or nonparticipation in political agreements, play the key role in the world economy.[3] It was the leading producer of coal, pig iron, and petroleum, creditor of most of Europe, and investor in enterprises which ringed the globe. The nation's economic nationalism—its insistence on war debt payments[4] and towering tariff barriers—was a reflection perhaps, not of isolationism, but of an intervention in world affairs based on cash returns rather than democratic ideals.

Despite the Wilsonian cry for self-determination in the peace treaties, the United States was established as a dominant power in the Caribbean, having purchased the Virgin Islands during the war, possessing a naval base in Cuba, and exercising such control over the Republic of Panama, Nicaragua, Haiti, and the Dominican Republic as to make them "virtual protectorates."[5] Furthermore, American influence in the Far East extended from the Aleutian Islands to Hawaii and across the western Pacific to the Philippines. If the nation was really "isolationist" in the twenties, the term was most applicable in relation to Europe.[6] The over-all

---

opponents of the League, like Lodge and Borah, did not base their opposition on isolationist grounds. Usually, students of foreign policy have demeaned the anti-isolationist significance of the Washington Conference of 1922, but Charles Evans Hughes's biographer believes it "brought the United States back into world councils for the first time since the tragic debacle over the Treaty of Versailles" (Merlo J. Pusey, *Charles Evans Hughes* [New York, 1951], 522).

[3] Foster Rhea Dulles, *America's Rise to World Power* (New York, 1954), 128, says: "The implications of its new power could not be brushed aside by President Harding's strictures against 'internationality.' "

[4] The State Department, throughout the twenties, exercised strong influence on private loans to other nations, chiefly in order to apply pressure for the payment of war debts, but also in order to ensure political "stability" in certain areas, like the Caribbean. Herbert Feis writes that in this period: "We acted as banker to the whole needy world. Private capital provided the funds. But the American Government concerned itself with the lending operations" (*The Diplomacy of the Dollar 1919–1932* [Baltimore, 1950], 4–25).

[5] Dulles, *America's Rise,* 134.

[6] And even here, it may be argued, there was no great overt crisis to demand American action. Perhaps "intervention" is more accurately measured in relative terms—that is, in relation to the extent of crisis demanding action.

American position in the world was such that Reinhold Niebuhr could write in early 1930 of the nation's "awkward imperialism." [7]

LaGuardia's position in the twenties, for nonintervention in Latin America and for activity in Europe, cannot easily be viewed through the traditional concepts of "interventionism" versus "isolationism." He was concerned about ends, not means, and hewed rigorously to the aim of creating independent and democratic nations, whether such results could be brought about in a particular instance by intervening or by desisting from intervention.

It was a moralistic interventionism which had led LaGuardia to support World War I, to urge encouragement of the Russian revolutionaries in 1917, and to attempt to foment revolutions in Central Europe during the war. In the 1920's this spirit found a base of operations in Ireland. When the British imprisoned the American-born Irish nationalist leader Eamon de Valera in early 1924, LaGuardia introduced a resolution in the House declaring that de Valera's imprisonment without trial was "against the morals, custom, and policy of liberty-loving people in this advanced age." He asked that the Secretary of State protest to the English government.[8] Telegrams of thanks to LaGuardia for his stand came from mass meetings of the American Association for Recognition of the Irish Republic, held in various parts of the country. De Valera's mother, living in Rochester, New York, wrote to LaGuardia:

Honorable Sir: I could not let the opportunity pass without expressing my gratitude to you for the generosity you have shown in behalf of my son Eamon De Valera. You well described him as languishing in prison. Let us hope he is not tortured as well. Poor fellow he has done nothing. Only loved Ireland. I hope your kind resolution will bear fruit. I thank you with all the sincerity of a heartbroken mother.[9]

She added a postscript: "You were the only one of many."

When several months passed and still no action had been taken, LaGuardia once again addressed the House, saying: "I think that

[7] "Awkward Imperialists," *Atlantic Monthly*, CXLV (May, 1930), 670–675.
[8] H.R. 208, March 5, 1924; reprint of speech in Congress May 21, 1924, LaG. Papers.
[9] March 8, 1924, *ibid.*

this great Republic of ours has established a record in the history of the world as being ready at all times to assist any people who are striving to attain independence. It is as natural for an American to sympathize with the cause of liberty as it is for a mother to love her own child." [10] LaGuardia was challenged by Representative Holaday, and the following exchange took place:

MR. HOLADAY: Does the gentleman believe that if an American citizen leaves this country and goes to another country, encourages an insurrection or a civil war, becomes a candidate for president of that country, and is elected or defeated, gets in trouble, is entitled to claim the protection of the American government?

MR. LAGUARDIA: I claim . . . it is proper for this House to give its moral support to any people any place in the world who are seeking to govern themselves and seeking to overthrow any foreign sovereign oppression.[11]

The State Department did not act. De Valera was eventually released by the British, only to be imprisoned again in 1929. LaGuardia appeared at a mass protest meeting in New York City and told his audience:

I came here tonight to join with you in protest against another of the many outrages against decency which have been perpetrated by the so-called "Government" of the Northern Six Counties of Ireland. . . . There can be no such thing as a compromise with liberty. . . . When the Irish revolutionists—how I love that word!—when the Irish revolutionists needed money to carry on the war, the people of America responded and . . . I am sure that America will respond again.[12]

LaGuardia's vociferous protest about the situation in Ireland was not matched by any equal activity in connection with the Mussolini regime in Italy, which had come to power in 1922. Throughout the 1920's, many Italian-Americans were attracted to the nationalism of Il Duce, and a schism developed in the Italian community of New York between Fascist supporters and others who were bitterly opposed to the Mussolini government.[13] LaGuardia made no attempt in this period to make clear where

---

[10] *Congress. Rec.*, 68:1, May 21, 1924, 9119.   [11] *Ibid.*
[12] *Irish World*, Feb. 23, 1929, LaG. Papers.
[13] On Decoration Day, 1927, two men were killed in a clash between pro- and anti-Fascists in New York (Federal Writers' Project, *The Italians of New York* [New York, 1938], 101).

he stood on the question. His concern for de Valera's imprisonment in 1924 was not matched, for instance, by any expressed
attitude toward the murder of Socialist deputy Matteotti in the
same year. Norman Thomas has said that "LaGuardia as a politician never wanted to lose the Italian vote, and if you look
through the records you will find that he never really denounced
Italian fascism." [14] Marie Fischer LaGuardia claims, on the other
hand, that LaGuardia was opposed to Mussolini from the start
and was denouncing him at a time when others were saying how
much good he was doing for Italy.[15]

Mrs. LaGuardia may be right, but there is nothing in the
record to prove it, and it seems fair to conclude that, at the least,
LaGuardia was circumspect on this issue for a man who was
forthright on so many others. It is hard to believe that he was not
sensitive to the extent of pro-Mussolini feeling among New York
Italians and aware of how many votes he stood to lose by openly
attacking the Fascist regime. And silence on this would not lose
Jewish support, for there was no such active animosity among
Jews toward Mussolini as existed later toward Hitler. It may be
argued, in defense of LaGuardia, that there was no specific issue
in relation to Fascist Italy which at this time engaged the attention of more than a small handful of Americans.

While, throughout the twenties, the United States seemed
cautious about political intervention in Europe, it displayed no
such hesitation in regard to Latin America. At the same time that
the Coolidge administration was taking halting steps toward the
League of Nations, it was acting with force and determination to
protect American investments and political power in the Caribbean area. By 1924 the finances of half of the twenty Latin-
American states were being directed to some extent by the United
States.[16] When other tactics did not work to assure that the desires
of the American government would be fulfilled, marines were

[14] Interview with Norman Thomas, in Oral History Project, Columbia
University. Thomas says LaGuardia "was magnificent about German naziism,
but never about Italian fascism, although he wasn't a Fascist." As late as
1935, when Italy invaded Ethiopia, Thomas says, he had to argue hard with
LaGuardia not to attend a Madison Square Garden meeting for Italian
relief.

[15] Interview with Mrs. LaGuardia, Aug., 1956.

[16] Bailey, *Diplomatic History*, 711.

dispatched—to Haiti, the Dominican Republic, and Nicaragua. Fiorello LaGuardia was very much aware of the difference between the actual state of affairs and the promise Coolidge had made in his inaugural address, when he said: "America seeks no earthly empire built on blood and force. . . . The legions which she sends forth are armed, not with the sword, but with the cross." [17]

Nicaragua was the focal point of marine diplomacy in the twenties. Her proximity to Panama, and the ever-present possibility of a trans-Nicaraguan canal, gave Nicaragua a special place in the plans of the State Department, while fruit and lumber investments gave American private business groups a sphere of interest there. Ever since 1909, when a United States–aided revolution had overthrown the Liberal Zelaya government, a pattern of Yankee intervention had been established, with bank credits and marines standing guard alternately over shaky conservative governments.[18]

After the withdrawal of the legation guard of marines in 1925, a Liberal revolution got under way, and when rebel forces pushed on toward Managua in spite of progovernment actions by United States naval forces, "American fruit and lumber companies sent daily protests to the State Department." [19] On January 8, 1927, American marines were ordered to station themselves in Fort Loma, commanding the Nicaraguan capital, and two days later Coolidge sent a special message to Congress, saying:

I am sure it is not the desire of the United States to intervene in the internal affairs of Nicaragua or of any other Central American repub-

---

[17] Claude Fuess, *Calvin Coolidge* (Boston, 1940), 362.

[18] Two Americans aiding the rebels had executed the Liberal Zelaya in 1909. In 1911, U.S. warships patrolled both coasts against revolutionary activity. In that year also, the State Department interested American bankers in Nicaragua. In 1912, eight U.S. warships frustrated an attempt to overthrow President Díaz, and the following year a treaty gave the United States exclusive canal rights and naval bases, for three million dollars. Elihu Root commented in 1915 that "the present government with which we are making this treaty is really maintained in office by the presence of the United States marines in Nicaragua." From 1912 to 1925 a legation guard of American marines stood watch over the government (Council on Foreign Relations, *Survey of American Foreign Relations* [New Haven, 1929], 167–197).

[19] *Ibid.*, 192.

lic. Nevertheless, it must be said, that we have a very definite and special interest in the maintenance of order and good government in Nicaragua at the present time.[20]

By February 20, 1927, five thousand United States troops had landed, and several days later the United States gave the Díaz government three thousand rifles, two hundred machine guns, and three million rounds of ammunition.[21]

LaGuardia went into action almost as quickly as had the marines, writing letters to the Secretary of State, issuing releases to the press, taking the floor of the House, keeping up a constant correspondence on the question with constituents. On all these fronts his cry was the same, that American troops must withdraw from Nicaragua.[22] In the Senate, a similar campaign was waged by William E. Borah.[23]

Secretary of State Frank Kellogg explained to the Senate Foreign Relations Committee that the threat of Communist influences in Nicaragua had brought on American intervention. LaGuardia, asked to comment on this statement by the New York *Evening Graphic*, called it "aldermanic stuff." There was no proof of Communist activity in Nicaragua, he said, adding: "The protection of American life and property in Nicaragua does not require the formidable naval and marine forces operating there now. Give me fifty New York cops and I can guarantee full protection." [24] LaGuardia wrote a constituent that Kellogg, back in November, had planted the story of Communist activities in the press by asking various wire services to print such a story

[20] Ruhl J. Bartlett, *The Record of American Diplomacy* (New York, 1954), 546. Graham H. Stuart, *Latin America and the United States* (New York, 1955), 332, says: "The first landing of troops was declared to be solely for the protection of American lives and property, but there was little evidence that American lives and property were in jeopardy."

[21] A government publication, *Relations between the United States and Nicaragua* (Washington, 1928), 43, says: "In entering into the transaction the United States government followed its customary policy of lending encouragement and moral support to constitutional governments beset by revolutionary movements intended to overthrow the established order."

[22] New York *Evening Graphic,* Jan. 14, 1927.

[23] Borah had written two years earlier that the Monroe Doctrine "does not give us the right . . . to invade territory, to tear down governments and set up others" (*Collier's,* LXXV [Jan. 31, 1925], 25).

[24] Jan. 13, 1927, LaG. Papers.

(only Associated Press complied).[25] When LaGuardia made this accusation publicly, the State Department denied it, and when LaGuardia said that he had conferred with Kellogg and had gotten the impression that no forces would be sent to Nicaragua, Kellogg denied the conference had taken place.[26]

Emile Gauvreau, editor of the New York *Daily Mirror,* publicized LaGuardia's position on Nicaragua in this period. LaGuardia wired the *Mirror,* shortly after the marines were sent, that the action could only "play into the hands of people slimy with oil, greedy, and having only their own selfish interests in mind, who are seeking to embroil this country into armed conflict with our sister republics of the south." [27]

In April, 1927, Coolidge, harassed by a nationwide barrage of criticism, ordered Colonel Henry L. Stimson to negotiate peace between the rival factions in Nicaragua.[28] Stimson reported later how he met rebel leader Moncada under "a large black thorn tree" and in thirty minutes reached an agreement on peace terms.[29] This included American supervision of elections to be held in 1929, the appointment of Liberal governors in six of the country's thirteen departments, and the maintenance of marines in Nicaragua.[30]

Following this agreement, LaGuardia kept up a constant barrage of criticism of the provision for the supervision of the elections by marines, suggesting that if supervision were necessary, civilians should be sent. He wrote to the Secretary of State on October 5, 1927:

[25] Letter of Jan. 19, 1927, *ibid.*   [26] LaGuardia to Kellogg, *ibid.*
[27] *Ibid.*

[28] It might be pertinent at this point to wonder to what extent the "isolationism" of the twenties represented a deplorable retreat from international responsibilities (as it has usually been viewed) and to what extent it represented a laudable pacifism and revulsion against interventionism.

[29] Coolidge Papers, Library of Congress, Washington, D.C.

[30] Moncada's willingness to negotiate was born mostly of a sense of futility in the face of overwhelming power. As he stated at the time of his acceptance of the peace terms: "I am not inhuman. For a noble and generous cause I would put myself at the front of the constitutional forces, but I cannot advise the nation to shed all its patriotic blood for our liberty, because in spite of this new sacrifice, this liberty would succumb before infinitely greater forces and the country would sink more deeply within the claws of the North American eagle" (Council on Foreign Relations, *op. cit.,* 195).

May I suggest that this Government assign a group of experienced, sincere, and impartial Americans, unspoiled by diplomatic training and bare of side arms, gatlings, and bombs? Strange as it may seem, it is not the minority down in Nicaragua who need the protection, but it is the majority who want an opportunity to vote without intimidation and molestation. Neither the gold braid of the navy or the spurred boot of the army can assure that confidence of a fair and impartial election necessary to the successful conduct of a democratic government.[31]

Kellogg, treating LaGuardia gingerly as always, replied that the idea would be considered. When, several months later, newspapers reported that an army general, aided by marines, would supervise the elections, LaGuardia wrote again to Kellogg: "Permit me to state, Mr. Secretary, that universal suffrage and the secret ballot are absolutely inconsistent with uniformed marines and fixed bayonets. The two cannot be harmonized." [32]

Stimson, on the other hand, felt that the United States had "no cause to be ashamed" of its effort "to do an unselfish service to a weak and sorely beset Central American State." His argument that the United States had not transgressed upon Nicaraguan sovereignty was based on his belief that every step taken was upon the request of the Nicaraguan government.[33]

The 1929 elections put a Liberal in power in Nicaragua, and, from that point on, relations with the United States, though not ideal, improved somewhat. This process of amelioration in the last years of the Coolidge administration, an adumbration of the "good neighbor" policy, has often been attributed to the wisdom

[31] New York *Times,* Oct. 10, 1927.

[32] *Congress. Rec.,* 70:1, March 23, 1928, 5251–5252. On the other side of the Capitol, George Norris also struck hard at administration policy in Nicaragua. He had written to a constituent: "We are in Nicaragua, sustaining in power a government there that in reality we originally put in power. We are there without the consent of the people of Nicaragua, and, as far as I know, without any right, moral or legal" (Norris to O. D. Shaner, Feb. 14, 1928, Norris Papers, Library of Congress, Washington, D.C.).

[33] Henry L. Stimson, *American Policy in Nicaragua* (New York, 1927), 116, 127. A third viewpoint is that the United States was well meaning but blundering in its policy toward Nicaragua, because it was trying to accomplish two irreconcilable objectives: to supervise Nicaraguan conduct, and to refrain from violating its political integrity (Harold N. Denny, *Dollars for Bullets* [New York, 1929], 384–391).

of the President and his State Department, without giving credit to the salutary prodding by LaGuardia and other American progressives.

During the Coolidge administration, Mexican relations also reached a critical stage. The new Mexican constitution of 1917 had vested ownership of all mineral and oil resources in the Mexican nation. As a result, American recognition of the Republic was delayed until 1923, when Mexico agreed that American rights acquired before 1917 would not be abrogated. When Calles became president in 1924, he insisted that the confiscation provisions of the constitution applied retroactively. The American reaction to this has been described as follows:

The outside world, specifically the United States, was generally unsympathetic, even unfriendly, to the aims of the Revolution. It was viewed narrowly as an unscrupulous attempt to redefine and limit property and contractual rights in a way that not only threatened particular American vested interests in oil, mining and agriculture, but which clashed head-on with an economic internationalism characteristic of the Western World since the 16th century.[34]

On January 12, 1927, Secretary of State Kellogg told the Senate that Bolshevik influences were at work in Mexico, and the press began to talk of American intervention.[35] The reaction of progressives on Capitol Hill was immediate. LaGuardia charged that oil was behind the Mexican war talk, Borah demanded arbitration of the Mexican mineral lands controversy, and Norris got the Senate to pass a resolution (February 3, 1927) asking the Secretary of State for information on United States pre-1917 oil holdings in Mexico.[36] John Rankin of Mississippi noted on the floor of the House that only 22 of the 666 American companies in Mexico had refused to comply with Mexican law, and these were mostly Sinclair and Doheny interests, the same ones that had been involved in Teapot Dome. LaGuardia supported Rankin in this accusation.[37]

While the Coolidge administration was pondering its policy, progressives continued their pressure. LaGuardia wired the *Eve-*

---

[34] Cline, *op. cit.*, 194.   [35] Bailey, *Diplomatic History*, 713.
[36] Copy of Norris resolution of Feb. 3, 1927, LaG. Papers.
[37] *Congress. Rec.*, 69:2, Feb. 2, 1927, 2826.

ning Graphic: "There are some interests anxious to jockey this country into a break with Mexico. It is the oil interests and these people will use anyone and anything to serve their selfish and sordid purpose." [38] George Norris' position was later expressed to a constituent: "We should never forget that the right of revolution is, after all, a rather sacred right. We owe our very governmental existence to a revolution and . . . we should keep our hands off of revolution in foreign countries." [39]

It is difficult to determine precisely how much this kind of criticism from progressives had to do with Coolidge's decision, in September, 1927, to send the tactful and broad-minded Dwight Morrow to arrange a peaceful settlement with Mexico. However, it seems reasonable to assume that it constituted one important element in the complex of influences acting upon Coolidge at this time.

LaGuardia also criticized American activities in Haiti, where something close to a protectorate had existed since the landing of marines in 1915.[40] In a series of articles in the New York *Evening Graphic*, he assessed the results of the fourteen-year United States occupation. While noting that the Department of Agriculture and the Public Health Service had instituted many beneficial innovations, LaGuardia believed that the population still felt the "sting of intervention," and he urged that it come to an end. "Continuing the present oppression," he said, "while permitting the development of corporate-owned plantations, will only continue the exploitation of the unhappy masses of the island." [41] Other progressives also had criticized American intervention in Haiti, notably William Borah; [42] but it was not until the Hoover administration that steps were taken for the removal of American troops from Haiti.

LaGuardia's insistence on nonintervention in the Caribbean

[38] March 3, 1927, LaG. Papers.
[39] Letter of March 22, 1929, Norris Papers.   [40] Stuart, *op. cit.*, 283.
[41] Stuart, *op. cit.*, ch. xiii, confirms this ambivalence in American policy in Haiti, citing the welfare work by Americans in health and sanitation, along with lack of political freedom, illegal arrests, and arbitrary executions.
[42] Borah fought this issue throughout the twenties. See letter of June 28, 1922 to constituents, letters of thanks from Haitians, and letter of congratulation from *Nation* editor Ernest Gruening for his anti-imperialist speech in the Senate, Borah Papers.

extended to the island of Puerto Rico. He introduced a bill in the Seventieth Congress for the popular election of the Governor of Puerto Rico and received telegrams of thanks from the Senate and House of Representatives of that island.[43] LaGuardia told Puerto Rican officials that his bill was "the first step toward complete autonomy." [44] There is little doubt that the vocal Puerto Rican minority in LaGuardia's Twentieth District had a good deal to do with his militancy on this question. In this period Vito Marcantonio was back in the district, handling many rent cases for Puerto Rican families and keeping LaGuardia in touch with the situation there. LaGuardia assured the Puerto Rican Brotherhood of America, on 115th Street, that he would oppose in the House a bill giving American sugar companies tax advantages in Puerto Rico. He told them: "It seems to me that the sugar companies are getting a little too much down there and I am exceedingly anxious to do everything that is possible to protect the native of Puerto Rico against exploitation." [45]

He testified on his bill for the popular election of the Puerto Rican governor before the House's Committee on Insular Affairs and was questioned closely by committee members:

MR. HOOPER: Do you think that the hand of the Federal Government here rests very heavily upon Porto Rico in any manner whatever?

MR. LAGUARDIA: . . . Put yourself in the position of a Porto Rican. That hand rests heavily, no matter how lightly, in fact, when it rests on a people without their choice or consent. . . .

MR. RAGON: If we should grant this privilege to the island of Porto Rico, we would have twelve million people in the Philippine Islands on our necks.

MR. LAGUARDIA: I would give the Philippines complete independence. Have we not promised it to them? . . .

MR. KIESS: Has not Porto Rico done well under American rule?

MR. LAGUARDIA: Yes; they have in dollars and cents, but how about human liberty? [46]

The bill was bottled up in committee, with the Coolidge administration cool toward any change in the *status quo*,[47] and it was

---

[43] Wire of March 20, 1928, LaG. Papers.

[44] Wire of March 17, 1928, *ibid.*   [45] Letter of March 20, 1928, *ibid.*

[46] Copy of hearings on May 16, 1928, of House Committee on Insular Affairs, LaG. Papers.

[47] Coolidge had told Governor Towner of Puerto Rico that "Porto Rico

not until the coming of Franklin D. Roosevelt that LaGuardia's wishes for greater Puerto Rican autonomy were fulfilled.

His interest in Filipino independence led to a long friendship with Manuel Quezon, then President of the Senate in the Philippines. Quezon wrote to LaGuardia in early 1928, warning of a pending attempt in Congress to amend the Jones Act in a way that would decrease the powers of the Philippine legislature. LaGuardia assured him that he would be on guard.[48] That summer Quezon sent LaGuardia some souvenirs, and in response LaGuardia told of a conversation with the son of Emilio Aguinaldo, who had led the Philippine rebellion against American rule after the Spanish-American War:

I am sure you will be amused to hear about a chat that I had with young Aguinaldo a few nights ago. As you know, he resigned from the Military Academy and has held a position with the Harriman Bank. He is now returning to the Philippines as secretary of one of the bank's subsidiary corporations. The youngster, out of caution, I believe, tried to appear as very conservative. By the end of the evening, I had him rooting for complete Philippine independence.[49]

The Kellogg-Briand Pact of August 27, 1928, renouncing war as an instrument of national policy, owed much to the agitation of pacifists, Progressives, and internationally minded conservatives. Specifically, William E. Borah, Nicholas Murray Butler, Fiorello LaGuardia, and Professor James Shotwell deserve a good part of the credit, the first three for helping to arouse public opinion in support of the idea, the last-named for inducing French Foreign Minister Briand to take the initiative.[50]

LaGuardia shared the revulsion against war which swept through the nation after the Armistice and told two hundred stu-

---

had a greater degree of sovereignty over its internal affairs than does the government of any State or Territory of the United States" (Stuart, *op. cit.*, 243).

[48] Quezon to LaGuardia, Feb. 23, 1928, LaG. Papers.

[49] LaGuardia to Quezon, June 22, 1928, *ibid.*

[50] Robert H. Ferrell seems to credit "those two irrepressible volunteer diplomats"—Nicholas Murray Butler and James Shotwell, who in 1926 and 1927, respectively, broached the idea to Briand (*Peace in Our Time* [New Haven, 1952], 66–67, 85). He finds the Pact the result of a confluence of French power politics with American naïveté, and he names Borah, Stephen Wise, and Jane Addams among other "unsophisticated" Americans who saw in the Pact a bar to war (*ibid.*, 118, 163).

dents of the Brooklyn Law School in early 1923: "I want to go down in history as 100% pacifist. I went through one war and I want to do everything in my power to keep my country out of another one." [51] About this same time, LaGuardia wrote: "Now is the time for . . . the expression by the American people of their determination not to permit the jingoists, junkers and war profiteers to get this country involved in the century-old Balkan squabble. . . . A war would be welcome to the tottering monarchs and the exploiting classes of Europe. . . . A new war would mean another cleanup for the English and French bankers. It would mean more profits for the war profiteers." [52]

In May, 1924, LaGuardia and Borah introduced resolutions in their respective branches of Congress directing the President to invite the other powers of the world to join in a conference "for the purpose of outlawing war as an institution." [53] The Borah-LaGuardia joint resolution went beyond the later Kellogg-Briand Pact by asking the proposed conference to "obtain an agreement or treaty from every nation to make war a public crime and to bind itself to indict and punish its own international war breeders or instigators and war profiteers." [54] Fundamentally, the progressives placed a great deal of emphasis on the economic motivation for war. No mere agreement, they believed, would end war; only the radical step of removing the economic roots of war could bring results.

This approach differentiated the thinking of leading progressives from the declaration that was ultimately embodied in the Pact of Paris. LaGuardia revealed this in December of 1928, when the Senate was about to ratify the Pact. He supported ratification, but pointed to the futility of such a declaration while the great powers of the world were engaging in a reckless armaments race. He wrote:

While the Secretary of State urges Congress to act on these great peace measures, comes the Secretary of the Navy asking for great weapons of war. . . . The two propositions are irreconcilable. If we are to have

[51] Brooklyn *Eagle,* March 17, 1923.
[52] Undated copy of a LaGuardia speech, LaG. Papers.
[53] New York *Times,* May 18, 1924.
[54] Copy of House Joint Resolution 265, introduced May 17, 1924, LaG. Papers.

peace, if the great powerful United States is to take leadership in the world in the movement for peace, the justification for this tremendous new and additional armament cannot be explained. . . . It was competitive armament which brought about the ruinous World War.[55]

He had fought all that year against increased naval armaments. Answering the pleas of three ministers to oppose a big naval program, he said:

Rest assured that I will oppose, fight against, and vote against the increased Naval Program Bill. I agree with what you say and I too hope to see the time when Christians will be willing to apply Christianity to their national as well as international affairs. I am looking forward to the time when our nitrate plants may be turned into fertilizer plants and our tanks into tractors.[56]

He carried out his promise on the floor of Congress, telling the House that he opposed huge expenditures for war, but if war were to be waged to control the Mississippi Valley, he would vote three or four hundred million dollars for that purpose, because that would be a "war for humanity." [57]

LaGuardia believed strongly in world organization. He was among the House members resolving that the United States should join the Permanent Court of International Justice.[58] Also, he was a vigorous supporter of the Interparliamentary Union, which had been trying vainly to achieve international co-operation since the turn of the century. In the summer of 1928, LaGuardia sailed for Germany and in the flower-bedecked Reichstag, where six hundred representatives of thirty-seven nations sat (and where five years later the swastika would rule), told the assembly, speaking in German, that the key to peace was a disarmament program, carried out by "peace experts" rather than military men. "Weak navies make strong friendships," he told the conference, in a speech that would have made his old idol, Theodore Roosevelt, stir with anger.[59] The spirit of the Rough Rider, it seemed, was no longer riding the crest of the progressive wave.

[55] New York *Evening Graphic,* Dec. 13, 1928.
[56] LaGuardia to Rev. Lee H. Ball, Jan., 1928, LaG. Papers.
[57] *Congress. Rec.,* March 16, 1928, 5025.
[58] *Ibid.,* March 3, 1925, 5413. Progressives split on this issue, with John Nelson of Wisconsin opposing the resolution, Cooper of Wisconsin supporting it, and Minnesota Progressives Kvale and Schall abstaining.
[59] New York *Times,* Aug. 24, 1928.

10 · The Battle for Public Power
in the Twenties

THE establishment of the Tennessee Valley Authority in 1933—leading to an achievement so monumental that one economist has called it a "social resurrection" [1]—owed a great deal to political ground-clearing actions undertaken in the 1920's. One of these actions was the frustrating of efforts to lease the Muscle Shoals dam and plants in the Tennessee Valley to private interests. Another was the laying of plans, the preparation of public opinion, and the introduction of legislation for government operation of power projects in the Tennessee Valley and on the Colorado River. Both of these accomplishments can be attributed in large part to the perserverance of two legislators: George Norris in the Senate and Fiorello LaGuardia in the House of Representatives.

At Muscle Shoals, Alabama, in the denuded and neglected Tennessee Valley, by turns flooded and arid, the government had begun building a dam and two nitrate plants during the war in order to increase the production of explosives.[2] When the war ended, and after $150,000,000 had been spent, Congress cut off funds for the unfinished dam, and a number of private companies, seeing immense possibilities in the Valley, began to bid for the right to develop the site. By 1924 the leading contender was the Henry

[1] Broadus Mitchell, *Depression Decade* (New York, 1947), 340.
[2] Section 124 of the National Defense Act of 1916 authorized this. See Preston Hubbard, "The Muscle Shoals Controversy" (Ph.D. dissertation, Vanderbilt University, 1955), 2.

Ford Company, and for the next two years the battle raged—between administration efforts to lease the site to Ford and the resistance movement of a small, stubborn band in Congress.[3]

The attitude of the Coolidge administration was from the first favorable to private development. In reply to a letter from a resident of Tennessee, the President's secretary said: "Mr. Ford is still disposed to bid on the Muscle Shoals development and there seems to be a very fair chance that the works will ultimately be turned over to him under an arrangement satisfactory to both him and the Government." [4] Several weeks after this letter was dispatched, Coolidge recommended to Congress that the property be sold, saying that the price of purchase was not too important.[5] Accordingly, an administration-supported bill was introduced in the Senate directing the Secretary of War to accept Ford's offer to lease for one hundred years dam and power properties on the Tennessee River and to buy nitrate plants and properties at Muscle Shoals.

While Norris went into action in the Senate to battle this plan,[6] LaGuardia opened his campaign in the House and during a five-day debate in early March of 1924 led the attack on the Ford offer. He pointed out that the language of the bill (H.R. 518), as reported out of committee, was precisely the language of the Ford request. "Ford wrote this bill," he told the House, "and you cannot get away from that, and he has told you that you must pass it just as it is written." Replying to the American Farm Bureau Federation, which was supporting the bill, LaGuardia said the bill would not guarantee cheap fertilizer for the farmer, and he urged that the Department of Agriculture be permitted to manufacture such fertilizer. LaGuardia noted that Ford was guaranteed 8 per cent on the total cost of production of $100,000,000, although his actual initial investment was only $15,000,000, so that his actual profit would be more than 50 per cent on the initial investment. "Talk about profiteering, and it is right here under your nose. . . . You

[3] Outside Congress, Gifford Pinchot was the most severe critic of the proposal, *ibid.,* 53.

[4] Letter of Nov. 15, 1923, Coolidge Papers.   [5] *Ibid.*

[6] After sharply querying Secretary of War Weeks on his position, Norris got Weeks to say that he agreed to a fifty-year lease and competitive bidding (Weeks to Norris, Jan. 30, 1924, LaG. Papers). Norris had, on May 11, 1922, introduced his first bill for government development of Muscle Shoals on a multipurpose basis (Hubbard, *op. cit.,* 122).

are bowing to money . . . and if you pass this bill you should replace that flag on the wall of this house with a great big dollar sign. . . . Why Gentlemen, this proposition makes the Teapot Dome look like petty larceny." [7]

LaGuardia seized upon Ford's known anti-Semitic activities [8] to buttress his argument, calling him a man with "hatred in his heart . . . based on his ignorance of history, literature and religion. . . . The wealth and ignorance of Henry Ford combined have made it possible for vicious men to carry on a nefarious warfare against the Jews not only of America but of the whole world." [9] Immediate support for LaGuardia's stand came from Jewish newspapers and organizations all over the country.[10] In response to a letter from the editor of the American *Israelite,* suggesting that the administration be asked to act against Ford's anti-Semitic activities, LaGuardia wrote: "To seek at this time an expression of official attitude toward Mr. Ford, I believe, is entirely useless and unnecessary." He referred to "recent conferences, statements, and exchanges of mutual expressions of admiration" between administration officials and Ford.[11]

His attack on the Ford offer brought forth an indignant letter from a New Yorker who apparently had served with the congressman during the war a1d now wrote:

What in the world has happened to you and your associates in Washington? Have you all suddenly gone insane or has it been gradually coming on you in the strain of your efforts . . . and weakened your minds so that you are not only physically unfit to carry on but mentally sick. . . . I have just read your speech in Congress yesterday against Henry Ford's bid for Muscle Shoals. . . . Don't spoil all of

[7] *Congress. Rec.,* March 6, 1924, 3706–3709.

[8] Gustavus Myers, *History of Bigotry in the United States* (New York, 1943), 333–369, discusses Ford's activities and says (p. 333): "Parallel to certain years of the Ku Klux Klan a centralized and intensive agitation was carried on exclusively against Jews by a publication owned and financed by one of the richest and most conspicuous of American industrialists." He is referring to Ford's *Dearborn Independent,* which published the forged "Protocols of the Wise Men of Zion." In 1927, Ford retracted his statements about the Jews, and by 1942 he was speaking out forcefully against anti-Semitism (*ibid.,* 367).

[9] *Congress. Rec.,* March 6, 1924, 3708.   [10] *The Day,* March 8, 1924.

[11] LaGuardia to Isaac Wise, April 30, 1924, LaG. Papers.

your good work now making foolish speeches. . . . He is the only man
capable of handling the situation at Muscle Shoals and Wall Street
only wants it for a stock-jobbing proposition.[12]

LaGuardia replied:

Please don't get excited. . . . I do not know what information you
have on Muscle Shoals, but I can assure you that in twenty years of
public life I have never seen anything as brazen as the proposition
before us. . . . As to being with Wall Street, why, my dear boy, all the
fight in New York against me is now and always has been prompted,
directed and paid for by the big Wall Street interests, and it is this
same interest, while they personally do not like Henry Ford, would
like to see the Ford offer accepted, because it will establish a precedent
for . . . the continued exploitation by public utilities corporations
of the natural resources of this country.

Making it plain to Congress that he was not only against Ford's
offer but against any offer by private companies to produce fertilizer and power in the Tennessee Valley, LaGuardia said: "I am not
for the Alabama Power Company offer [13] and I am not for the operation of this great plant by anyone or any corporation except the
United States Government." [14] To support his stand for government ownership of the power and nitrate properties, LaGuardia
compared the results of private and public control of natural resources:

The two engineering feats which may be compared to Muscle Shoals
are the Niagara water power and the Panama Canal. The Niagara
power was grabbed by greedy, selfish corporations, assisted by favored
legislation, and this gift of nature, this great water power, is turned
into dividends for these companies, and the people must pay excessive
rates for power, current, and light. The Panama Canal, on the other
hand, stands as a monument to government operation.[15]

[12] Correspondence between LaGuardia and R. N. Estey, March 7, 1924
(*ibid.*). Ford's diatribes against Wall Street and his antiwar activities led a
number of progressives to support his offer and even to boom him for the
1924 presidency (Hubbard, *op. cit.*, 172).

[13] In Jan., 1924, the Alabama Power Company and eight other southern
power companies submitted a joint bid on Muscle Shoals (Hubbard, *op. cit.*,
182).

[14] *Congress. Rec.*, March 6, 1924, 3704.   [15] *Ibid.*, March 10, 1924, 3838.

LaGuardia kept up the battle against the bill for five days of wearying debate, while the House members pushing for passage grew more and more impatient. Finally, on March 10, 1924, the House voted to close debate on all amendments. LaGuardia rose to his feet with still another amendment, and as he began to speak for it, cries of "Vote! Vote! Vote!" came from all sides of the House. Refusing to yield, LaGuardia cried: "Oh you can holler vote as much as you like. You can laugh the amendment down if you desire, but you will live to rue the day that you railroaded and jammed the bill through the House.[16]

The Muscle Shoals bill passed the House that same day, but in the Senate the opposition of a determined group led by George Norris prevented its passage. The Senate Agricultural Committee, now dominated by Norris, Brookhart, and other progressives, began extensive hearings in April on Muscle Shoals, including an investigation of an alleged Coolidge-Ford "deal" for the presidency.[17] At these hearings expert after expert condemned Muscle Shoals as unsuitable for fertilizer production, which had been the avowed chief purpose of the Ford program. In addition, the hearings revealed widespread opposition to Ford by southern manufacturers, who feared competition from new, electrically powered Ford enterprises in the South. As a result, the Ford offer was buried in the Senate committee with hardly a trace of mourning.[18] Norris, instead, offered his own substitute proposition—government ownership and operation of the Muscle Shoals properties—and battled for it all through the session. He told the Senate:

You can trace the electric light in Omaha, and the electric light in the South and they both wind up in Wall Street. . . . We are not legislating for today, Senators; we are setting up a milepost in the history, not only of our country, but of civilization. We are going to say by our action on this bill when we get through with it whether

[16] *Congress. Rec.,* March 10, 1924, 3904–3905.

[17] In December, 1923, Ford and Coolidge had met at the White House, after which Coolidge sent a message to Congress outlining a plan for the sale of Muscle Shoals property and development rights to a private lessee under terms fitting the Ford offer. When, on Dec. 19, 1923, Ford punctured his own presidential bubble and declared himself for Coolidge for President, talk began to spread of an arrangement between the two men (Hubbard, *op. cit.,* 172–175).

[18] *Ibid.,* 205–225.

it shall be a marker for human progress, more happiness, and greater democracy, or whether we are going to relegate ourselves and our prosperity to the control of combinations and trusts.[19]

With the Norris bill under debate in the Senate, LaGuardia grew more and more insistent in the House on government ownership, saying:

I say that the policy of the control of water power must be sooner or later decided by Congress. The quicker we decide to take God's gift to the people of America and operate it for the enjoyment of all the people instead of for the profit of private corporations, the better it will be for the people of this country. I do not want to hesitate. I am ready to go on record for the government operation of Muscle Shoals today.[20]

Proponents of private operation of the Muscle Shoals properties claimed that this would aid the farmer, but LaGuardia insisted that this was only intended to delude the agricultural producers of the nation.[21] The production of fertilizer, he pointed out, was really incidental to the project, and the manufacture of power was the all-important thing. "Muscle Shoals," he declared, "is a water-power project first, and incidentally a nitrogen plant. There is no use fooling ourselves, and there is no use continuing to fool the farmer."

The original aim of the Muscle Shoals project had been to produce nitrates for war. With the end of the war, the production of fertilizer for peacetime agriculture became the predominant issue. By 1924, however, it was becoming more and more clear that electrical power was the overriding, crucial factor in the Muscle Shoals controversy. The Norris committee hearings that year indicated that Ford, ostensibly concerned with fertilizer, was really interested in electrical power. Between 1921 and 1924 a "virtual

---

[19] Norris speech, Dec. 17, 1924, LaG. Papers.

[20] *Congress. Rec.*, 68:2, Jan. 27, 1925, 2542–2543.

[21] *Ibid.*, March 2, 1925, 5181. The American Farm Bureau Federation, saying the bill would put cheap fertilizer and electrical power within reach of the farmer, asked for passage of the bill (LaG. Papers). The Farmers Na tional Council, represented in Washington by Benjamin C. Marsh, testified against the Ford offer and for the Norris bill. The Council claimed to represent 800,000 farmers, one-third of them farm laborers (Hubbard, *op. cit.*, 191).

electrical revolution" took place in the United States, with the formation of huge interstate power systems. Thus, by early 1925 the emphasis had definitely shifted to the power possibilities of the Muscle Shoals development.[22]

With the Ford offer dead and the Norris bill stymied in the Senate, Coolidge set up a board of inquiry in March, 1925, and out of it came another bill setting up a joint committee of Congress authorized to lease the site. LaGuardia, Norris, and their allies would not relent. LaGuardia said: "You cannot find any corporation in business for love, for philanthropy, or for patriotism. The lessee will want to make money and they will make it on the farmers and the consumers. The lessee corporation will make money and the farmers will pay." [23]

By late 1926 the effort to dispose of the dam and plants to private interests had collapsed, and the failure of the joint committee's proposals, coming on top of the Ford withdrawal, boosted the stock of the Norris plan. Furthermore, the election of 1926 strengthened the farm bloc in Congress, and this was the heart of the pro-public-power group in Congress.[24] The way was thus clear for Norris and LaGuardia in early 1928 to introduce a joint resolution for government development of Muscle Shoals for the production of both power and fertilizer.[25] LaGuardia, testifying for the resolution before the House Committee on Military Affairs, said:

Let us be perfectly frank about it, Mr. Chairman. Muscle Shoals is the greatest power plant in the country, and this is what makes it attractive. . . . That being so, why should the Government part with this priceless possession. . . . Whoever gets control of Muscle Shoals

[22] Hubbard, *op. cit.*, 233–238.

[23] *Congress. Rec.*, 69:1, March 11, 1926, 5438–5439.

[24] Hubbard, *op. cit.*, 233–238.

[25] Section Two of the joint resolution called for sale of power by the government to "states, counties, municipalities, partnerships, or individuals," and Governor Al Smith of New York suggested a compromise to the effect that the government would sell to power companies who would then become the middlemen. LaGuardia told the committee: "I know that neither this committee, nor Congress, nor the country is prepared for the broad scope of Section Two, but just as sure as we are here this morning, conditions are going to be such in this country that we will have to come to that, just as we did when we took over the supply of fresh water" (copy of the joint resolution, LaG. Papers).

will have the absolute control of the industry of that whole section of the country, within the radius of the transmission of power. Congress cannot afford to give that power to any one group of men.

I am not afraid of this talk of the Government going into business, of the Government being paternalistic, and of the Government depriving private business of what they should have. There is nothing in that. I remember the time and you all do, when it was considered socialistic for a municipality to have its own water supply. . . . Gentlemen, times are changing.

. . . My resolution would provide for the Government to keep that plant, and it would be a model power plant for the whole United States, and it would start a new era in this country. . . . Just as municipalities, just as states, took over the water supply from private companies, so eventually will the states and the Federal Government have to take over the distribution of hydraulic power all over this country.[26]

He was unperturbed by the expressed fears of committee members that private power companies would thereby be put out of business. The following exchange took place:

MR. RANSLEY: . . . Do you not practically put the Government into the power business?

MR. LAGUARDIA: Oh yes.

MR. RANSLEY: Do you realize that that means they will paralyze all opposition?

MR. LAGUARDIA: Yes.

MR. RANSLEY: No one, of course, can compete with the Government if the Government is in the power business.

MR. LAGUARDIA: Yes.

When it was proposed to amend his resolution to replace the word "fertilizer" by "nitrogen products" LaGuardia became angry over what he considered a ruse by fertilizer companies to prevent government production of fertilizer. "I want to say gentlemen," he declared, "that the conduct of the lobby of the Power Trust and the conduct of the lobby of the Fertilizer Trust is living proof that the world's oldest profession is not limited to any one sex." [27]

On March 13, 1928, the Norris resolution passed the Senate by a vote of 48 to 25. Southern and western senators from the farming

[26] Hearings, Feb. 7, 1928; copy in LaG. Papers.
[27] *Congress. Rec.*, 70:1, May 16, 1928, 8879.

states had united to support the measure.[28] It was not that the farm bloc was pro-public power; it was simply pro-power, and the stubbornness of the Progressive forces, aided by disunity among the various business interests fighting for control of the Muscle Shoals region, led to a situation where the farm bloc had to back the Norris-LaGuardia resolution or face total inaction on development of the region. The resulting combination of southern Democrats and western Republicans was enough to assure success for the proposal.

By this time it was clear that the development of Muscle Shoals would not bring maximum advantage to the region unless it were linked with a comprehensive plan for the entire Tennessee Valley. However, for tactical reasons Norris limited his resolution to Muscle Shoals. The power of the public utilities interests was formidable. At this time ten huge systems sold 75 per cent of all electrical power in the country. The vast Insull holding-company empire alone had assets of two and a half billion dollars and produced nearly one-eighth of the nation's power.[29]

The House of Representatives now went into action, passing by a vote of 251–165 a substitute for LaGuardia's bill offered by Congressman Morin of Pennsylvania. The farm bloc here too supplied the bulk of support.[30] Three days before adjournment, the Norris-Morin bill went to the White House for presidential action. Coolidge listened patiently to the pleas of Borah, who went to the White House to urge passage of the measure, and then pocket-vetoed the bill.[31] Norris and LaGuardia cried that a pocket veto was not valid between sessions of Congress, only between Congresses,[32] but the argument made no headway.[33]

[28] Hubbard, *op. cit.*, 379.   [29] Soule, *op. cit.*, 184–185.

[30] The passage of the bill at this time, though surprising in view of the strong anti-public-power sentiment in Congress up to 1927, was aided by the fact that 1928 was an election year and that the Federal Trade Commission's investigation of the power industry had been highly publicized. See note 35.

[31] Claude Fuess says Coolidge's presidential accomplishments were "chiefly negative. . . . He was a safe pilot, not a brilliant one." Irving Stone puts it differently: "Calvin Coolidge believed that the least government was the best government; he aspired to become the least president the country has ever had; he attained his desire" (Isabel Leighton, ed., *The Aspirin Age* [New York, 1949]), 130.

[32] New York *Times,* June 8, 1928.

[33] A year later, a Supreme Court ruling approved such vetoes.

Despite this setback, LaGuardia continued to publicize the propaganda activities of the power trust, for every day the Federal Trade Commission was disclosing new evidence of the rewriting of textbooks [34] and control over the press.[35] He kept harping on the statement of a utilities official to a Birmingham convention of the National Electric Light Association: "Don't be afraid of the expense. The public pays the expenses." [36] While Walsh was asking the Senate to investigate the extent of financial interest in newspapers by the International Paper and Power Company, LaGuardia introduced three House bills aimed at preventing the acquisition of newspapers by public utilities.[37]

LaGuardia particularly attacked the activities of the power trust in New York City, where gas and electric interests were now seeking a merger; he wrote in the New York *Evening Graphic* of the "avariciousness of the Power Trust, its uncouth methods of obtaining legislation to exploit the people, its underhanded system of thwarting and distorting the minds of students by controlling education and textbooks." [38]

[34] Ernest Gruening, *The Public Pays* (New York, 1931), 82–107.

[35] *Ibid.*, 160–210. The power companies had been waging a tremendous campaign against government ownership of electrical power resources. Montana's Senator Thomas Walsh proposed in 1927 to investigate holding-company control in the power and light industry and efforts of the power industry to influence public opinion. He wanted to probe, Walsh said, "the most formidable lobby ever brought together . . . representing capital to the amount of nearly ten billion dollars." The Senate thought it was weakening the Walsh resolution by finally turning the investigation over to the Federal Trade Commission, but the Commission did a thorough job, unearthing in its hearings some startling facts about the influencing of public opinion in support of the private power companies. These findings included the following: As early as 1921, Samuel Insull had told a meeting of the Public Policy Committee of the National Electric Light Association of the need for a campaign of education in the colleges. A dean of Ohio State University was hired, during a sabbatical leave, at $15,000 plus expenses to direct the Association's Committee on Cooperation with Educational Institutions, and soon the Association was receiving reports on public utilities courses taught at various institutions. One of its consultants, after sitting in on a Pennsylvania State University course which had been fathered by the utilities, submitted a critique of the course, saying: "I do not think it is advisable to use the word 'profit' as is so frequently done in the course, since in the utility business, in a sense, there are no profits" (*ibid.*, 7–53).

[36] *Ibid.*, 235.   [37] New York *Times*, May 7, 1929.

[38] Undated article from the *Evening Graphic*, LaG. Papers.

The issue of public power arose again in 1927–1928 over the Swing-Johnson bill for government construction of Boulder Dam on the Colorado River. Thousands of businessmen in the Far West were in back of the bill,[39] but the power lobby opposed government action, and Representative Leatherwood of Utah told a House committee that it was "a power project under the guise of a flood control and irrigation measure . . . a dangerous, dishonest, and unsound proposal." [40] Decrying the "sordid, selfish opposition" to the dam, LaGuardia told the House:

This project surpasses the Panama canal. It will be a monument to the civilization of this era. . . . The question may properly arise, Why are you, from New York, thousands of miles away from Boulder Dam, interested?—and I will tell you why. We are interested in Boulder Dam because we are suffering under the exploitation of the Power Trust in the East and the Boulder Dam project will demonstrate how cheaply power can be generated and once we demonstrate how nature may be harnessed and power generated at a low cost, it will break the control of the Power Trust and it will bring relief . . . to the entire country.[41]

He had with him at this time figures showing that in Ontario, where power was publicly owned and distributed, it cost less than one-half of what it cost New York consumers,[42] and he said:

Why just think of it! In this day and age we transport coal hundreds of miles into a city to generate electricity, when God Almighty has been so generous to the people of this country in giving us natural water power from which we could generate electricity, and without the exploitation of the power companies we could send current into the homes and light, to heat, to wash, and to cook at a very small cost. I am more interested in the welfare of the women than I am in the dividends of the power companies.[43]

The Boulder Dam was tied up in committee at this time, and LaGuardia cited this as proof of the need to liberalize the House rules. "I am ready," he told his colleagues, "to join in a filibuster with anyone in this House, under the very severe rules under which

---

[39] Wire to LaGuardia, Feb. 24, 1927, from California investors' group, and hundreds of letters from manufacturers, LaG. Papers.

[40] *Ibid.*   [41] *Congress. Rec.*, 69:2, Feb. 25, 1927, 4845.

[42] Bulletin of National Popular Government League, Feb. 24, 1927, LaG. Papers.

[43] *Congress. Rec.*, 69:2, Feb. 25, 1927, 4845.

we operate, and absolutely go on a legislative strike, until this bill is brought before us." [44] There was no response to his offer, however.

Pressure against the Swing-Johnson bill mounted. A resolution adopted unanimously by the New York State Chamber of Commerce told of "the blighting influences of government ownership." [45] An editorial in the New York *Sun* urged a de-emphasis on power distribution and a concentration on the less controversial flood-control aspects of the bill.[46] The New York *World* offered a compromise based on Governor Al Smith's idea of using private interests as middlemen, but still retaining the principle of government ownership. [47]

With both sides lined up for a fight to the finish, La Guardia took the floor of the House in May, 1928, and made one of the most powerful speeches of his congressional career.[48] He dismissed talk of engineering difficulties with the statement: "Such timidity, such fear, such doubts, and such evil forebodings always accompany the initial steps of great undertakings." Constitutional arguments had been leveled at the Boulder Dam proposal on the ground that congressional authority to control navigation did not include the right to produce and distribute electrical power.[49] LaGuardia's answer was: "Anyone serving in this House will know that the cry of unconstitutionality is always raised in opposition to measures where logical, sound, or economic reasons are not available." In an argument that sounds much like later New Deal argumentation, he said: "Constitutional limitations must necessarily be construed in the light of changed conditions. It is left for each age to say what the laws of that age shall be."

He called upon the imagination of his colleagues to visualize the results of the Boulder Dam project:

Imagine this huge canyon to be dammed by a wall over six hundred feet high, creating a gigantic natural reservoir site impounding twenty-six million acre-feet of water. Millions and millions of horsepower now

[44] *Ibid.*, Feb. 25, 1927, 4846.   [45] LaG. Papers, May 3, 1928.
[46] April 16, 1928.   [47] Dec. 27, 1927.
[48] *Congress. Rec.*, 70:1, May 24, 1928, 9773–9777.
[49] The same doctrine of states' rights would later be invoked in connection with the development of the Connecticut River basin, resulting in "a chronicle of failure" (William E. Leuchtenburg, *Flood Control Politics* [Cambridge, 1953], 257).

going to waste year after year will be harnessed and utilized to generate electricity which will be sent hundreds of miles and bring cheer, comfort, and move the wheels of industry. Just think of . . . a magnificent stream, with a daily uniform flow of water throughout the year to be utilized as a great artery of commerce for that region of the country. The Imperial Valley, now threatened by flood, to be secured in its safety. . . . The project is thrilling.

Now he lashed out at one of "the most vicious, disgraceful venal lobbies that ever existed in the history of the world." Fifteen holding and operating companies, he charged, controlled 80 per cent of the national production of gas and electricity.[50] As his colleagues leaned forward and people in the galleries strained to see, LaGuardia held up the evidence of the lobby's activities—photostatic copies of checks made out by the National Electric Light Association to various people and institutions in the educational world. He quoted a letter from an Association official which enclosed plans of public utilities courses and said: "The plan was put across in the usual way. We laid the groundwork circumspectedly and with care so that the actual suggestion that such courses be started came from the faculties of the institutions themselves. The rest was routine." LaGuardia noted the tampering with textbooks, and commented, "Why, this bribery in the form of subsidies, this method of reaching the textbooks, would make a student an illegitimate alumnus of an immoral alma mater" (laughter and applause).

The only immediate result, however, was the passage of a bill, signed by Coolidge in December, 1928, which provided for government construction of Boulder Dam but left to the Secretary of the Interior the decision on whether the government or private companies should operate the power stations. The era of the T.V.A. was still several years off.

---

[50] Later, testimony before the Senate Banking and Currency Committee revealed that in 1930 the combined assets of five holding-company groups totaled two and a half billion dollars (Ferdinand Pecora, *Wall Street under Oath* [New York, 1939], 227).

11 · The "Other Half" in the New Gilded Age

IN Calvin Coolidge's autobiography, written early in 1929, he said that his administration had "encouraged enterprise, made possible the highest rate of wages which has ever existed, returned large profits, brought to the homes of the people the greatest economic benefits they ever enjoyed, and given to the country as a whole an unexampled era of prosperity." [1]

Throughout the twenties, however, Fiorello LaGuardia found it necessary to spend most of his time and energy battling against the high cost of food and rent, for the rights of wage earners on strike, for a redistribution of wealth through taxation, and in general for government aid to that part of the population which was bypassed in the national rush toward better living. In the course of these conflicts the plastic of his social and economic philosophy hardened, took more definite form, and, in the era of greatest triumph for laissez faire, pointed unhesitantly and challengingly toward the concept of the welfare state.

Shortly after LaGuardia took his seat in the Sixty-eighth Congress, in early 1924, the House began to consider extension of the rent controls which had been established in the District of Columbia in wartime to curb rent profiteering. The original imposition of controls had been greeted with fierce indignation on the part of exponents of "rugged individualism" like Congressman James T. Begg of Ohio, who had said:

[1] *Autobiography* (New York, 1929), 183.

Why, the wildest-eyed Bolshevik that ever spoke from a soapbox in New York City never advocated a wilder doctrine than this. . . . If there is a thing that America is going to be confronted with . . . it is a showdown between the man who through perseverance and industry and economy has saved out of a mere pittance to acquire something, and the profligate and waster who has spent his all and today has nothing.[2]

Facing the same kind of argument in 1924, LaGuardia told the House that at hearings on the New York rent law, he had heard landlords raise the same cries, asking protection of their "constitutional right" to set whatever rents they wished. They had used college professors and legal experts to support their stand against rent control, he said:

but gentlemen, with all of their experts, with all of their professors, with all of their legal talent, there is no argument that can prevail when a man with a weekly income and a family to support is compelled to pay out of his income such a large proportion that there is not sufficient left to properly care for and nourish his children. That is the condition in New York City; that is the condition in Washington, D.C. . . .

As long as landlords are determined to exact a pound of flesh from their tenants, as long as landlords insist upon the right to increase rent, limited only by their own greed . . . an emergency exists and I for one do not hesitate to say, as I have stated before, it is part of the duty of the government to protect its people in providing regulatory provisions for the people's shelter as we regulate their food, health, transportation and safety.[3]

The bill was passed, but a year later the question of renewal came up, and LaGuardia received a letter from the general counsel for the New York Life Insurance Company, asking him to vote against rent control, warning that if the bill passed his company would refuse to invest in mortgages in the District of Columbia. The attorney said he had on his desk a request for a $90,000 loan and that he was delaying action on it pending the decision by Congress on the bill.[4] LaGuardia replied: "You have permitted yourself to become part of a vicious, unwarranted and organized propaganda carried on throughout the country where rent laws have become

[2] *Congress. Rec.*, 68:1, April 28, 1924, 7387.   [3] *Ibid.*, 7391–7392.
[4] Harry Bottome to LaGuardia, Jan. 28, 1925, LaG. Papers.

necessary." Citing the letter as a "veiled threat" to call in mortgages and hold up future investments in the District, he promised
to expose this to the public.[5]

When the Real Estate Board of New York asked LaGuardia to
vote against the recent control bill, terming it "one of the most
radical ever introduced," he answered:

> I have read the arguments contained in your memorandum and it is
> the same old whining, cringing pleas presented by the New York land-
> lords who have thrived on the housing situation. . . . Nothing better
> in support of the bill could have reached the memberships of Congress
> than a protest from the landlords of New York City. Please keep up
> your good work.

Coolidge had backed the Rent Law, and LaGuardia called it "the
outstanding act of his administration to date." [6]

While the twenties saw the passage of no significant piece of social welfare legislation, the economic relief measure that came
closest to fruition was the McNary-Haugen plan.[7] This proposed
to aid the farmer by having the government dump farm surpluses
abroad in order to keep domestic farm prices high. In the many
times that this proposal came up for discussion in the House, La-
Guardia never tired of pointing to its inadequacy as an aid to the
farmer.[8] He noted, furthermore, that while the farmer was plagued
by low prices the consumer was paying high prices and that it
would take more fundamental action than the kind provided in
the McNary-Haugen plan to solve that problem.

In May of 1924, LaGuardia took the floor of the House to deliver a major address on the McNary-Haugen bill. At this time, his
break with the Republican party, and his line-up with the Progressive party, were imminent. He was being called a radical in the

[5] New York *Times,* Jan. 30, 1925.

[6] Letter of Jan. 8, 1925, LaG. Papers.

[7] There were five McNary-Haugen bills introduced from 1924 to 1928,
one each year. The last two passed both houses and were vetoed by Coolidge.
They are discussed at length in Murray R. Benedict, *Farm Policies of the
United States 1790–1950* (New York, 1953).

[8] Benedict, after a detailed study of the McNary-Haugen bills, concludes
that they had important flaws, but would probably have helped in assuaging
the crisis faced by the farmer (*op. cit.,* 236). John D. Black, *Agricultural
Reform in the United States* (New York, 1929), 232–254, discusses the proposals sympathetically.

press, in his mail, and on the floor of Congress, and he decided to
take this opportunity to reply.

Gentlemen, I am a progressive in every sense of the word. Some of my
friends sometimes refer to me as a radical. If by that they mean that I
am seeking radical changes in the very conditions which brought about
the disparity between the exorbitant retail prices of food and the
starvation prices paid to the farmer, I am not at all shocked by being
called a radical. . . . Something is radically wrong when a condition
exists that permits the manipulation of prices, the creation of monopolies on food to the extent of driving the farmer off his farm by foreclosures and having thousands of underfed and ill-nourished children
in the public schools of our cities.[9]

Cutting beneath what he considered a superficial layer of futile
ameliorative legislation for the farmer, LaGuardia hit hard at
what he believed lay at the root of both the farmer's and the consumer's problems: "a vicious, unfair, unbalanced economic system"
favoring neither of these two major groups, but catering to the
special interests of the banker, the railroad, the middleman. "At
this late date," he said, "Congress is asked to give the farmer relief
without disturbing the real cause of his evils." [10]

The "toilless, unproductive end of industry," he maintained,
was taking an "undue and disproportionate share to that which it
contributes" and the McNary-Haugen bill would simply increase
farm prices, thus hurting the consumer, without protecting both
groups from the gas trusts, the farm machine trusts, the leather
trusts. "Don't you see," he cried, "that you are only going half-
way?" What was needed, LaGuardia said, was comprehensive legislation establishing national regulation of transportation, marketing, and money. The laws had not kept up with the development
of the modern industrial system. "You have protected the dollar
and disregarded the producers. You have protected property and
forgotten the human being, with the result that we have legalized
a cruel system of exploitation. Now we are approaching the time
when a real change is necessary." [11]

It was a speech which could be considered a testament of the
Populist-Progressive movement, with strong foreshadowings of the
New Deal philosophy, and a definite undercurrent of socialist

[9] *Congress. Rec.*, 68:1, May 23, 1924, 9351–9352.
[10] *Ibid.*   [11] *Ibid.*

theory. It indicated that, if there was a wing of the Progressive movement which sought a return to the golden age of competition, there was another wing which looked forward to comprehensive regulation of the economic structure. Together with all of La-Guardia's actions and statements in the twenties, the speech would seem to show that if the Eastern progressivism of the Wilson era was (as Hofstadter has said) "a mild and judicious" movement, its leading spokesman in the twenties had converted it into a bold and militant one.[12]

His colleagues recognized the strong coloring of socialism in La-Guardia's position. When Representative Tincher of Kansas asked LaGuardia if he had a remedy for the problems of the farmer and the consumer, he quickly replied: "Take control of all transportation of the country, take all the elevators and storages, and eliminate entirely the middleman and banking industry." Tincher said: "I was laboring under a misapprehension. I thought Mr. Berger had the sole honor of representing his party in Congress." [13] (He was referring to Socialist Victor Berger.)

Concern about the price of food made LaGuardia an active participant in the debates over the McNary-Haugen bill all through the Coolidge administration: In the spring of 1926 and again in early 1927, LaGuardia introduced an amendment to the bill. His amendment was almost verbatim, as he told the House, Section Four of the wartime Lever Food Control Act. That section punished by a maximum five-year imprisonment and $5,000 fine any one of a series of acts tending to raise the price, restrict the supply, hoard or monopolize, or set any unreasonable charge for farm products. This, LaGuardia pointed out, would enable action against trusts which unnecessarily increased the prices of bread and meat. "The only purpose of the amendment," he said, "is to protect the consumer against gougers, profiteers, monopolies, food

12 Richard Hofstadter, *The Age of Reform* (New York, 1955), 163, says that Eastern progressivism before the war aimed at "not a sharp change in the social structure, but rather the formation of a responsible elite which was to take charge of the popular impulse toward change and direct it into moderate . . . channels." That there were still such important elements among Eastern progressives in the twenties, there is no doubt, but the mannered arguments of this conservative group were often lost in the tumult created by the congressman from the Twentieth District.

13 *Congress. Rec.*, 68:1, May 22, 1924, 9204.

manipulators, speculators and gamblers." [14] Congressman Haugen of Iowa opposed it, however, and the House voted it down quickly. A year later LaGuardia introduced it again, and once more it was shunted aside.

Nevertheless, LaGuardia, pounding away constantly on the theme that the farmer and the consumer were both victimized by monopolies, refused to take a sectional stand against the farm relief bills supported by the Midwest. He clashed on this issue with his fellow congressman from New York, Hamilton Fish, Jr. Fish told the House that anyone for the McNary-Haugen bill was betraying his constituents, and LaGuardia retorted by referring to Fish as the "short-distance progressive" who could not speak for the laboring man. "He might," LaGuardia said, "be able to speak for the strongly-entrenched insurance interests who have made the burden of the farmer harder, but he cannot speak for the laboring people of New York City." [15] Several days after this exchange, LaGuardia voted for the bill to establish a Federal Farm Board, while Fish voted against it.[16]

During debate on the Cooperative Marketing bill in early 1925, LaGuardia commented on the irony of a situation where the nation could produce such huge quantities of bread, meat, potatoes, and milk, and yet the prices of these necessities were so high that many urban workers were not able to buy all that they needed to feed their families. Furthermore, he noted, the farmer was getting an infinitesimal portion of these high prices. "The hand that lifts the tape of the ticker makes more than the hand that pushes the plow," LaGuardia declared. Again, he called for "the courage to admit that our economic system needs readjustment." [17]

In the year 1925 the real-estate boom in Florida was reaching its dizziest peak, and perhaps two million Americans had enough leisure (and enough money) to play golf, spending about half a million dollars that year on the game. It was a year when millions of people in the lower-middle-income brackets, if they could not afford to join the country clubs which were by this time symbols of upper-middle-class revelry, could jam the huge sports arenas to

[14] *Ibid.*, 69:1, May 20, 1926, 9773.   [15] *Ibid.*, 69:2, Feb. 14, 1927, 4063.
[16] *Ibid.*, 69:2, Feb. 17, 1927, 4099.
[17] Printed copy of remarks, Feb. 26, 1925, LaG. Papers.

watch Red Grange or Jack Dempsey or Babe Ruth.[18] Yet, in the late summer and fall of 1925, Fiorello LaGuardia, and hundreds of thousands of people in the city of New York, were concerned about the price of meat.

The retail price of meat jumped nine to ten cents in August, 1925, and a city-wide committee representing tenant associations, community councils, and civic organizations asked LaGuardia to study the meat situation and initiate some action.[19] A meeting of community leaders took place in LaGuardia's office in the district, discussing the advisability of organizing a meat strike in New York.[20] LaGuardia contacted the Retail Grocers Association of Manhattan and the Bronx, asking their co-operation in the meat strike.[21] Letters came from all over the city offering co-operation in the strike.[22] Senator Royal S. Copeland, at LaGuardia's request, presided over a meeting of community organizations on September 10, 1925, after which the press was told: "All in the conference agreed that the present prices place an undue burden upon the poor. These cheaper varieties of meat are the ones consumed by the great masses of the people of the city. They simply cannot afford to serve meat with the prevailing prices." [23] While Copeland was handling the New York meeting, LaGuardia hurried to Chicago to confer with the meat packers, but could get no satisfaction.[24]

He had sent a batch of wires to congressmen from the cattle-producing regions, to confirm his suspicion that cattle raisers were not getting the benefit of the increased prices. A letter from Tom Connally told of drought in his section and "a serious business depression." He received a bill of sale from Congressman Mansfield of Texas showing three cows sold at 1.5 cents a pound, purchased by one of the largest packers in the country. New York was paying twenty-eight cents a pound for sirloin and thirteen cents for hamburger at this time.[25] Mansfield said that prices for beef on the hoof were so low that cattlemen could not afford to feed their stock.

[18] Frederick Lewis Allen, *Only Yesterday* (New York, 1931), 233–234.
[19] LaGuardia to Alfred McCann, Sept. 2, 1925, LaG. Papers.
[20] Letters of Aug. 27, 1925, *ibid.*   [21] Aug. 31, 1925, *ibid.*
[22] John Gratz to LaGuardia, Sept., 1925, *ibid.*
[23] Press release, Sept. 10, 1925, *ibid.*
[24] Press release, Sept. 11, 1925, *ibid.*
[25] Bill of sale, Sept. 5, 1925, *ibid.*

LaGuardia passed this information on to the press, saying, "New York City is to be a city of vegetables, fruit, and fish, until meat exploitation stops." [26]

In response to a request by LaGuardia for an investigation, Secretary of Agriculture William Jardine wrote: "An investigation of this subject, such as you suggest, would entail a great deal of time and expense, and I regret that we are not in a position to undertake a study of this kind." [27] He enclosed a bulletin on the economical use of meat and received a blistering reply from the New York congressman, who said:

I asked for help and you send me a bulletin. The people of New York City cannot feed their children on Department bulletins. . . . Your bulletins . . . are of no use to the tenement dwellers of this great city. The housewives of New York have been trained by hard experience on the economical use of meat. What we want is the help of your department . . . to bring the pressure of the United States government on the meat profiteers who are keeping the hard-working people of this city from obtaining proper nourishment.[28]

The threatened strike did not come off, but LaGuardia continued his campaign against the high price of meat. When the House began discussion on a bill enabling the Department of Agriculture to set up a division of co-operative marketing, LaGuardia took the floor: "Mr. Chairman and gentlemen, now that the House is engaged in its favorite indoor sport of fooling the farmer, I want to take the opportunity to say just a few words for the consumer." Once again he denounced the jobbers, commission merchants, bankers, railroads, canning companies, and food monopolies and asked for a basic change in the system of distributing food. He noted that, as punishment for his break from the Republican party, he had been put on the Alcoholic Liquor Traffic Committee and said: "I am more interested in food than in booze." [29]

He told the House of his investigation of meat prices in New York the past summer and of his request for aid from the Department of Agriculture. "*This* is the help I got," he said, holding up the pamphlet on the economical use of meat. His colleagues

[26] New York *Times,* Sept. 5, 1925.   [27] LaG. Papers, Oct. 6, 1925.
[28] LaGuardia to Jardine, Oct. 14, 1925, *ibid.*
[29] *Congress. Rec.,* 69:1, Jan. 26, 1926, 2772–2773.

laughed. The department had also sent him a pamphlet on "Lamb and Mutton and Their Uses in the Diet," despite the fact, he told the House, that 90 per cent of the people in New York could not afford lamb chops.

"Why, I have right here with me . . ." LaGuardia said, and pulled out of his vest pocket a rather scrawny lamb chop. This had cost thirty cents in New York, he said. Then he reached into another pocket and pulled out a steak, saying: "Here is $1.75 worth of steak." Then, out of another pocket, a roast, commenting: "Now here is a roast—three dollars worth of roast. What working man's family can afford to pay three dollars for a roast of this size?" The cattle grazer, he noted, was getting 2 and a half to 5 and a half cents a pound, while the consumer paid 75 to 80 cents a pound. This meant, he concluded, that the packing-house monopolies were making unjustifiably large profits and could afford to cut prices substantially while continuing to make adequate returns.[30]

LaGuardia's figures were questioned by the Institute of American Meat Packers, and he replied:

Both of your letters display the arrogant attitude of the packers. . . . I maintain now as I told the people in Chicago that the packers have it in their power to reduce the retail cost of meat in New York City from 25% to 33½%. Some of these days we will simply stop eating meat in New York City and perhaps then we may arrive at a fair level of prices.[31]

It was true that LaGuardia's figures were not always accurate. He had spoken at times of the packers being able to cut prices 40 per cent and sometimes he had used the figure 25 per cent. When criticism was leveled at him, he shrugged it off impatiently. His principles, he believed, were fundamentally sound even if his statistics were not always accurate.[32]

Throughout the Coolidge years LaGuardia kept up a running

[30] *Ibid.,* Jan. 30, 1926, 3052, 3053.

[31] LaGuardia to Norman Draper, March 26, 1926, LaG. Papers.

[32] Government figures disputed LaGuardia's contentions about eighty-cents-a-pound roast. They show that the retail price of rib roast climbed from 21.8 cents in 1913 to 38.6 cents in 1927 and reached a high of 44.1 cents in 1928 (U.S. Department of Labor, Bureau of Labor Statistics, *Retail Prices 1890–1928* [Washington, 1929], 116–117).

battle for action against what he termed the "bread trust." [33] He charged that the Ward interests, headed by "Bread King" William B. Ward controlled the three leading baking companies in the industry and expressed shock that the Federal Trade Commission had voted to end its investigation of the four-hundred-million-dollar combine. (The probe had been ordered in 1924 by a Senate resolution.) Basil Manly's People's Legislative Service came to LaGuardia's aid by carrying on a pressure campaign among members of Congress, and on the other side of the Capitol, Burton Wheeler and other Progressives called for action.[34]

LaGuardia sent letters to various community leaders in Manhattan, asking for information on bread prices, sizes of loaves, and price changes, saying, "I need this information in my fight on the formation of a gigantic bread trust in this country." [35] He also

[33] If there was any issue on which the Populist and Progressive movements concentrated their heaviest fire (even if the ferocity was to a great extent only verbal), it was the iniquity of the trusts. The results were often picayune, but the fervor carried over into other issues and undoubtedly helped create the general climate of reform in twentieth-century America. The inactivity of the Coolidge regime was particularly evident in this area. Antitrust laws were not strictly enforced, only seventy-five cases being initiated between 1925 and 1929, and the Federal Trade Commission "adopted the policy of keeping secret the charges against business interests, minimizing cease and desist orders, and relying mainly on trade practice conferences, in which business agreed upon its own rules." The appointment of W. E. Humphrey, a lumber company attorney, to the Federal Trade Commission in 1925 gave the administration supporters a majority and led to a policy of easing up on antitrust action. In those rare instances when recommendations were made to the Justice Department, the Attorney General did not act (Soule, *op. cit.*, 134–138).

By the end of the decade the two hundred largest nonbanking corporations had combined assets of eighty-one billion dollars, nearly half of all corporate wealth in the nation, and received 43.2 per cent of the income of all nonbanking corporations. These two hundred giants represented .07 per cent of the total number of corporations in the United States. Between 1919 and 1929 their assets increased from 43.7 billion to 81 billion dollars (Adolf A. Berle and Gardiner C. Means, *The Modern Corporation and Private Property* [New York, 1937], 29–33). Thousands of firms disappeared in mergers, and holding-company empires came to dominate the economy. At the start of 1929, 93 of the 9 largest corporations were either wholly or in part holding companies (Soule, *op. cit.*, 143).

[34] Copy of remarks in Senate by Burton K. Wheeler, Feb. 10, 1926, LaG. Papers.

[35] LaGuardia to Mrs. Simkovitch, Feb. 15, 1926, *ibid.*

wrote to various retail bakers for data and on February 1, 1926, introduced two resolutions in the House, one calling on the Federal Trade Commission to determine whether or not the Ward Food Products Corporation was a combination in restraint of trade, the other asking the Department of Justice if it had taken any action against the Ward corporation.[36] The bills were buried in committee, and Speaker Longworth sustained a point of order against a LaGuardia motion to discharge his resolution from committee.[37] At a mass meeting in Carnegie Hall, LaGuardia told the audience: "A monopoly of bread is not only unlawful, but cruel and sinful. Where is the greed of the food manipulators going to end? It certainly is a critical time in our country when people are exploited on the very basic necessities of life." [38]

The Justice Department was finally prodded into action, and in April of 1928 a consent decree was entered in Federal Court ending the two-billion-dollar Ward Food Products Corporation.[39] However, Ward and others continued to maintain their control over the separate units in trust. The result was in keeping with the historic pattern of antitrust action, where so often intense struggles culminated in petty victories.

The decline of trade union membership from about five million to about three and a half million members in the twenties [40] reflected a consolidation of craft union organization, with a resultant bettering of conditions in those unions. However, millions of workers in the mass-production industries remained unorganized, their meager earnings averaged out with the augmented wages of the aristocrats of labor to give a favorable picture in the statistical totals. Furthermore, even among the organized workers, the fruits of prosperity were uneven, with the result that certain industries, notably the textile and mining industries, faced prolonged and bitter strikes through the decade. The activities of Congressman Fiorello LaGuardia in this period were vivid proof of the fact that certain important groups in the laboring population were suffering hardships amid the general well-being.

Following his sharp criticism of the use of the labor injunction

[36] New York *Herald Tribune,* Feb. 1, 1926.
[37] New York *Times,* Feb. 12, 1926.
[38] Press release, March 31, 1926, LaG. Papers.
[39] People's Legislative Service Bulletin of May 11, 1926, *ibid.*
[40] Soule, *op. cit.,* 227.

in the 1922 coal mine and railroad strikes, LaGuardia appeared on a dozen different sectors of the labor front throughout the twenties, wherever he thought his strident voice could have some effect. He walked the picket line and then spoke at a Madison Square Garden meeting protesting the use of an antipicketing injunction in the 1926 garment strike in New York,[41] and several months later he aided striking paper-box makers. He denounced the use of "kidnapped" Chinese strikebreakers to replace striking American sailors [42] and attacked the Pullman Company for preventing the organization of 12,000 Pullman porters.[43] He fought for pay raises for government workers [44] and even made the sports pages by denouncing "baseball slavery" and calling for the unionization of baseball players.[45] Testifying before the House Civil Service Committee, LaGuardia declared that women earning $1,200 a year in government service could not attend church on Sunday because they had to stay home and do their own washing. "They talk about Andrew Mellon being a great financier," he said. "Gentlemen, it is easy to play with hundreds of millions of dollars, but a woman who can keep her family clean and decent on $1200 a year is a real financier." [46]

When anthracite miners in eastern Pennsylvania went on strike in August, 1925, LaGuardia wrote a column for the New York *Evening Graphic* condemning the "arbitrary, brazen and wilful refusal of the operators" to accept Governor Gifford Pinchot's terms for settlement. He concluded with a plea for government ownership of the mines:

There seems to be one solution only. This country is blessed with a rich supply of coal. It is not the invention of any one man, it is God's gift to the people of America. It requires only human labor to dig the coal, bring it from the bowels of the earth so it may be used for the benefit of mankind. The American people all have an interest in this coal. The government should step in at this time, compel a settlement of existing differences and immediately commence a survey of available coal fields now in operation and take such actions as eventually will put the government in possession of the gift of God that

---

[41] New York *Times*, Sept. 21, 1926.   [42] *Ibid.*, July 16, 17, 1927.
[43] *Ibid.*, July 16, 1927.   [44] New York *Evening Journal*, May 4, 1925.
[45] Bill of Feb. 2, 1925; copy in LaG. Papers.
[46] Washington *News*, March 20, 1928.

surely was intended to be used for the benefit of all American people.[47]

The strike ended in February, 1926, but LaGuardia continued to take every opportunity to tell Congress that the coal resources were God's gift to the American people and should be nationalized.[48]

Two years later, in February, 1928, when another strike, this time against a series of wage cuts, tied up the Pennsylvania coal fields,[49] LaGuardia visited the strike area at the invitation of *News* editor Lowell Limpus. He interviewed strikers, their wives, and children, and his anger reached the boiling point. Once again he saw the labor injunction in action when a group of men, women, and girls were arrested by state police for mass picketing in violation of a federal court injunction.[50] After watching children hide under their beds in miners' shacks (strikebreakers had the day before poured volley after volley of bullets through the windows of the school at Broughton just before the 350 school children were to be dismissed),[51] LaGuardia told newspapermen:

I have never seen such thought-out, deliberate cruelty in my life as that displayed against the unfortunate strikers by the coal operators and their army of coal and iron police. Imagine, gentlemen, a private army, with its private jails, where the miners are unlawfully detained and viciously assaulted! . . . I have been preaching Americanism as I understand it, where justice and freedom and law and order prevail, but these miners and their families don't even get a shadow of it. . . . Asbestos will not hold the statements I shall make on the floor of the House.[52]

[47] New York *Evening Graphic,* Dec. 2, 1925. He had, a year before, urged the same solution on Congress (*Congress. Rec.,* 68:1, Jan. 3, 1924, 520).

[48] *Congress. Rec.,* 69:1, June 17, 1926, 11472.

[49] The entire bituminous coal industry in that period was generally acknowledged to be a "sick" industry, facing deadly competition from other power sources, and it often tried to solve its problem by cutting labor costs (Dulles, *Labor in America,* 247).

[50] Pittsburgh *Sun-Telegraph,* Feb. 4, 1928.

[51] New York *Daily News,* Feb. 3, 1928.

[52] Pittsburgh *Sun-Telegraph,* Feb. 4, 1928. LaGuardia sent a telegram to the House of Representatives asking the passage of a resolution to investigate the strike. He submitted an affidavit signed by a strikebreaker, swearing that this miner and another strikebreaker had been paid $25 each

Senator Burton K. Wheeler followed LaGuardia into the mine district and then told the press:

> It seems inconceivable to me that Secretary of the Treasury Andrew W. Mellon, with all his millions, should not have relieved the horrible misery and suffering which I have found so abundant right here in his own back yard. All day long I have listened to heartrending stories of women evicted from their homes by the coal companies. I heard pitiful pleas of little children crying for bread. I stood aghast as I heard most amazing stories from men brutally beaten by private police-men. It has been a shocking and nerve-racking experience.
>
> I have been familiar with industrial strife for twenty-five years. I have called mining camps my home for twenty-two of those years. Yet I never in all my experience have seen anything which might approach the horror of the situation here. . . . I am going back to Washington tonight, prepared to demand action and prompt action.[53]

Meanwhile Hiram Johnson introduced a resolution in the Senate calling for an investigation of the strike, while LaGuardia and Pennsylvania Congressman Casey asked the House to act.[54]

Holding a sheaf of photographs and affidavits in his hand, La-Guardia spoke at length in the House on the Pennsylvania coal strike.[55] He used the opportunity to denounce the use of the in-junction in labor disputes and noted that in this case it barred the union from retaining attorneys, paying strike benefits, and even from singing hymns. Several months later, writing about the strike in the *Nation,* LaGuardia urged the government to "step in and take possession of all natural resources, coal, oil, water and gas." [56]

---

by coal and iron police for firing into the miners' barracks (*Congress. Rec.,* 70:1, Feb. 4, 1928, 2470).

[53] New York *Daily News,* Feb. 6, 1928.

[54] New York *Times,* Feb. 9, 1928.

[55] *Congress. Rec.,* 70:1, Feb. 8, 1928, 2734–2737.

[56] "The Government Must Act." *The Nation,* CXXVI (April 4, 1928), 378–379. The Senate Committee on Interstate Commerce had been investigat ing the troubles of the coal industry, and ended up with 3,414 pages of con-tradictory testimony from miners and operators. There was enough evidence of general distress, however, for committee chairman James E. Watson of Indiana to introduce a bill licensing of coal operators in interstate com-merce, enabling the formation of mergers, and recognizing labor's right to organize and bargain collectively. The bill, however, did not get anywhere (McAlister Coleman, *Men and Coal* [New York, 1943], 132–135).

Throughout the Coolidge era, budget-balancing and tax reduction (particularly in the higher brackets) became almost obsessive administration policies, while LaGuardia kept saying that the burden of taxation should be lifted from the lower-income groups of the nation. His pursuit of this idea led to a long conflict, covering most of the decade, between the blunt-talking congressman from the tenement districts of New York and one of America's richest men, Secretary of the Treasury Andrew Mellon.

The slight, seventy-year-old Andrew W. Mellon, according to William Allen White, was "President Coolidge's bad angel," whose millions of dollars "spoke gospel to Coolidge." As Secretary of the Treasury he was the "guardian angel of all that the Chamber of Commerce held sacred in its white marble palace." [57] Samuel Hopkins Adams has said, "As one of the world's richest men, Mr. Mellon logically and conscientiously conceived his official duty to be the conservation and protection of wealth." [58] The vast Mellon empire included coal, coke, gas, oil, and aluminum. "No other Croesus," Mellon's biographer says, "has levied toll on so many articles and services." War contracts boosted further the already considerable Mellon fortune, which one day would reach two billion dollars.[59] One hundred Mellon companies were connected through a two-hundred-and-fifty-million-dollar banking institution, Union Trust.

Mellon's first report in 1921 to the House Ways and Means Committee and the Senate Finance Committee recommended the repeal of the wartime excess-profits tax and a cut in income surtaxes from a 73 per cent ceiling to a 40 per cent ceiling. There would be no tax cuts below the $66,000 a year level. To make up for the loss in revenue, Mellon proposed a higher documentary-stamp tax, a two-cent postal card, a license tax on motor vehicles, and several other taxes. When Bob La Follette attacked his proposals, the Secretary of the Treasury replied:

Any man of energy and initiative in this country can get what he wants out of life. But when that initiative is crippled by legislation or by a tax system which denies him the right to receive a reasonable share of his earnings, then he will no longer exert himself, and the

[57] *A Puritan in Babylon* (New York, 1938), 395–396.
[58] *Incredible Era* (Boston, 1939), 227.
[59] Harvey O'Connor, *Mellon's Millions* (New York, 1933), xi-xv.

country will be deprived of the energy on which its continued great-ness depends.[60]

Accepting the bulk of Mellon's ideas, Congress removed the excess-profits tax and cut the top surtax to 50 per cent.

On November 10, 1923, a few months after LaGuardia's return to Congress, the "Mellon Plan" was presented, calling for a reduc-tion of the top income surtax from 50 per cent to 25 per cent. In-comes under $8,000 were to have their tax rates lowered from 8 per cent to 6 per cent and incomes under $4,000 from 4 per cent to 3 per cent.[61] When the Democratic caucus decided to battle for a 44 per cent surtax ceiling and the administration insisted on Mel-lon's 25 per cent, the House became involved in a long debate.

Taking the floor in the midst of this deadlock, LaGuardia said he was more interested in the tax on low incomes, which he be-lieved should be lowered to 4 per cent on incomes under $8,000 and 2 per cent on incomes under $4,000 (a rather mild suggestion for LaGuardia, apparently born of a feeling that the tax on in-comes under $4,000 could not be completely eliminated under the existing line-up of forces in Congress). He insisted on discussing the tax program in terms of fundamental principle, which was in this instance, he believed, that of "social taxation," deliberately conceived as a weapon for redistribution of the wealth. He told the House:

When you are taxing income and you run into 25, 35, and 40 percent, it is no longer a revenue, scientific, or a progressive tax. It is a social tax, and I am in favor of it, and I am not afraid to say that I believe in a social tax. It is consistent with the progress of the Republic. Let us be frank about this. . . . The danger of the concentration of enormous fortunes in a few hands is quite obvious—we are now wit-nesses to a national scandal, the result of enormous fortunes. [He was referring to the Teapot Dome disclosures.] [62]

Mellon's idea of reducing taxes to encourage business was based on a historical untruth, LaGuardia said, because the men of wealth never took genuine risks; they let others, including the govern-ment, initiate hazardous ventures before moving in; and even then stockholders incurred the risk while the men behind the enterprise

[60] *Ibid.*, 126–128.   [61] *Ibid.*, 131.
[62] *Congress. Rec.*, 68:1, Feb. 16, 1924, 2602–2603.

held bonds, backed by the physical properties of the enterprise.[63]

Ogden Mills supported the "Mellon Plan," and when he expressed his viewpoint in writing to a stenographer who was a member of the Women's National Republican Club she expressed her appreciation, telling him that his letter was especially welcome in view of one she had received from LaGuardia, which had said, with rather ungallant sarcasm: "I can readily understand your anxiety and that of your co-workers on the taxes over $200,000 a year. I was a stenographer once and I remember how much I had to worry about my income over $200,000 a year." [64]

The House finally passed the Mellon tax plan over the objections of a handful of progressives, with the Democrats yielding to Republican strength. In the Senate, a Progressive-Democratic coalition forced the adoption of a substitute bill, and the final result was a reduction of the top surtax to 40 per cent, coupled with an increase in the inheritance tax from 25 per cent to 40 per cent. The latter change displeased Mellon, who said, "Estate taxes, carried to an excess, in no way differ from the methods of the revolutionists in Russia.[65]

In spite of the watering down of the "Mellon Plan" by stubborn opposition, the result was a victory for those asking eased taxes on higher incomes. Mellon was feted and praised and hailed as the greatest Secretary of the Treasury since Hamilton. Nicholas Murray Butler wrote happily to Republican leader Samuel Koenig: "I am just back from Pittsburgh where on Saturday night there took place at the Chamber of Commerce dinner the most magnificent demonstration in favor of Secretary Mellon that it is possible to imagine. . . . It was really a great occasion." [66]

LaGuardia did not confine his attacks on the Mellon philosophy to the halls of Congress. When Federal Judge George English of the New York District "punished" a New Jersey Central Railroad official (who had been convicted of defrauding the government of

[63] Mellon said, on the other hand, "I have never viewed taxation as a means of rewarding one class of taxpayers or punishing another" (Andrew W. Mellon, *Taxation: The People's Business* [New York, 1924], 11). Higher taxation on the rich was ultimately borne by the consumer, Mellon said. His was, in a sense, the "trickle-down" theory in converse (*ibid.,* 21).

[64] LaGuardia to Miss Clara Artus, Feb. 18, 1924, Ogden Mills Papers, Library of Congress, Washington, D.C.

[65] O'Connor, *op. cit.,* 135–136.   [66] April 14, 1924, Butler Papers.

more than one million dollars) by fining him $12,500, with no jail sentence, LaGuardia was furious. He told the newspapers:

On this day that the whole nation with bowed heads [it was Memorial Day] are uttering prayers and paying tribute to the men who have given their all for the sake of the country, we read the disgusting announcement that a weak judge, or perhaps influenced, failed to send a reptile of a profiteer to jail on the plea that the profiteer had a "weak heart". . . . If Joyce with a weak heart stole a million dollars, what would he have done if he had had a strong heart? [67]

In October of 1925, Mellon presented a new tax program to Congress, lowering the maximum surtax on high incomes to 20 per cent, establishing a basic 5 per cent rate on low incomes, reducing and eventually repealing the inheritance tax, and repealing the gift tax. The House Ways and Means Committee emerged with unanimous support for these proposals, and LaGuardia sprang to the attack, wondering how John Garner of Texas, for one, could reconcile his backing for the "Mellon Plan" at this time with his previous opposition to it. Once again he declared that the basic purpose of the progressive income tax was to prevent the concentration of wealth in the hands of a few families. "I do not want to destroy wealth," LaGuardia said, "but I do want to abolish poverty." He took sarcastic note of Coolidge's presidential message pleading for charity to dependent widows and orphans, while his Secretary of the Treasury took steps to reduce by $7,961,165 the taxes of the six men who had made over four million dollars each in 1924.[68]

Mellon's new program also eliminated the publicity clause, which had required the government to reveal the amount of taxes paid by each taxpayer, and LaGuardia sharply attacked this change,[69] engaging in a spirited floor debate with Ogden Mills, whose keen mind forced LaGuardia several times to retreat from exaggerations.

Some of his colleagues from working-class districts took the floor to support LaGuardia's tirades against the "Mellon Plan." Congressman William P. Connery of Massachusetts told the House:

[67] New York *Times,* May 31, 1924.
[68] Press release, Dec. 10, 1925, LaG. Papers.
[69] *Congress. Rec.,* 69:1, Dec. 15, 1925, 889.

I am not going to have my people who work in the shoe factories of Lynn and in the mills in Lawrence and the leather industry of Peabody, in these days of so-called Republican prosperity when they are working but three days in the week, think that I am in accord with the provisions of this bill. In Lawrence they have worked so little in the mills that they do not know what a week's work looks like. When I see a provision in this Mellon tax bill which is going to save Mr. Mellon himself $800,000 on his income tax and his brother $600,000 on his, I cannot give it my support.[70]

Finally, the House, anxious for quick action, moved to limit debate on the tax bill, and LaGuardia, restraining his anger with unusual external calm, rose to decry the limitation: ". . . and I say now in the best of humor and in all kindliness that if this condition continues, well then the fight is on. We will keep a quorum here and make objection to every unanimous consent request made." [71] When the tax bill came up for final passage with all the essential features of the original Mellon proposal intact, and even a more drastic reduction in the surtax than the administration had asked, the House approved it overwhelmingly, 355 to 28.[72] Among the handful opposing the bill were LaGuardia and fellow Progressives Kvale of Minnesota, and Nelson and Schafer of Wisconsin. Thus in early 1926 the "Mellon Plan" became law.

Two years later Mellon once again proposed tax reductions for high incomes. LaGuardia countered with an amendment establishing a 30 per cent surtax on incomes over $1,500,000. It was quickly rejected by the House.[73] When the bill passed several days later by a vote of 366–24, LaGuardia, Kvale, and Nelson were again among the progressives opposing it, joined this time by Wisconsin's Frear.[74]

As Coolidge prepared to leave the White House, business interests could look back with satisfaction on the six years of operation of the Mellon program. Persons receiving $5,000 a year had benefited from tax reduction to the extent of a 1 per cent gain in income after taxes; for higher incomes the gains were progressively larger until those with incomes of one million dollars saved 31 per cent

[70] *Ibid.*, Dec. 17, 1925, 1031–1032.
[71] *Ibid.*
[72] *Ibid.*, Feb. 23, 1926, 4443.
[73] *Ibid.*, Dec. 12, 1927, 500.
[74] *Ibid.*, Dec. 15, 1927, 717–718.

after taxes. As the decade came to a close, 25 per cent of the nation's annual income was earned by 5 per cent of the population.[75] La-Guardia's stand against the maldistribution of wealth had crumbled before the big guns of Mellon and prosperity.

All of the welfare issues of the 1920's, however, were pushed into the back pages by the highly publicized furore over prohibition. The columns of the New York *Times* in the 1920's devoted proportionately far more space to LaGuardia's views on prohibition than to his views on any of the important economic questions of the time; yet, his own activity on prohibition both inside Congress and out never matched the energy and time he devoted to issues like profits, prices, labor, taxes. If LaGuardia's tirades against prohibition were more publicized than his criticisms of big business, that was because, in Hofstadter's words, "Prohibition was a pseudo-reform, a pinched, parochial substitute for reform." [76] It was a side show, but so long as the nation's press kept the lights darkened on the main show, it was bound to appear as the chief attraction.

The issue, however, was not wholly a sham, for there were other aspects to prohibition than that of bluenosed Puritanism trying to reform personal habits by legal proscription. For one thing, it involved the issue of governmental corruption by moneyed interests. As LaGuardia said to the House in February, 1925:

Gentlemen, what is the use of closing our eyes to the existing conditions? The importation of liquor into this country is of such magnitude, it comes in such enormous quantities, involving use of a fleet of steamers, involving enormous banking operations, involving hundreds of millions of dollars, that it could not carry on without the knowledge if not the connivance of the authorities entrusted with the enforcement of the law.[77]

LaGuardia pointed his finger at the Department of Justice and noted that one of its "ace" enforcement officers named Franklin L. Dodge had confiscated $200,000 worth of liquor for his own use and then got the Department to prosecute the man from whom he had taken it, one George Remus. A good place to start enforcement, LaGuardia declared, would be in the Department of Jus-

[75] Soule, *op. cit.,* 317.   [76] *Age of Reform,* 287.
[77] *Congress. Rec.,* 68:2, Feb. 7, 1925, 3276.

tice.[78] In a long speech in the House in early 1927, he charged govenment agents with unlawfully operating a whiskey-selling Bridge-Whist club in New York, a whiskey-selling poolroom in Norfolk, Virginia, and a distillery at Elizabeth City, North Carolina.[79]

Prohibition involved class and economic issues, and LaGuardia was quick to seize upon this. Fashionable Atlantic luxury liners, he told the House, were doing rumrunning, delivering Europes's finest liquors to New York customers who had enough money to pay for them. The business, he said, amounted to $500,000 a week and was conducted by a syndicate traffic manager at 32 Broadway. The rumrunning was accomplished, he disclosed, by the simple expedient of buying and attaching to the liquor cargo stamps which indicated passage by customs inspectors.[80] Thus, LaGuardia charged, the lower-class urban immigrant was hounded by the law, while wealthy men and women drank their liquor undisturbed.

To demonstrate the ineptness of the Volstead Act, LaGuardia publicly combined two legal drinks to create an illegal one, and the New York *Times* reported jovially:

Representative Fiorello H. LaGuardia will walk into a drug store at 95 Lenox Avenue, near 115th Street, at nine o'clock this morning and there purchase a bottle of malt extract, 3.5 percent alcohol, and a bottle of near-beer. He will mix the two at the soda fountain and drink the concoction. Then he will stand by and wait to be arrested.[81]

Behind the clowning, however, LaGuardia kept pointing to deeper questions. Civil liberties—the usurpation of power by police officials—was one of them. In the spring of 1929, LaGuardia expressed his disgust at the applause that erupted in the House of Representatives when a member described the shooting by police of a Volstead Act violator. He asked the House to remove the word "applause" from the record, for he thought its insertion a shameful commentary on the chamber. Denouncing the shooting of suspects

[78] *Ibid.*, 69:1, March 24, 1926, 6175.
[79] *Ibid.*, 69:2, Jan. 20, 1927, 2018–2022.
[80] New York *World*, Dec. 17, 1927. One month later, his charges were substantiated by secret service men of the Treasury Department (New York *Telegram*, Jan. 14, 1928).
[81] June 17, 1926.

in prohibition cases, he declared that police were using killings as a smoke screen for their own activities. Arbitrary powers, he insisted, should not be placed "in the hands of every thieving, grasping, murderous police officer who spends half of his time hi-jacking and the other half of his time enforcing the prohibition law." [82]

Throughout his congressional vigil, LaGuardia kept in touch with affairs back in the Twentieth District. Hundreds of letters came to him asking for aid in getting jobs, in securing rent decreases, in filling out naturalization papers. He referred many of them to Vito Marcantonio, who was on duty at Harlem House on 116th Street,[83] and answered many letters himself, keeping in personal touch this way with community groups, asking often for data on prices, rents, and other conditions.

Municipal problems, particularly those affecting the "bread-and-butter" needs of low-income groups were constantly on LaGuardia's mind. A court decision allowing the I.R.T. to raise its fare to seven cents [84] drew an immediate verbal attack from him, and he introduced a bill to prevent federal courts from aiding "greedy public service corporations." [85] He denounced the establishment of "an exclusive club for exclusive people in Central Park," noting that "out of season fruit from distant tropics, rare species of fish specially imported and choice morsels to tickle the tongue of the fastidious gourmand were menued and their high prices featured. Not since Nero banqueted and fiddled while Rome was burning has such contempt for the rights, comfort and feelings of the people been shown." [86]

Commenting bitterly on the huge fortunes being made in the Jazz Age, while ordinary people struggled for bare necessities, LaGuardia wrote:

It is true that Mr. Mellon, Mr. Ford, Mr. Rosenwald, Mr. Schwab, Mr. Morgan and a great many others not only manage to keep their enormous fortunes intact, but increase their fortunes every year. . . . But can any one of them improve on the financial genius of Mrs. Maria Esposito or Mrs. Rebecca Epstein or Mrs. Maggie Flynn who is keeping

---

[82] *Congress. Rec.*, 71:1, May 1, 1929, 754.

[83] Interview with Miriam Marcantonio, Aug., 1956; also various letters in LaG. Papers.

[84] New York *Times*, May 13, 1928.   [85] *Ibid.*, May 21, 1928.

[86] Clipping from New York *Graphic* article of 1928 in LaG. Papers.

house in a New York tenement raising five or six children on a weekly envelope of thirty dollars a week, paying thirty and thirty-five dollars a month rent, trying to send the children to school warmly clad and properly nourished, paying exorbitant gas and electric bills and trying to provide meat at least once a day for the family? [87]

As 1928 drew to a close, LaGuardia accompanied a New York *American* reporter on a tour of homes in the poorer districts of the city in connection with the newspaper's annual relief fund and reported: "I confess I was not prepared for what I actually saw. It seemed almost incredible that such conditions of poverty could really exist." [88] The article was lost amid reports of a city dancing, singing, and shouting with joy to usher in the year 1929.

[87] *Ibid.*   [88] New York *American,* Jan. 1, 1929.

12 · LaGuardia and Progressive

Politics, 1924-1929

FOR some Progressives the defeat of La Follette in 1924 was further evidence of, as H. L. Mencken put it (though he was not a Progressive), the American people's "congenital incapacity for the elemental duties of citizens in a civilized state." [1] Others took hope from the nearly five million votes, but returned, weary and disappointed, to the between-elections lethargy that often marks middle-class liberals in days of middle-class prosperity. Still others, sharply or vaguely aware of discontent in the midst of plenty, or moved by some inner turbine that functioned through defeat as well as victory, refused to relinquish their battle regalia. LaGuardia and a handful of Progressives in and out of Congress were among these.

First, they had to face the calm but efficient retribution of the victor. When the Republican caucus in the House of Representatives convened in January, 1925, thirteen Progressives, including LaGuardia, were not on the invitation list.[2] In a stormy House debate, Representative Wood of Indiana, speaking for the Republican party, declared the outcasts could not come to the caucus unless they "appeared as penitents." [3] Protesting this action, Wis-

[1] Notes on Democracy, 100–101.
[2] Besides LaGuardia, those excluded were Keller of Minnesota, Sinclair of North Dakota, and Cooper, Veight, Nelson, Schafer, Lampert, Beck, Browne, Schneider, Frear, and Peavey, all of Wisconsin (New York Times, Jan. 30, 1925).
[3] Ibid.

consin's Frear pointed out that Theodore Roosevelt, Nicholas Longworth's father-in-law, had broken from the Republicans in 1912, yet had not been excommunicated by the party; but the Republican decision stood. It meant that the Progressives, including Henry Allen Cooper, oldest Republican member of the House, would be barred from the important House committees. Nicholas Longworth took the floor on January 30, 1925, and delivered a twenty-minute sermon on party regularity, scolding the insurgents as a father would scold an errant son, but promising, magnanimously: "We will welcome them back at the first opportunity when they evince any desire to come back and qualify as Republicans." [4]

LaGuardia was not to be humbled into repentance and retorted by pointing to the haste with which regular Republicans in New York had accepted Progressive endorsement at election time. He warned his punishers: "I serve notice now that I shall fight in New York City and they can keep me out of their caucus, but I can keep them out of the City Hall in New York City. We have our own conditions there, Mr. Floorleader." LaGuardia turned to reassure his Progressive colleagues: "I hope that my Progressive friends will not worry unduly. If these Republicans will not invite us to their conference or caucus we will not invite them to ours." He would not retreat an inch from the position he had taken in the campaign, he said, and did not regret for one moment his support for the La Follette ticket, taunting the Republican victors with these words: "The record of Senator La Follette as a statesman and economist and legislator will stand out and live long after many inconspicuous and colorless representatives dragged into office by a party emblem will have been entirely forgotten." [5]

In February, 1925, the remnants of the group that had with wild enthusiasm designated La Follette and Wheeler six months before gathered disconsolately in Chicago to declare the end of the Conference for Progressive Political Action. Eugene Debs, who had but a few months to live, urged that the delegates not lose hope, saying, "Do you know that all the progress in the whole world's history has been made by minorities?" [6] Some delegates remained and set up a committee authorized to call a third-party convention

[4] *Congress. Rec.*, 68:2, Jan. 30, 1925, 2712–2715.
[5] *Ibid.*, Jan. 10, 1925, 1638.   [6] MacKay, *op. cit.*, 234.

in the fall, but this never materialized and the committee held desperately to life, maintaining tenuous liaison with state and local progressive groups until the end of 1927.[7] New York, for instance, held a Progressive convention in the spring of 1925, led by Arthur Garfield Hays, and Oswald Garrison Villard, but little was accomplished.[8]

While the national and state movements struggled feebly to keep alive, local groups in a few areas maintained their vitality. One of these was in the Twentieth Congressional District, where a number of meetings of the "Progressive Party of the 20th Congressional District" were held in February and March of 1925.[9] Even here, however, the bitterness of the 1924 campaign had left a rift which could not be healed.

In the course of his campaign as a Progressive with Socialist backing, LaGuardia had built up a retinue of active workers who were not tied to the regular political machine, but came straight out of the tenements of his district. Vito Marcantonio and Nick Saldiveri had organized them into a cohesive and disciplined force, tied together by personal loyalty to LaGuardia and devotion to the ideals he championed. They regarded the regular political machine with deep distrust. As Saldiveri said, "to practically every one who has joined our movement the word Leader and Executive Member seems poison." [10]

When the election of 1924 was over and LaGuardia returned to Washington, the regular machine moved back into the district to take over, with the county committee appointing its own precinct captains over the heads of the rank-and-file in the district. "It seemed," Saldiveri complained to LaGuardia, "as if everything that took place . . . had to have the sanction from Downtown." He and his friends did not want to be "cogs in a wheel which was to be run by unseen powers." [11] Therefore, they resigned from the regular club in the district, and, led by Vito Marcantonio, Charles Rappina, and Louis Pisa (who were affectionately dubbed "The Three Rebels"), began to hold their own meetings at Socialist headquarters in the district. LaGuardia encouraged them and

[7] *Ibid.*, 238.   [8] Call for convention, April 22, 1925, LaG. Papers.
[9] *Ibid.*   [10] Saldiveri to LaGuardia, March 2, 1925, *ibid.*
[11] *Ibid.*

wrote to Marcantonio about a future meeting "to talk on the situation and possibilities of the progressive party." [12] While in Washington, he maintained contact with the problems of the people in the district, referring letters asking for aid to Marcantonio. "Marc," as LaGuardia called him, handled hundreds of tenants' cases in the New York courts during this period.[13]

In March of 1925, LaGuardia made his annual report to constituents, who jammed the Star Casino on 107th Street to hear him. Lambasting the Coolidge administration, he declared that Mellon seemed to take as his guide the twenty-fifth verse of the fourth chapter of St. Mark: "For he that hath, to him shall be given: and he that hath not, from him shall be taken even that which he hath." He noted the discrepancy between Coolidge's talk of economy and huge expenditures for armaments. Hitting at an issue particularly close to his listeners, LaGuardia commented on the refusal of Congress to ease the immigration law. He promised to return to Congress "to prevent the majority party going wild in its determination to legislate for the benefit of the few at the cost and expense of the great masses of the American people." [14]

He could win the applause of his constituents, organize a Progressive club in the district, and defy Longworth on the floor of Congress; yet, from the standpoint of orthodox political tactics, LaGuardia was in a serious predicament. With the Republican party having disowned him, and with the Progressives disbanded, he would face the 1926 election with no national organization behind him. An exchange of letters in the spring of 1925 between Wisconsin Progressive John M. Nelson and New York Progressive J. A. H. Hopkins (of the Committee of Forty-eight, and now chairman of a "Provisional Committee" of the Progressive party) revealed this problem as it applied, not only to LaGuardia, but to all congressional progressives. Hopkins wanted the insurgents in Congress to come out with a "ringing declaration" of allegiance to a new Progressive party (which at this time existed mostly in Hopkins' imagination) and pledge to run on the Progressive line in 1926 and 1928. He was contemptuous of their "intention to crawl back into the Republican party." He claimed that it was this timidity which had held the progressive movement back at every crucial turn.[15]

Nelson's argument was based, he claimed, on practicality; for Progressive congressmen to commit themselves at this point to a new party would be "political suicide." All of his friends had told him, Nelson explained patiently, that they could not win on a Progressive ticket in an off-year election. "How would it help the progressive movement if we lost our strength in the House and in the Senate?" he asked. He pinpointed the situation in Hopkins' own state:

Now, my dear Hopkins, just consider the case of LaGuardia. He has to use some present available party organization. To run as a Progressive will mean sure defeat—for there is no such party organization and until some great issue is at stake or some national personality is a candidate for president, success will be very doubtful. Let us be practical; it is folly to build on shifting sands and idle dreams.[16]

If Nelson's logic was sound, if LaGuardia was to be guided by "practical" political considerations and seek at least a temporary reconciliation with the Republican regulars, then his actions between the spring of 1925 and the fall of 1926 were most strange.

In April, 1925, he traveled to Brooklyn to attend services for the martyrs of the Easter uprising in Ireland and drew prolonged applause when the chairman, introducing him, said: "We have here a man, who is, like ourselves, a rebel. A man who is noted for the fact that he admits no one as his master." [17] Ten days later he was at a Rotary Club in Asbury Park, denouncing both Republican and Democratic parties, saying that "there is no party division in Congress on matters involving more than a million dollars and there is no definable difference between the Republican and Democratic Parties." [18]

In September he went to Wisconsin to help Robert La Follette, Jr., campaign for the seat made vacant by the death of his father that summer. To many requests for support from Republican

[15] Hopkins to Nelson, May 11, 1925, LaG. Papers.
[16] Nelson to Hopkins, April 24, 1925, *ibid.*
[17] Brooklyn *Daily Times*, April 13, 1925.
[18] Asbury Park *Evening Press*, April 23, 1925.

candidates running in the New York municipal elections in 1925, LaGuardia wrote: "Surely the Republican Party does not want an endorsement from one whom they have so recently cancelled from their membership." [19] He was following through on the warning he had given to Longworth in January, that the Republicans could punish him in Congress but he could hurt them in New York.

He made this especially clear in the 1925 mayoralty race in New York. State Senator James J. Walker, backed by Tammany, defeated John Hylan, backed by Hearst, for the Democratic nomination. LaGuardia had been mentioned as an independent candidate, but he quickly declined, making a remarkably prescient statement: "Senator Walker in all likelihood will be elected. The people of New York City will receive a liberal education in public utilities ruling the city . . . and a real 'everybody-getting-his' administration." [20] The New York *Times* commented on the absence of a Progressive ticket and the excellent prospects for Tammany: "It will be remembered that when the Cheshire Cat vanished, it left its grin behind. But the only third-party grin which is at present visible is on the face of the Tiger." [21]

LaGuardia proceeded to endorse for mayor the Socialist candidate, Norman Thomas, writing him: "I shall support your platform and the entire Board of Estimate and Apportionment. I agree with you that it is the best means of political education available to Progressives and Liberals." [22] A week before election he spoke at a Brooklyn mass meeting for Thomas. Walker won the election with ease.

Throughout 1926, LaGuardia maintained contact with John M. Nelson, J. A. H. Hopkins and other Progressive leaders. A "Progressive Research Bureau" was formed with Nelson as chairman and LaGuardia as secretary, aiming to organize the progressive Republicans in Congress. LaGuardia was invited in February to a dinner intended to effect a liaison between New York progressives and those in Congress; Oswald Garrison Villard, La Follette, Jr., Wheeler, Norris, Borah, Frear, and Shipstead were among the guests.[23] Meanwhile the persevering executive committee set up

[19] LaGuardia to Hugh F. Flaherty, Oct. 22, 1925, LaG. Papers.
[20] Press release, *ibid.*   [21] Sept. 22, 1925.
[22] Sept. 22, 1925, LaG. Papers.
[23] Gilson Gardner to LaGuardia, Feb. 5, 1925, *ibid.*

by the 1925 national Progressive convention kept grinding out desperate messages of hope, professing to see the signs of growing disillusionment with conservative politics.[24]

LaGuardia reported to his constituents at the Star Casino in the summer of 1926, telling the crowded meeting hall: "Congress has just passed through a crime wave. Ruled by the Ku Klux Klan and the trust bosses, the legislative body of the United States government is but a travesty of what it should be." He asked for the nationalization of coal and oil resources and added: "If that is radicalism, put me down as a radical." [25]

His most significant comments at the meeting were reserved for the problem of political parties and the forthcoming election. Pointing to the existence of progressives and conservatives within both parties he called for a new realignment of the major parties to preserve American democracy. In accord with this view, he announced to the cheering crowd that he would run for Congress in November on an independent ticket.

LaGuardia, it appeared, was flaunting his progressivism with almost insulting disdain for the traditional niceties of political compromise. Yet one month later the Republican candidate for Congress in the Twentieth District, by decision of the county committee, withdrew from the race, and LaGuardia's name was substituted as the sole Republican nominee.[26] It was an astounding climax. By any "sober" estimate, by any "practical" view, LaGuardia had marched deliberately toward the precipice of political suicide. He had bolted the party, denounced its candidates, excoriated its program, hobnobbed with Socialists, called for the nationalization of basic industries, and with perfectly infuriating aplomb had virtually spat in the faces of the Republican leaders. At the critical moment, however, they had, with at least outward poise, designated him as their candidate. And he, with equal nonchalance, had accepted.

His bold independence between the 1924 and 1926 elections can be explained by his indomitable courage, by that hot flame of principle that burned inside him. Such an explanation would be accurate; but it would not tell the whole truth. The fact was that

[24] Bulletin, July 1, 1926, *ibid.*
[25] New York *Evening Graphic,* July 20, 1926.
[26] New York *Times,* Aug. 25, 1926.

LaGuardia, with his own independent organization in the district, masterminded by the brilliant Marcantonio, with the enthusiastic support of the tenement-dwelling Italians, Jews, and Irish, who saw him as one of their own, felt confident of victory with or without Republican support. He knew, too, that the Republican party needed him—more, probably, than he needed them. They wanted the votes of the low-income national minorities which LaGuardia would bring into the Republican columns if he were on the ticket.[27] The Republican party endorsed LaGuardia, said the New York *Times,* because he

has dazzled and irritated alternately the Republicans since he ran like hotcakes for President of the Board of Aldermen. They have never been able to depend on his staying hitched. He is unstable, flighty, airy, too confounded independent. . . . Party labels mean nothing to him. . . . Mr. Koenig was forced to adopt Mr. LaGuardia, not for the latter's sake, but in the hope to increase the Republican vote in the Harlem section of Manhattan and to bring about the election of one more Republican representative from New York City.[28]

For LaGuardia, it was a beautiful wedding of politics and principle, and it worked.

The congressional race was close; LaGuardia won another of his hairbreadth victories, getting 63 votes more than his Democratic opponent, a district leader named H. Warren Hubbard.[29] The Democrats made important gains in New York State, electing Al Smith as Governor for the fourth time and sending Robert F. Wagner to the Senate to replace the defeated Wadsworth. LaGuardia was now the only Republican congressman from New York City and told reporters he would call a caucus of New York City Republicans if he could "find a convenient telephone booth." [30]

[27] Drew Pearson and Robert S. Allen, *Washington Merry-Go-Round* (New York, 1931), 246, confirm this picture, saying: "In 1926, none of the parties wanted him. He was preparing to run as an independent when the Republicans, finding themselves hard-pressed in their local campaign, persuaded him to run on their ticket."

[28] Aug. 26, 1926.

[29] LaGuardia received 9,121 votes, Hubbard 9,058, Socialist Dobsevage 1,049.

[30] New York *Times,* Nov. 3, 1926.

Back in the House after the election, he gave no indication of having made any "deal" for the Republican nomination. Although the *Times* had reported during the campaign that LaGuardia had promised to support the Coolidge administration,[31] this was far from the truth, for he continuel his attacks on administration policy. In February, 1927, he reiterated his progressive faith, paying tribute on the House floor to the dead La Follette and promising to continue his "fight against special privilege." [32] A month later, he reported to his constituents at the Star Casino, denouncing the Senate filibuster against the Boulder Dam project, charging that the Ku Klux Klan was working openly in Congress against changing the immigration laws, and sharply attacking the armaments program of the administration.[33]

In June, 1927, he received warm tribute in a feature article by Duff Gilfond in the *American Mercury,* in whose pages H. L. Mencken had been, through the decade, stabbing at Congress with his pitiless pen.[34] Gilfond called LaGuardia "a splotch of color on a gray scene" and reported that after listening to the pompous and continual use by hypocritical congressmen of the word "great," it was refreshing to hear LaGuardia's favorite adjective—"lousy." He described LaGuardia in the House:

Short, spry and round, he bounces in and out of his seat, waking the somnolent gentlemen about him in his efforts to catch the Speaker's eye. His arm waving frantically for recognition, he seems like a grown-up school boy trying to answer teacher's question. He offers as many, if not more amendments to pending legislation than any member of the House. He has an astounding acquaintance with a great variety of legislation, and a way of seeing points that most men miss.[35]

The local elections that took place in the fall of 1927 saw him once again ignore blithely his recent support by the Republican machine. He endorsed Socialist-supported Jacob Panken in his race for Municipal Court judgeship, saying: "It is indeed reassuring to

[31] *Ibid.,* Aug. 25, 1926. [32] *Congress. Rec.,* 69:2, Feb. 20, 1927, 4263.
[33] Press release, March 17, 1927, LaG. Papers.
[34] H. L. Mencken, *Notes on Democracy* (New York, 1926), 124, refers to the House as a "depressing gang of incompetents, mainly petty lawyers and small-town bankers . . . in intelligence, information and integrity . . . comparable to a gang of bootleggers."
[35] *American Mercury,* XI (June, 1927), 152–158.

find that there is no corporation owning real estate and operating tenements that have the name of Judge Panken as part of their corporate name." [36] (His grammatical singulars and plurals, as in the foregoing quotation, often became hopelessly mixed, but his ideological syntax remained intact.) When asked to endorse a Republican candidate for local judicial office, he replied: "If Cohen is all right on the Rent Laws and is in no way tied up with real estate holdings or apartment house operators, such as some of the dogs who call themselves judges, I shall be glad to go on his committee." [37]

With the bitterness of 1924 having dissipated somewhat by 1927, and with the close division of strength in the new House requiring careful nurturing of those holding the balance of power, LaGuardia was taken out of solitary confinement and given a post in the Seventieth Congress on the important Judiciary Committee of the House. There seems to be no way of knowing with certainty if there was a connection between this and his actions in January of 1928. However, his behavior that month did indicate one thing clearly: he was not an absolute teetotaler at the bar of political patronage. On January 12, he introduced the kind of bill that good organization men have been introducing in Congresses since the days of the Founding Fathers—a bill creating three additional judgeships for the United States District Court in the Southern District of New York.[38] And the following day he wrote a hand-cupped-on-one-side-of-the-mouth letter to County Chairman Samuel Koenig:

Now this is the lay of the land. . . . We have Tammany on record by Senator Wagner introducing a similar bill in the Senate. Today big stiff Carew . . . asked me not to call up the bill. . . . I told him I could not do that. . . . He then said he was opposed to the bill and would defeat it again unless satisfactory arrangements could be made. Perhaps they have in mind to have Wagner's bill considered in the Senate first in the hope that the Senator may make some arrangement as to appointments. . . . In the meantime it might be well if you got some publicity on the need of additional judges in New York. . . . Besides these judges, hope to have several hundred jobs for you before long. Had a very satisfactory talk with Ogden yesterday. Will tell you all about it when I see you.[39]

[36] Statement of Sept., 1927, LaG. Papers.   [37] Sept. 2, 1927, *ibid.*
[38] H.R. 9200, Jan. 12, 1928, *ibid.*   [39] Jan. 13, 1928, *ibid.*

A year later, after Tammany obstruction designed to win a voice in the appointments had been overcome, the bill for additional judgeships passed.[40]

LaGuardia now received a letter from Colonel Arthur W. Little, a prominent Republican in New York. "As you and I know," Little wrote, "things do not happen, but must be made to occur. This is my opening shot with you for your 1929 campaign for the mayoralty." Little was interested in securing the 1928 Republican presidential nomination for Frank Lowden, former Illinois congressman and governor, who had been a leading contender in 1920. If LaGuardia could help him become a delegate to the national convention from New York, Little wrote, the two would work together for Lowden's nomination against Hoover. "With Lowden elected, I have the best of reasons to believe that you and I would not be without influence at the White House." This "in" with the White House, Little assured LaGuardia, would get him the nomination for mayor in 1929.[41] It is hard to say whether or not LaGuardia intended to go along with this plan. The two men conferred shortly after this letter,[42] but the Lowden boom never materialized.

The uneasy alliance of convenience between LaGuardia and the Republican party continued; he did not stop flaying the Coolidge administration on the floor of Congress and speaking his mind on whatever issue he chose; nor did he refuse to co-operate with party leaders when they faced a common problem or when he could assuage their antagonism at small sacrifice. When the 1928 presidential campaign got under way with no third-party candidate in sight,[43] LaGuardia scrupulously refrained from supporting either Republican candidate Herbert Hoover or Democratic candidate Al Smith, although there is no doubt that Smith's political views

[40] LaGuardia wire to Charles Tuttle, Jan. 15, 1929, *ibid.*

[41] Little to LaGuardia, Jan. 16, 1928, *ibid.*

[42] LaGuardia wire to Little, Jan. 19, 1928, *ibid.*

[43] John Dewey headed, in 1928, a newly formed League of Independent Political Action, in which economist Paul Douglas and others joined, but not until 1932 did it take active part in the presidential campaign, supporting Socialist candidates in that year (MacKay, *op. cit.*, 255). Oswald Garrison Villard, *Fighting Years* (New York, 1939), 504, believes that La Follette's death was important in keeping the Progressive party dormant in 1928.

were much closer to his own than Hoover's. He conducted his congressional campaign on his own platform, after trying unsuccessfully to get the Republican party to adopt a number of his planks.[44]

Throughout the campaign, he maintained lines of communication with all political groups. Frederic C. Howe wrote to him on behalf of the Progressive League for Alfred E. Smith, which was headed by Frank P. Walsh and David K. Niles, saying: "We are digging in here for Governor Smith and are making substantial headway." [45] A Socialist Assembly candidate in Brooklyn received LaGuardia's endorsement.[46] His relations with the Republican oligarchy remained cool, and he kept complaining in letters to Republican friends that the national leadership was making it dificult, because of its conservative program, for local Republicans to win in New York. He told Republican National Committeeman John Tilson, "Damn it all, I want to do what I can but a lot of sons of female dogs in Washington are going out of their way to make things hard for us here in New York." [47]

Nicholas Murray Butler, disgusted with the nomination of Hoover and the Republican stand for the Eighteenth Amendment, forgot old differences and endorsed LaGuardia's candidacy in the Twentieth District, saying:

In this welter of unreason, intolerance, bigotry and hypocrisy through which we are passing, it is a pleasure to find a Republican candidate who is a genuine liberal and who at the fortunate cost of alienating the bigots, the intolerants and the persecutors, will stand for American principles of government and social order, for the historic teachings and ideals of the Republican Party and in favor of those truly pro-

[44] New York *Times,* June 12, 1928. He fought for inclusion of six planks in the Republican platform: a modification of the prohibition law, action against the power trust, the exclusion of federal courts from local utility problems, the outlawry of war, political autonomy for Puerto Rico, and limitations on the use of injunctions in labor disputes.

[45] The League was a thinly disguised adjunct of the Democratic party, it seemed, for Howe's letter was originally written on stationery of the Democratic National Committee—of which he was executive-secretary—after which he apologized, sending along the Progressive League letterhead (Howe to LaGuardia, LaG. Papers).

[46] New York *Times,* Nov. 1, 1928.

[47] LaGuardia to Tilson, Oct. 5, 1928, LaG. Papers.

gressive policies upon which the opportunity of the individual man and the lasting prosperity of the country can alone depend. I greatly hope that LaGuardia will be elected by a substantial majority.[48]

LaGuardia, relying mainly on his own political organization, defeated his Democratic opponent by 1,200 votes [49] and wrote Butler a letter of thanks for his endorsement.[50] The relations between the two men were warmer now than they had ever been, and, the campaign over, LaGuardia returned to his congressional duties in Washington.

During the Christmas holiday, while Congress observed a brief recess, LaGuardia quietly became engaged to Marie Fischer, his secretary since 1917 and constant ally through the past twelve years of hectic activity, and on February 28, 1929, they were married. The engagement and wedding had come as a surprise to even their close friends.[51] It had been a long companionship and a quick courtship. Congressman Kvale of Minnesota, a Lutheran minister, performed the ceremony, and the happy couple took an apartment in an ordinary tenement on 109th Street near Madison Avenue. In the coming years they would alternate between this and a tiny apartment in Washington. The new Mrs. LaGuardia gave up her duties as his secretary, took some courses at Columbia University, and spent much of her new leisure time reading, while continuing to counsel her husband in his political moves.[52]

In the spring of 1929, with LaGuardia's obvious encouragement, there began a boom to secure for him the Republican nomination in the November mayoralty race. As early as April, a committee was appointed by the Columbian Republican League to work for his nomination. Support began to come from various quarters: the New York Young Republican Club; the Kings County League of Italian-American Republican Clubs; a group of Brooklyn county committeemen. More and more Samuel Koenig seemed to look favorably on LaGuardia's candidacy. The reason was clear: he was the candidate most likely to succeed. His following among Italian

[48] New York *Times,* Nov. 1, 1928.

[49] Dickheiser, Democrat, got 10,878 votes, and Caspe, Socialist, 377 votes (New York *Times,* Nov. 8, 1928).

[50] Nov. 16, 1928, Butler Papers.   [51] New York *Times,* March 1, 1929.

[52] Limpus, and Leyson, *op. cit.,* 273–276; also, New York *Evening Journal,* April 10, 1929.

and other national groups in the city was huge.[53] Koenig had looked around hard for a good conservative candidate,[54] but had not found one, and decided in favor of LaGuardia. There was a brief splurge of opposition by the perennial antimachine conservative William J. Bennett,[55] but it did not get far. On August 1, 1929, an unofficial Republican city convention named LaGuardia the Republican candidate for mayor, with the blessing of Samuel Koenig, who said that the decision "represents the desires of the rank and file of the party and of the plain people." [56]

The nomination was one thing; real support from the Republican party was another.[57] To too many conservatives in Republican ranks, LaGuardia was still anathema, and they could not bring themselves to campaign for him or to contribute money for his expenses.[58] One observer of that campaign, Ed Flynn, has said, "It is interesting to note that hundreds of people who had no interest in Socialism seemed to regard LaGuardia with more fear and suspicion than they did the outright Socialist candidate." [59]

While conservatives in his party could not back him because of his progressive views, liberals shied away because the Republican machine had nominated him. Their coolness toward LaGuardia was due also to the fact that the Socialist party had a capable and forceful candidate, Norman Thomas. *The Nation,* while praising LaGuardia for his "independence, courage, true liberalism," backed Thomas because "the Republican machine is not one whit better and is far less able than Tammany Hall." [60]

Heading the list of obstacles to a LaGuardia victory in 1929 was

[53] *Columbian Republican,* June 1929, in LaG. Papers.

[54] New York *Telegram,* Feb. 8, 1929.

[55] LaGuardia says Bennett had not wanted to be a candidate but was led to sign a statement during a drinking session with a newspaperman (*Making of an Insurgent,* 79).

[56] New York *Times,* Aug. 2, 1929. Koenig said later, "I was roundly abused for having nominated Mr. LaGuardia, and one important individual said we were disgracing the party" (Oral History Project, Columbia University).

[57] Samuel Koenig later noted that "LaGuardia ran his own campaign in 1929" (*ibid.*). Frank Freidel says LaGuardia was "weighed down by a foolish and incompetent Republican organization existing on what crumbs it could pick up from Prohibition and corruption" (*Franklin D. Roosevelt: The Triumph* [Boston, 1956], 91–92).

[58] *Ibid.*   [59] Edward Flynn, *You're the Boss* (New York, 1947), 55.

[60] Oct. 23, 1929.

the simple fact that his Democratic opponent was James J. Walker. One year older than the forty-seven-year-old LaGuardia, born in Greenwich Village into an Irish family tied to Tammany (his father had been a Tammany alderman, assemblyman, and ward leader), Walker had moved nimbly up the political ladder, from law school to the Assembly and then the State Senate—guided by the experienced hands of Charles F. Murphy himself. In the legislature he voted with the machine and made many warm personal friends.[61]

LaGuardia was, thus, operating under great handicaps, but he campaigned like a man out to win. He stormed from one end of the city to the other, concentrating on the issues closest to the needs of the city's slum dwellers: food, housing, schools, parks, sunlight, and dirty politics. After an intensive study of the food situation in New York City, he told audiences in every borough of his findings. The methods of food distribution, he disclosed, were chaotic and wasteful, for food went from farmer to commission merchant to wholesaler to jobber to retailer to consumer, and the result was high prices. A three-hundred-page report on this situation had been made in 1912 by a committee set up under Mayor Gaynor, and the committee (which followed a barrel of spinach and found it was loaded and unloaded nine times from farmer to consumer) recommended the construction of large terminal markets. Under Hylan the Bronx Terminal Market had been built for freight cars and steamships to unload their produce directly into proper storage areas where retailers could secure their produce. However, LaGuardia charged, Walker had taken no step to open this market or to build new ones. New Yorkers were paying, he reminded his audiences, forty-three cents out of every hard-earned dollar for food.[62]

Speaking in the slum-ridden Bedford-Stuyvesant section of Brooklyn, LaGuardia pointed to the "thousands of sunless, fire-exposed homes with yard toilets and dark and ill-kept public halls"

[61] Norman Thomas and Paul Blanshard, *What's the Matter with New York* (New York, 1932), 159–160. Grover Whalen (whom he later appointed police commissioner) said of Walker: "What a charm the man had. . . . You couldn't help but like him" (Grover Whalen, *Mr. New York: The Autobiography of Grover Whalen* [New York, 1955], 133).

[62] Undated copy of speech, LaG. Papers.

which, he said, were "an everlasting disgrace to the richest city in the world." Walker had fought, he noted, against the Multiple Dwelling bill, which set up standards for improving tenements, and after the bill became law Walker's Corporation Counsel had joined realty interests in attacking the bill in the courts.[63] In regard to housing, he told his listeners that "the Walker administration has made a record of callous indifference and malevolent sabotage unequalled by any administration in the history of the city." [64]

Both Norman Thomas and LaGuardia were merciless in their attacks on Tammany Hall and its long history of graft and corruption, which, they claimed, were being continued and extended in the Walker administration. They kept insisting that Governor Franklin D. Roosevelt should use his powers of investigation to clean up New York City, and Roosevelt's own associations with Tammany were, by implication, drawn into the charges. However, Roosevelt did not act, and Thomas and LaGuardia did not press the charges further, thus leaving their assault "fiery but inconclusive." [65]

In the last days of the campaign, speaking to Irish audiences, La-Guardia showed signs of desperation. He pointed to the fact that a "British peeress," one Lady Armstrong, was on the Walker committee and charged that in Walker's apartment there was an autographed photograph of the Prince of Wales. (What better proof could be offered of Walker's infidelity to the Irish Republic?) Going far afield from his usual concentration on important issues, he descended to a discussion of Walker's reputation as a well-dressed man, telling members of the Irish Republican League:

He is not a well-dressed man, according to the standards of American gentlemen. He is a loudly-dressed man—displaying all the bad taste and vanity of the political parvenu who got rich quick. . . . He is the loudly-dressed man according to the styles of the English fop or the Paris gigolo.[66]

[63] Oct. 15, 1929, *ibid.*   [64] Speech of Oct. 16, 1929, *ibid.*
[65] Freidel, *op. cit.*, 91–92. Freidel says that Roosevelt offered to act if LaGuardia and Thomas would present specific facts to him. Since they did not go further than their original charges, he was, Freidel believes, politically safe in not acting. Of course, "politically safe" does not bear upon the question of ethics.
[66] Speech of Oct. 26, 1929, LaG. Papers.

Walker was equal to the occasion, responding gracefully and chidingly that "until we have an ordinance to the contrary, I shall
bathe frequently, as is my custom; and change my linen often, as
is my perhaps eccentric desire; and patronize the tailor of my own
choice." [67]

Four days later, as the campaign reached its low point in personal
vilification, LaGuardia read to his audience an editorial on Walker
printed years before by Hearst's New York *American,* which now
was backing Walker. The editorial, replying to Walker's request
to look at his record, retorted:

Which record do you mean, smelly little Jimmie? Do you mean the
record of your grandiose speeches at Albany? Or do you mean the
records you were making for the putrid meat sellers in the courts of
New York? Do you mean your lip service to the five-cent fare? Or do
you mean the bills you introduced quietly to give perpetual franchises
to certain bus companies at ten-cent fares? Which record are you
standing on, smelly little Jimmy? [68]

Such tactics apparently did not help LaGuardia.[69] When the
final tallies were in on election day, Jimmy Walker had won a
sweeping victory, with 865,549 votes against 368,384 for LaGuardia
and 174,931 for Thomas. The *Times* commented: "No one could
have been surprised—not even Major LaGuardia really—at the reelection of Mayor Walker. If ever there was a foregone conclusion
it was this one. The stars in their courses fought for Mr. Walker." [70]

LaGuardia returned now to Congress. A week before the New
York mayoralty election, the stock market had collapsed in a wave
of wild panic, and, though few people realized it at this time, the
nation was entering upon a new era.

[67] Gene Fowler, *Beau James: The Life and Times of Jimmy Walker* (New
York, 1949), 246.

[68] Sept. 11, 1925.

[69] Norman Thomas, who shared platforms with LaGuardia several times
in the course of the campaign and debated the issues with him, has said:
"I never thought he made a very brilliant campaign in 1929. . . . He played
very much under wraps for LaGuardia" (interview with Norman Thomas,
Oral History Project, Columbia University).

[70] Nov. 6, 1929.

13 · *Hunger vs. Private Enterprise:*

First Round

FROM the nation's leaders in business and government, the 1929 crash and ensuing depression drew, in erratic succession, shocked disbelief, forced optimism, grudging recognition, and, finally, the slow gathering of remedial efforts. When Wall Street collapsed, the reaction of the President, his cabinet, and the nation's leading financiers was that the storm would soon blow over; only courage and confidence were needed.[1] Whistling in the dark became widespread: Mayor Jimmy Walker of New York asked motion picture theaters to show only cheerful films, *True Story Magazine* advised wage earners to buy more luxury items on credit, and a new song was copyrighted in November entitled "Happy Days Are Here Again."[2]

To Fiorello LaGuardia and other progressives, the convulsions of October, 1929, did not come, as to the financial world, mysteriously and suddenly out of a monolithic prosperity, for they had been recording the seismic signals throughout the twenties.[3] More-

[1] In Washington, Andrew Mellon, whom Hoover had retained at his Treasury post, gave the press a cheerful New Year's prediction of "steady progress," while the President said that business could have "greater assurance" for the coming year. New York's leading bankers and merchants were also optimistic, seeing a return of prosperity in 1930 (Mitchell, *op. cit.*, 31).

[2] Dixon Wecter, *The Age of the Great Depression* (New York, 1948), 12–13.

[3] Many of the letters of complaint to LaGuardia were from people who had been jobless even before the market crash. In October, for instance,

over, they had access to instruments, which, if not as refined as
those of the Stock Exchange, were perhaps better gauges of the
depth of the economic disorder. Letters from constituents in growing number testified to the seriousness of the situation. While stock
prices were tumbling furiously in Wall Street in the first days of
the crisis, LaGuardia was reading a letter from a woman in his
district:

I am asking you a favor. My husband is out of work for the last four
weeks and I have seven children none able to work and we are certainly down and out up against the rent and everything. Now Mr.
LaGuardia what I want to ask you is to try and get my husband a job
of any kind as he is a man not afraid of any kind of work so we could
get on our feet.[4]

President Hoover, despite his public assurances, soon began to
view the situation as a serious one. On November 21, 1929, he
called a meeting of business leaders at the White House, urging
that employment and wage levels be maintained on both economic
and humanitarian grounds. That same afternoon he conferred with
leaders of the American Federation of Labor and the Railroad
Brotherhoods and asked them to co-operate in restraining demands for wage increases.[5]

It was soon evident, however, that the program of voluntary

he received a letter signed by four sons, asking aid in obtaining a job for
their father, who had been out of work for three years (Oct. 27, 1929, LaG.
Papers). The precrash rise of economic distress is attested to by Lillian
Wald, who watched the growing signs from her Henry Street "window."
She tells of the winter of 1928–1929 when the children were sitting in the
kindergarten drinking milk. One little boy said he would be a carpenter
when he grew up, whereupon a four-year-old spoke up soberly: "Miss Wald,
the carpenter that lives in our house ain't got any work" (*Windows on
Henry Street* [Boston, 1924], 227–228). The general situation on the East
Side became serious enough in February of 1929 to warrant a special meeting at the settlement house (*ibid.*).

[4] Letter of Oct. 21, 1929, LaG. Papers.

[5] Hoover's first annual message to the Seventy-first Congress on December
3 recognized that "uncontrolled speculation" had brought plummeting farm
prices and unemployment, and pointed to his efforts in stimulating state
and local governments and private business leaders to bolster productive
activity. He also recommended an increase in the public works program,
banking reform, and administrative reorganization for economy purposes
(W. S. Myers and W. H. Newton, *The Hoover Administration* [New York,
1936], 26–27).

action to maintain purchasing power levels was not working satisfactorily. Industry found it impossible to keep its assurance to expand employment; indeed, its operations contracted considerably. The promise not to cut wages was broken elsewhere, although dividends continued to be paid at high levels for two years.[6] In November, Hoover had wired governors and mayors asking expansion of public works programs, and now the responses came, "cordial but vague." [7]

In November and December of 1929, while Hoover was placing primary reliance on his voluntary method and Governor Roosevelt of New York was apparently even less active,[8] LaGuardia was rushing about, trying to dig up data about past depressions and planning legislation of a long-term character to prevent unemployment. He studied British laws on unemployed insurance and began working on a public works program based on federal aid to the states.[9]

His office kept receiving letters from constituents asking for help. A tenement dweller on 113th Street wrote:

> You know my condition is bad. I used to get pension from the government and they stopped. It is now nearly seven months I am out of work. I hope you will try to do something for me. . . . I have four children who are in need of clothes and food. . . . My daughter who is eight is very ill and not recovering. My rent is due two months and I am afraid of being put out.[10]

The letters poured in, scrawled on cheap note paper in Italian or in English, and LaGuardia had to reply helplessly that the entire country was in a crisis and there were no jobs to be found.[11]

---

[6] Mitchell, *op. cit.*, 84.

[7] *Ibid.*, 85. Governor Franklin D. Roosevelt of New York replied that he expected to recommend a public works program to the legislature "limited only by estimated receipts from revenues without increasing taxes" (Myers and Newton, *op. cit.*, 29).

[8] Roosevelt's annual message to the legislature on Jan. 1, 1930, "contained not a single reference to rising unemployment nor to increasing privations of the people," and it was not until the appearance of public soup kitchens and a deluge of letters pleading for aid that he moved swiftly into action (Bernard Bellush, *Franklin D. Roosevelt as Governor of New York* [New York, 1955], 128).

[9] Letter of Dec. 3, 1929 to W. E. Walling, LaG. Papers.

[10] Letter of Feb. 14, 1930, *ibid.*

[11] As conditions worsened in New York City, with soup lines becoming

When Governor Franklin Roosevelt ordered a survey of unemployment in the state, it was found that in some industrial centers 75 per cent of the labor force was jobless. Factory employment had decreased 10 per cent since October. Roosevelt then set up a joint business-labor commission to work out methods for the future control of unemployment.[12] He did not believe that the depression would last, but thought it important to anticipate future economic difficulties by remedial legislation.[13] In a statement much like Hoover's, he called upon the "good will" of New York industrialists to curb unemployment.[14]

Meanwhile, the first unemployment census in the nation's history, taken in April of 1930, showed three million unemployed, with 180,000 people jobless in Manhattan alone,[15] but the rate at which unemployment was increasing made these statistics obsolete almost as soon as they were tabulated. Nine months later, a special census showed six million unemployed.[16]

In the early months of 1930, LaGuardia worked feverishly to get House action on several bills authored by Senator Robert F. Wagner of New York, which had already been approved by the Senate. One of the measures proposed a free national employment service, managed locally, to serve as a clearing house for jobs and jobseekers. After a stubborn fight in the House Judiciary Committee to force the bill onto the floor,[17] LaGuardia led the campaign for

---

more frequent and the furniture of evicted families beginning to appear on the sidewalks, radical groups were quick to point to all this as evidence of the breakdown of the capitalist system. The Communist-connected Trade Union Unity League called for a huge demonstration on March 6, 1930, advancing a program of public works, unemployment insurance, the halting of evictions, and calling for a "Revolutionary Workers" government (*ibid.*).

[12] Bellush, *op. cit.*, 129.   [13] *Ibid.*   [14] *Ibid.*

[15] U.S. Department of Commerce, Bureau of the Census, *Fifteenth Census of the United States: 1930, Unemployment* (Washington, 1932), II, 2, 379.

[16] Wecter, *op. cit.*, 18–19. The extent to which the January, 1930, census underestimated unemployment is discussed by Mitchell, *op. cit.*, 92.

[17] Committee chairman George Graham's minority report said: "To me the establishment of another bureau in Washington with its multitude of employees and its contribution to centralization is exceedingly offensive and objectionable." According to Pearson and Allen, *op. cit.*, 247, only a threat to destroy the Republican majority by organizing a bolt of dissident Republicans brought the bill onto the floor.

its adoption. The National Association of Manufacturers contended that the bill constituted a violation of states rights, and LaGuardia countered by pointing to other federal activities carried on within state boundaries, like flood control, farm relief, and the public health service. The new age of giant industry, he told the House, had nationalized the economy and thus demanded federal regulation of activities heretofore considered local. He said:

States' rights, I am sorry to say, has too often been used as a weapon to prevent progressive legislation. In this instance many exploiters of labor may be found raising a cry of states' rights and the constitution in order to prevent the enactment of necessary legislation to control and abolish unemployment. . . . Unemployment in one state is a matter which concerns every other state. I believe it is one of the most important functions of government to deal with the question of employment and unemployment.[18]

In this speech LaGuardia reiterated what he had been saying for years, that the economic system had to be revamped to meet new conditions. "There is no more justification for unemployment in this day and age than there is for epidemics of preventable diseases," he declared.[19]

However, LaGuardia did not feel that at this time the nation was prepared to accept, from a constitutional point of view, federal action in matters which the states had been handling for over a century. In view of the difficulty of securing constitutional amendments, he proposed instead that a governors' conference be called to secure uniform state legislation dealing with child labor, old-age pensions, unemployment insurance, and wages and hours.[20]

While the House debated the Wagner proposal for a national employment agency, the House Judiciary Committee considered another bill initiated by the New York senator, setting up a permanent advisory board to recommend to the President long-range, planned programs of public works, forestalling economic crises. Prevention rather than cure was the objective. Andrew Mellon wrote to the chairman of the Judiciary Committee, commenting on proposed public works in his department, that "our present resources are strained to the utmost to keep up with the present

[18] *Congress. Rec.,* 71:2, June 10, 1930, 10407–10411.
[19] *Ibid.*   [20] *Ibid.*

work. For this reason, to carry out advanced planning for buildings . . . in addition to that now contemplated, is not feasible with our present resources." [21]

With such arguments from the administration, the Wagner Public Works bill emerged from committee only after it had been so emasculated that even the National Association of Manufacturers could approve it. Emanuel Celler of Brooklyn dissented from the majority report of the committee, objecting to the amendments which had cut the heart out of the bill. "There is a disposition," Celler said, "to minimize the present unemployment and business depression. Proclamation after proclamation is promulgated by the President and his cabinet officers reiterating that prosperity is in the offing, and with each proclamation unemployment and business adversity increase." The vital parts of the bill, calling for public works planning in advance, had been eliminated, he noted. Celler called attention to the fact that in the past Hoover had, on a number of occasions, expressed a favorable attitude toward public works, but that now, when action was badly needed, the president was renouncing his earlier position.[22]

LaGuardia issued his own minority report, supporting Celler, and flaying the amendments which would "cripple and destroy the purpose of the bill." [23] He contrasted what he called meticulous planning for war, with the refusal to embark on long-term programs for economic security. "If it is necessary for the War Department to prepare careful plans for wars which will probably never occur," he declared, "it is surely much more necessary to provide in advance for the relief of industrial depressions which are sure to come." [24]

The Wagner bills could not be expected to receive enthusiastic support so long as the administration, and many private groups, were still unconvinced of the severity of the economic dislocation. American Federation of Labor President William Green informed Hoover, while the Wagner bills were being debated in the House, of "improvement" in the employment situation, which he found "decidedly encouraging." [25] And Congress, after approving moder-

[21] Andrew Mellon to George S. Graham, June 13, 1930, LaG. Papers.
[22] Minority report of Congressman Celler, *ibid.*
[23] Minority report of LaGuardia, June 19, 1930, *ibid.*
[24] *Labor*, June 24, 1930.   [25] Myers and Newton, *op. cit.,* 39.

ate increases in public works appropriations, adjourned in July, 1930. The following month William Green issued another rather optimistic statement, saying that Hoover's policies were beginning to have a stabilizing effect.[26]

Toward the end of the summer of 1930,[27] LaGuardia began to plan his re-election campaign. Tammany's new chieftain, John F. Curry, had planned a surprise for the race in the Twentieth District by picking a young Italian, Vincent Auletta, as the Democratic candidate against LaGuardia.[28] Curry was still enjoying his reminiscences of the Walker victory over LaGuardia in the 1929 mayoralty race and felt confident that Tammany's Number One irritant would now be ousted from his congressional seat.

In the fall of 1930, however, the fortunes of insurgency were riding high, lifted there by the depression. Hoover's efforts to meet the growing unemployment seemed more and more puny as the months went by, and the crisis deepened. His loss of popularity was so apparent even as early as May of 1930 that Louis Brandeis could write from his Supreme Court perch to Norman Hapgood, "Politically, things American have taken a great turn since May, 1929." [29]

Strengthened by the support of Nicholas Murray Butler, who also insisted that the New York State Republican party take a stand against the Eighteenth Amendment,[30] LaGuardia declared he was ready to defy the organization on this issue and run as an independent. This did not become necessary, for the Republican organization needed LaGuardia desperately at a time when its prestige was sinking daily. It was conscious, too, of the support for LaGuardia in many important circles, both Republican and Democrat. The New York *Times* was pointing to corruption in Jimmy Walker's administration as proof of LaGuardia's prescience and of his fitness to serve in Congress. "Representative

[26] *Ibid.*, 42.

[27] LaGuardia spent a good part of the summer of 1930 working on a scheme for unemployment insurance, after writing to the British Ministry of Labor for information on the insurance system in Britain. Then he sailed to London as a delegate to the Inter-Parliamentary Union, taking his wife Marie along and making the trip a second honeymoon.

[28] New York *Evening Journal*, April 23, 1930.

[29] Mason, *op. cit.*, 600.

[30] LaGuardia to Butler, Sept. 20, 1930, Butler Papers.

LaGuardia," the *Times* said, "has the right, if any man had, to stand up in New York City today and say 'I told you so.' Recent disclosures of corruption in the municipal government . . . seem to furnish full justification for the charges which Mr. LaGuardia freely made in the last Mayorality campaign." [31]

Prohibition became one of the important issues in the campaign. Nicholas Murray Butler had discussed with LaGuardia the strategy for prohibition repeal early in the year.[32] The issue crossed party lines, and Democrats like Robert F. Wagner stood firmly with LaGuardia against the drys.[33] Heywood Broun had noted LaGuardia's floor fight against prohibition, saying, "Some day the United States will honor LaGuardia for the persistent and skillful fight which he has made in Congress against Volsteadism." [34] LaGuardia kept pointing, in congressional debate, to the difference between breaking ordinary criminal laws and violating the prohibition statute. "An act which is inherently wrong," he said, "an act which involved moral turpitude, an act which indicates depravity, cannot be compared with an act which for 8,000 years has been legal and is now prohibited by statutory law." [35]

The campaign was conducted in an atmosphere of growing re-

[31] Aug. 30, 1930.

[32] Butler to LaGuardia, Dec. 24, 1929, and Jan. 21, 1930; LaGuardia to Butler, Jan. 24, 1930; Butler to LaGuardia, Jan. 27, 1930, Butler Papers. By 1930 certain key factors were making the position of the drys more and more untenable—almost universal disregard of the law, inaction by the state legislatures, reluctance on the part of the federal law enforcement agencies (Charles Merz, *The Dry Decade* [New York, 1930]).

[33] Washington *Herald,* Jan. 6, 1930.

[34] Washington *Daily News,* Jan. 10, 1930. LaGuardia's attacks on the Volstead law in the House were described by one reporter: "In debate on the floor he suggests a fighting cock more than a flower. He talks rapidly, his right arm working like a piston to emphasize every statement" *(ibid.,* Jan. 29, 1930).

[35] *Congress. Rec.,* 71:2, Feb. 15, 1930, 3732–3735. As the election campaign opened in the fall, LaGuardia suggested to Nicholas Murray Butler that Republican candidates come out openly against the Eighteenth Amendment, and Butler replied: "I applaud the suggestion. . . . The opposition is pretty well routed now, and a few more thrusts such as you gave them . . . will finish the business" (LaGuardia to Butler, Sept. 3, 1930; Butler to LaGuardia, Sept. 4, 1930, Butler Papers).

sentment by the working people of New York against the mounting toll of joblessness and of evictions, alongside the seeming
inability of government to stop the downhill movement. Families
were without food and fuel, and winter was coming. When the
International Apple Shippers Association offered fruit on credit
to the jobless to sell at five cents, there was a rush to accept, and
by November six thousand persons were selling apples on the
streets of New York.[36]

LaGuardia's battles against high prices and profiteering, his
constant exhortations for the protection of living standards, were
remembered by many of his constituents. In the last session of
Congress he had waged a powerful struggle on the House floor
for the adoption of the ill-fated Wagner bills to aid the jobless.
The New York *Evening Journal* counted 970 speeches which
LaGuardia had made during the eight-month session ending in
July, and noted: "On evenings of important social functions in
Washington which other public officials and their wives attend,
Congressman LaGuardia may be found in the Congressional
library, buried in books, digging for facts." As quickly as one
scheme or one bill was put down, it seemed, LaGuardia came up
with another. Some were well-thought-out plans for long-term
economic readjustment; others were spur-of-the-moment stopgap
measures.[37]

As the election neared, the New York *Daily Mirror* came out
in support of LaGuardia, saying:

It will be a tragic thing for the people of New York if Mr. LaGuardia
is defeated. He is the only real liberal in the delegation from this
state—one of the few in the whole House. He has maintained un-
ceasing vigilance against the plots of predatory wealth, food profiteers,
and grafters of all kinds. . . . He is incorruptible. Fiorello LaGuardia
is one of the outstanding and really effective Wet leaders in Congress.
. . . Citizens, do not let this worthy public servant be destroyed.[38]

[36] Wecter, *op. cit.,* 18–19.

[37] Some of the latter drew amused skepticism from the press, like La-
Guardia's suggestion that every man with a job should buy a suit for a
jobless man, who would buy a suit for another man when he secured a job.
To dramatize this, the congressman had a picture taken at Harlem House,
showing him buying a suit for an unemployed neighbor (New York *Daily
News,* Sept. 20, 1930).

[38] Oct. 24, 1930.

From a vacant store on 106th Street and Madison Avenue, La-
Guardia directed the campaign, paying, as usual, meticulous attention to every detail. Edward Corsi, Vito Marcantonio, and
Marie Fischer LaGuardia helped to weld together the organization which filled the neighborhood with placards and posters and
kept up the street-corner speeches through the night before the
election.[39]

LaGuardia defeated Auletta by a clear majority, 9,934 to 8,217
votes.[40] It was a particularly impressive fact in view of the Democratic landslide locally and nationally. Franklin D. Roosevelt re-
gained the governorship by a tremendous 700,000 plurality, and
so many Democrats ousted Republicans from their congressional
posts throughout the country that the administration was left
with a two-vote edge in the House. The New York *Times* head-
lined its story: "Stalemate Impends in New Congress. Leaders
Will Be Helpless. Legislative Chaos Likely." [41]

The new Congress would not convene, however, for another
year, and meanwhile December cold was in the air, and bread
lines were forming in the big cities of the nation. LaGuardia's
mail was piling high with pleas for aid and homemade solutions
for the crisis. One correspondent sent a mathematical formula to
alleviate unemployment. Another, who suggested the issuance of
purchasing power coupons by the post office, said: "As fantastic as
it may appear, I, an unrecognized student of political economy,
have solved this all-vital problem." Another, less optimistic, suggested government loans to workers, secured by future earnings.[42]

Some of these letters may still have been in LaGuardia's mind
when he took the floor at the start of the lame-duck session of the
Seventy-first Congress, delivering a long and powerful speech on
the seriousness of the depression and the need for immediate, bold
action. If the nation were threatened by foreign attack, he said,
there would be no question of its power to marshal all of its forces
to resist. "Yet we stand here as a Congress in despair and helpless

[39] Limpus and Leyson, *op. cit.*, 329–330.

[40] New York *Times*, Nov. 5, 1930. Socialist candidate Frank Porce received 849 votes.

[41] *Ibid.*, Nov. 9, 1930.

[42] Letters of Nov. 10, Nov. 20, and Dec. 10, 1930, LaG. Papers.

to know what to do to meet a crisis of unemployment so great that it may threaten the very safety of the Republic." [43]

Temporary measures would not solve a difficulty that was deep-rooted in the economic system, LaGuardia insisted. A permanent public works program, designed to keep employment and purchasing power at high levels in advance of any crisis, was needed. Again, he attacked the "states' rights" argument, pointing to the new interdependence brought by a highly industrialized society. As another long-term solution, he urged shorter hours. With many sections of the labor movement still striving for a forty-hour week, LaGuardia now boldly urged a thirty-hour standard. This would not, he said, anticipating the usual argument, lead to idleness; it would give the workingmen opportunities for education, recreation, and travel, all of which would create more job opportunities. The crisis, LaGuardia warned, would not adjust itself, as some people had confidently asserted, and a nationwide conference of states was an immediate necessity.[44]

Hoover's second annual message to Congress, on December 3, 1930, attributing the depression mainly to forces outside the United States, expressed a willingness to expand public works appropriations in the coming fiscal year to over $650,000,000. The year before, $520,000,000 had been appropriated. Beyond this, however, Hoover urged "rigid economy," saying that the Red Cross could relieve the cases of individual distress which were being reported in farm drought areas.[45]

LaGuardia spoke in the House on the inadequacy of the administration's public works appropriation. It would not result in the employment of even a thousand men in New York for any sizable period of time, he said. When a colleague pointed to the naval expenditures in the budget as increasing employment, LaGuardia replied angrily: "What do you want? Another war, to kill off a few more men? Is that the gentleman's solution of the unemployment situation? It is not mine." [46]

Two weeks later he was again on his feet, urging passage of his

[43] *Congress. Rec.*, 71:3, Dec. 3, 1930, 135–137.
[44] New York *World*, Dec. 4, 1930.
[45] Myers and Newton, *op. cit.*, 57–58.
[46] *Congress. Rec.*, 71:3, Dec. 9, 1930, 433–434.

bill for unemployment insurance. Based on the constitutional
right of the government to tax, his proposal was to tax every employee five cents a week and every employer ten cents to create
the fund from which unemployment benefits would be paid.
LaGuardia's bill would apply to farm and seasonal workers as well
as regular wage workers (thus, it went beyond the Social Security
measure passed in 1935). LaGuardia told his colleagues: "I suppose my bill will be criticized and I will be called a radical. I can
stand the abuse." [47]

The abuse he expected came, shortly after the New Year, in a
scathing editorial by the Chicago *Tribune*, which quoted scorn-
fully LaGuardia's insistence that the federal government act "to
eliminate suffering and hunger and want in the future." Said the
Tribune:

That is an assertion that would be heartily applauded in Moscow. It
represents a fallacy which has a good deal of popularity at this time
as in past times of stress. If it is not intelligently and strongly resisted,
it will produce results lastingly injurious to the nation's economic and
political welfare. . . . The notion that the government is an all-
powerful, all-wise, and all-beneficent agency to solve all our difficulties
and cure all our diseases, to push in a perambulator from the cradle
to the grave, is the folly of immature minds. . . . The short-sighted
and heedless expenditure of public funds means high taxes which for
years will retard the private enterprise essential to the prosperity of
the nation and will handicap it seriously at a time when its confidence,
its initiative, and its energy are most urgently needed. LaGuardia's
formula is nothing but socialism.[48]

What the Tribune denounced as socialism, the left-wing Socialists ridiculed as reformist beggary. The *Weekly People,* organ
of the Socialist Labor party, in an editorial entitled "A Question
to Congressman LaGuardia," charged that he was suggesting "a
bone be thrown to the American working class dog that has shown
disposition to growl and snarl from hunger and suffering." The
average worker, said the editorial, would respond: "To hell with
unemployment insurance! It is a beggars fee." The workers would
settle for nothing less than the fruits of their production, it concluded, and LaGuardia's proposal was therefore pitifully inadequate.[49]

[47] *Ibid.,* Dec. 16, 1930, 894.   [48] Jan. 6, 1931.   [49] Feb. 28, 1931.

Despite the New Year's assurance of the American Economic Association, drawing upon the nation's most learned academicians, that recovery by the spring "seemed assured," 1931 brought no change in the general picture of increasing distress.[50] Furthermore, a severe drought in the farm areas of the Southwest widened and tightened the hunger belt around the nation. In Arkansas food riots were reported, with five hundred cotton growers parading through one small town, their placards reading: "Give us food for our starving families." [51]

Alarm began to grow on Capitol Hill, and the House and the Senate moved quickly to pass drought-relief bills. At the last moment, however, when the House bill was due to go to conference for final modifications, it ran into a snag: upon a request for unanimous consent to give the bill to conference, Fiorello LaGuardia stood up defiantly and refused to go along. He would withhold his agreement, he told his amazed colleagues, until the sufferers in the cities were given relief equally with the drought-area farmers.[52] LaGuardia kept the bill out of conference for three days, holding stubbornly to his proposal that thirty million dollars be appropriated for food relief, half for the cities and half for the rural areas.[53]

LaGuardia's demands for relief for everyone was watched anxiously by people all over the nation, who saw him as one of the few men in Washington aware of the seriousness of the crisis. A man in Atlantic City wrote to him:

To refuse aid to the needy is to admit we have a government without a conscience. While thousands are starving physically millions more are starving mentally. Dozens are daily committing suicide driven by the lonesomeness of a helpless existence.[54]

Another letter came from Seattle. A fifty-five-year-old man with four children told how he had worked six years without a vacation

[50] Myers and Newton, *op. cit.,* 60. A new song appeared about this time called, "Life is Just a Bowl of Cherries" (Wecter, *op. cit.,* 18–19).

[51] Clipping from Winchester *Star,* Jan. 5, 1931, LaG. Papers.

[52] *Congress. Rec.,* 71:3, Jan. 8, 1931, 1618–1619.

[53] Baltimore *Sun,* Jan. 9, 1931. Congressman Wood of Indiana opposed relief measures for anyone, urban or rural, saying that local and private charities had the situation well in hand. Reports of a hunger riot in Arkansas were the work of Communist agitation, he said (*ibid.*).

[54] Jan. 9, 1931, LaG. Papers.

until the plant closed down on May 15, 1930. It was still closed
down. "Mr. Hamilton Fish," the man wrote, "will also have no
need to go round like the old witch doctors of Zululand smelling
out Communists for they are being made daily. I have a son aged
21, able-bodied and there is no more chance for him to work
either. . . . It appears to be a crime to live to be over 45, and a
worse crime to bring children into this gloomy-looking world." [55]

LaGuardia's mid-1930 proposal for a national conference of
governors to work out uniform labor legislation had been buried
in committee, but in January, 1931, Franklin D. Roosevelt invited
the governors of six northeastern states to a conference in Albany.
There they listened patiently to arguments for unemployment insurance by Professor Paul Douglas of the University of Chicago,
Professor Joseph P. Chamberlain of Columbia University, and Dr.
Leo Wolman of the Amalgamated Clothing Workers of America.[56] After the conference adjourned, Roosevelt received a wire
from LaGuardia, who congratulated him on his action and
reiterated the need for uniform state legislation.[57] Roosevelt himself had only recently come around to an unequivocal stand for
unemployment insurance.[58]

LaGuardia's obstruction on the drought-relief measure had
been a desperate effort to draw attention to the plight of the people in the cities, and when the bill came up for final approval on
February 9, 1931, LaGuardia told the House he would vote for it
because "it is time the residents of the rural districts and the
workers of the cities stood together in this common bond of misery
and poverty which united them." [59] He pleaded again, however,
for aid to the cities, pointing to conditions in New York. He had
just received a letter from the head of the Charity Organization
Society of New York, saying that it was spending $20,000 a month
in East Harlem alone. The Emergency Work Bureau in the city
was spending at the anual rate of $1,600,000, and funds would be
gone by the beginning of April. The number of New York City

[55] Jan. 11, 1931, *ibid.*   [56] Bellush, *op. cit.*, 185.
[57] LaGuardia to F. D. R., Franklin D. Roosevelt Papers, Hyde Park, New
York.
[58] Bellush, *op. cit.*, 182. In 1931, the A.F. of L. was still opposing jobless
insurance.
[59] *Congress. Rec.*, 71:3, Feb. 9, 1931, 4379–4381.

unemployed was reaching the half-million mark. A wire from Commissioner Frank Taylor of the New York City Department of Public Welfare reported that 400,000 were now getting municipal relief, with 90,000 more aided through private charities, and an indeterminate number were being kept alive by friends and relatives. LaGuardia recited these facts to his colleagues. "Gentlemen," he cried, "are we going to stand idly by in a condition of that kind, and discuss states' rights and argue about constitutional limitations?" [60]

His pleas for a basic re-evaluation of the economic system had recently received ideological support from an unexpected source, the Reverend Harry Emerson Fosdick, personal pastor of John D. Rockefeller and leader of the wealth-encrusted congregation which met at the Riverside Church in Manhattan. Fosdick told his church members in a searching sermon that the capitalist system was now on trial, that the "verbal damning of communism now prevalently popular in the United States will get us nowhere." One basic question had to be answered, he said: "Can capitalism adjust itself to this new age? Can it move out from its old individualism, dominated by the selfish profit motive, and so create a new cooperative epoch with social planning and social control?" Something was the matter, Fosdick insisted, with "a system that over the western world leaves millions upon millions of people out of work who want work and millions more in the sinister shadows of poverty."

LaGuardia read Fosdick's words to the House and then repeated his call for unemployment insurance, deriding the argument that this constituted "socialism." Workmen's compensation, he noted, had once been also considered paternalistic. It was ironic, LaGuardia said, that industrialists carefully oiled and housed their machinery when not in use, but would not take the same care of their unemployed workers.[61]

As if to point up his plea, a few days later a group of unemployed workers staged a noisy demonstration in the House gallery. Congressman Bachmann of West Virginia, a member of the Hamilton Fish's special committee to investigate Communist propaganda, called the demonstration a Communist tactic. He

[60] *Ibid.* [61] *Ibid.*

asked Congress to act upon the threat of communism, and La-Guardia retorted: "Give food to the hungry and work to the idle and you'll hear nothing about communism." [62]

After languishing for eight months on the House calendar, the Wagner bill for a federal employment agency was finally sent to the floor by the Rules Committee. It had already passed the Senate, and it was clear that the strategy of the House leaders had been to hold up the bill until very close to the end of the session, when it would have to race against time, and then even if passed could be pocket-vetoed by the President. All of LaGuardia's skill as a floor strategist could not maneuver the bill through the entangling net of House rules, and he knew that time was running out. He refused to surrender, however, and warned the House against further trickery to prevent passage in the last days before adjournment. After reading communications of support for the bill from the A.F. of L.'s William Green, the Railroad Brotherhood's A. F. Whitney, and the American Association for Labor Legislation, LaGuardia exclaimed, "I warn the House against a filibuster on this bill." [63]

Secretary of Labor William Doak made a last minute effort to hold up the Wagner bill, but with LaGuardia leading the floor fight for its passage it was enacted in the closing days of the session. The other Wagner bill, for a presidential commission to plan public works, had also been passed in emasculated form,[64] and now both measures went to President Hoover.

The position of the administration on federal action to relieve unemployment had already been made clear.[65] Hoover was willing

[62] New York *Times,* Jan. 9, 1931.

[63] Signers of the American Association for Labor Legislation letter included: banker Henry Bruere, economist Paul Douglas, Frances Perkins, Mary van Kleeck, Lillian Wald, Professor Taussig of Harvard, Broadus Mitchell, Irving Fisher, H. V. Kaltenborn, Sidney Hillman, Corliss Lamont, Stephen Wise.

[64] *Labor,* March 3, 1931, discusses the measures at that stage.

[65] Alice Roosevelt Longworth wrote of her husband, House Speaker Nicholas Longworth: "Nick was Speaker from the beginning of Coolidge's elected term through Hoover's first two years. . . . During those years Nick, one of whose major interests was government finance, used to talk with rising apprehension of the bill this country would eventually have to pay if the many proposals for spending money that were agitated in Congress should ever be passed" (*Crowded Hours* [New York, 1933], 328).

to increase to a certain extent public works appropriations, but was definitely opposed to the kind of bold spending program which Wagner, LaGuardia, James Mead, and Edward Costigan were asking. As for direct relief, he believed that "the spirit of charity and mutual self-help through voluntary giving" [66] would be sufficient to take care of hardship.[67] Accordingly, when the lame-duck session of the Seventy-first Congress ended in March, 1931, Hoover vetoed the two Wagner bills.[68] The issue of the welfare state philosophy versus the concept of rugged individualism had been squarely posed and decisively answered.

In the closing months of that same lame-duck session of Congress in the spring of 1931, there was a revival of the bitter Coolidge-era conflict over Muscle Shoals, and once again Norris and LaGuardia worked as a team in their respective houses to push through a bill for government operation of dams and power. Since the Coolidge veto of 1928, support had been slowly accumulating for government operation. Investigations of the power trust, both by the Federal Trade Commission and a Senate subcommittee, swung popular opinion toward public power and destroyed final hopes for leasing the Muscle Shoals area to private interests.[69] The 1930 elections saw antiutilities candidates win in state after state.[70] Congressman Swing of California was voicing the attitude of many congressmen when he said during debate on the new Norris bill in early 1931:

I am not prepared at this time to vote to have my government take over the power business of the country, but I am determined that the power business shall not take over the government of the country. If I must choose between the two, I will stand with my government.[71]

On February 20, 1931, under the constant prodding of LaGuardia and a few others, the House approved by a vote of 216–153 a bill authorizing the President to appoint a government corporation for administering a power project at Muscle Shoals.[72] In the

[66] Quoted in Karl Schriftgiesser, *This Was Normalcy* (Boston, 1948), 277.

[67] He refused, for instance, to sign a twenty-million-dollar appropriation for drought relief unless it were put in the form of a loan.

[68] Myers and Newton, *op. cit.*, 69.   [69] Hubbard, *op. cit.*, 450–452.

[70] New York *Times*, Nov. 7, 1930.

[71] *Congress. Rec.*, 71:3, Feb. 20, 1931, 5569.

[72] *Ibid.* The bill was confined to the Muscle Shoals area rather than pro-

Senate a coalition of southern Democrats and progressive Republicans brought passage by a vote of 55–28, and the Norris bill went
to the White House.

The public utility interests were laboring mightily to prevent
the Muscle Shoals measure from becoming law, and LaGuardia
took to the radio to attack his old enemies. He was not criticizing,
he told the radio audience, the technicians and engineers of the
power companies. His target was those interested, not in electricity as a public service, but in corporate control as a way of
making money.[73] These stock-manipulators, LaGuardia said,
"know more about the stock ticker than the dynamo." He went
on:

The Power Trust is not a myth. It is an existing, active, well-organized
combination of power, gas, electric and trolley corporations united in a
common purpose of keeping private control of public utilities—maintaining high rates, influencing legislation, and fighting public ownership.

This monopoly resulted in exorbitant costs for public utilities,
he said, and added, "There is not a mother keeping house in the
country but dreads the moment when the gas and electric bills
come." [74]

Nevertheless, on March 3, 1931, Herbert Hoover vetoed the
Muscle Shoals bill, saying, "I am firmly opposed to the government entering into any business, the major purpose of which is

---

viding for a comprehensive Valley project, and provided for public power
production and distribution along with leasing of nitrate plants to private
companies. It had been tied up in conference for almost a year, with a deadlock between an administration-sponsored bill by Representative Carroll
Reece of Tennessee and the Norris bill. On February 17, Reece's fellow
House conferees dramatically broke with him and accepted practically all
the Norris provisions (Hubbard, *op. cit.*, 487).

[73] To LaGuardia, the power fight was part of his general campaign against
big business. A year earlier he had attacked a court-approved rise in telephone rates as "judicial larceny" and called for federal regulation of the
industry (*Congress. Rec.*, 71:1, Jan. 27, 1930, 2484–2486). At the same time,
he lashed out at profiteering in the merchant marine, attacking what he
called unwarranted subsidies to shipping interests under the Jones-White
Act of 1928, and staging what was virtually a one-man stand against an
amendment increasing such subsidies (Washington *Post*, March 1, 1930).

[74] Speech in *Congress. Rec.*, 71:3, March 3, 1931, 6691–6692.

competition with our citizens." [75] Years later Hoover commented on the public-power controversy during his administration, insisting that "the distribution of the power by the government was pure socialism." Advocates of public power projects were "pseudo-liberals," he charged, and concluded, "Most of these pseudo-liberals also advocated government operation of the railways and no doubt hoped for the growth of Socialism inch by inch." [76] Not for another two years would the dream of George Norris and Fiorello LaGuardia be realized.[77]

Thus, in the battle for public power, as well as for relief, the first round was decisively taken by a combatant whose chief watchwords were economy, caution, and the sanctity of private enterprise. Fiorello LaGuardia, nursing his wounds, waited and prepared.

[75] Myers and Newton, *op. cit.*, 470.

[76] Herbert Hoover, *The Memoirs of Herbert Hoover: The Cabinet and the Presidency 1920–1933* (New York, 1952), II, 174.

[77] Eighteen months after the veto by Hoover, Franklin D. Roosevelt, in a campaign address at Portland, Ore., Sept. 21, 1932, set the tone for the reversal of the Hoover policy, talking of government development of the St. Lawrence, Tennessee, Colorado, and Columbia Rivers: "Each one of these, in each of the four quarters of the United States, will be forever a national yardstick to prevent extortion against the public and to encourage the wider use of that servant of the people—electric power" (Samuel Rosenman, ed., *The Public Papers and Addresses of Franklin D. Roosevelt* [New York, 1938], I, 727).

14 ⋆ Second Round: Relief,
Public Works, and Tear Gas

IN the eight months between the close of the lame-duck session
of March, 1931 and the opening of the Seventy-second Congress in
December, the depression worsened, and LaGuardia rushed from
one issue to the next, his anger mounting as he saw on the streets
of his own district increasing evidences of human suffering.[1]

Despite Hoover's plea for voluntary action by business in retaining employment at predepression levels, the Brooklyn Edison
Company in May of 1931 discharged 1,600 employees, and La-
Guardia moved to the attack. He wrote to Lieutenant-Governor
Herbert Lehman (Roosevelt was out of Albany) asking that the
state act to secure reinstatement of the laid-off men and a lowering of utility rates. Pointing to a $57,000,000 dividend paid by
the Brooklyn Edison Company and its affiliates in 1930, a 20 per
cent increase over 1929 payments, he told Lehman: "These semi-
public companies, enjoying franchises from the State giving them
a monopoly in the service which they sell, should not be per-

[1] It was particularly in such times of great tension that he was susceptible
to outbursts of rash behavior which added neither friends nor victories to
his cause. Shortly after his return to New York in the spring of 1931, a letter
from a veterans organization sent him headlong into conflict with General
Frank T. Hines of the Veterans Administration over alleged petty graft at
V.A. hospitals in New York. After an exchange of heated letters from La-
Guardia and mild replies from Hines, the issue petered out (LaGuardia to
Hines, March 30, 1931; LaGuardia to Limpus, April 2, 1931, LaG. Papers).

mitted to discharge a single solitary employee during this present depression. . . . "I sincerely hope that Governor Roosevelt will show his Rooseveltian mettle and wield the big stick over the Public Service Commission to reduce these exorbitant rates." [2] He went on:

Think of a company enjoying such monopolistic privileges and making such exorbitant profits, being able to turn a man out of work in the morning and cut off his light at night!

Please, Mr. Lehman, give this matter your serious consideration and do all that you can to have these unfortunate and innocent men, the victims of this greedy group, reemployed at the earliest possible moment.[3]

Roosevelt, back in Albany now, replied that he would ask the Public Service Commission to investigate LaGuardia's charges.[4]

Despite the constant rise in unemployment and privation through the summer of 1931, progressives, including both Franklin D. Roosevelt and LaGuardia, were still reluctant to push government spending beyond the limits of a balanced budget. Replying to a proposal by the Hearst newspapers that the government spend five billion dollars immediately to restore prosperity, LaGuardia said that public works should be financed out of current appropriations, bond issues, and taxes in the higher brackets. Increasing the national debt, he argued, would be "bad financing" and "bad statesmanship." [5]

In the fall of 1931 the knowledge that unemployment in New York State had reached the million mark, and that local relief efforts could no longer meet the need, led Franklin D. Roosevelt to call a special session of the state legislature. For the first time expounding the basic proposition that it was the duty of the government to prevent starvation, Roosevelt proposed to the legislature a program of unemployment relief and battled it through to final passage. The Wicks bill proposed to establish a Tempo-

[2] New York *Times,* June 3, 1931.

[3] LaGuardia to Lehman, June 1, 1931, F. D. R. Papers.

[4] Roosevelt to LaGuardia, June 3, 1931, *ibid.* The Brooklyn Edison Company said that the laid-off workers had only been hired temporarily and that a rate reduction would soon go into effect, saving the consumer six million dollars (New York *Times,* June 4, 1931).

[5] Letter of June 19, 1931, LaG. Papers.

rary Emergency Relief Administration for direct aid and work relief.[6]

LaGuardia followed the Roosevelt actions from the start of the special legislative session. After the program was presented to the legislature he urged Republicans to support it,[7] and upon its passage he wired the Governor:

Congratulations on passage relief measure stop your constructive program is first governmental step in right direction stop regrettable private employment agencies were not legislated out of existence stop your courageous stand on providing revenue from taxation to carry out program is indeed to be commended in these days of timidity to face issue and pass buck to Red Cross and Salvation.[8]

Roosevelt had insisted, over Republican opposition, that the twenty-million-dollar relief program would be financed out of an income tax increase, with the burden borne by those who "have benefited by our industrial and economic system." [9] Applauding this, LaGuardia told Roosevelt: "In the name of thousands of innocent victims of present depression with whom I am in contact thanks." [10]

The Seventy-second Congress opened in December, 1931, with the Democrats and Republicans so closely matched in strength that LaGuardia and his fellow Progressives found themselves with political power far beyond their numbers. In the Senate, 12 Progressives held the balance between 36 Republicans, 47 Democrats, and one Farmer-Labor man. In the House, the Democrats held a narrow majority, with 219 Democrats against 192 Republicans and 15 Progressives, and succeeded in electing John Garner of Texas as Speaker by a margin of 3 votes.

Hoover's message to Congress on December 8, 1931, placed the main responsibility for the depression on world-wide economic conditions, pointed to the actions taken by both govern-

---

[6] Bellush, *op. cit.*, 140–142.　　　　[7] New York *Times,* Sept. 11, 1931.

[8] Sept. 30, 1931, F. D. R. Papers.　　　[9] Bellush, *op. cit.*, 141.

[10] F. D. R. Papers. Both Republicans and Democrats in the legislature had favored the bill from the start, and it passed both houses unanimously. The act marked the first acceptance by any state of a significant share of responsibility for welfare and established work relief as a major method of public aid (Alexander Radomski, *Work Relief in New York State 1931–1935* [New York, 1947], 69–70, 314).

ment and private organizations to aid distressed persons, and made a number of proposals, with the greatest emphasis on improving the credit and financial structure of the nation. Anticipating the demands for large relief and public works expenditures, Hoover pointed to the fact that government expenditures on public works were already at an unprecedented level. He said:

We must avoid burdens upon the government which will create more unemployment in private industry than can be gained by further expansion of employment by the Federal Government . . . We can now stimulate employment and agriculture more effectually and speedily through the voluntary measures in progress, through the thawing out of credit, through the building up of stability abroad, through the Home Loan Discount Banks, through an emergency finance corporation and the rehabilitation of the railways and other such directions.[11]

A committee which Hoover had appointed to consider public works expansion sharply criticized a proposal by Senator Robert Wagner for a two-billion-dollar public works program, saying: "In the long run the real problem of unemployment must be met by private business interests if it is to be permanent. Problems of unemployment cannot be solved by any magic of appropriation from the public treasury." [12]

On the same day that the President's committee made this statement, Fiorello LaGuardia took the floor of the House to deliver a major address on the economic crisis, calling for immediate, bold action on a number of fronts. With reports coming every day from his district telling of people without food or coal to face the winter, he leveled his first attack on Assistant Secretary of Commerce Julius Klein, who had been giving the nation optimistic reports about the state of its economic health. "We are not going to get out of this depression or relieve the unemployment situation," LaGuardia said, "by pep talks given by the distinguished gentleman from the Department of Commerce, . . . the bed-time story teller of the Administration, Dr. Julius Klein." [13] Klein, he told smiling House members, was a "Baron Munchausen."

[11] Myers and Newton, *op. cit.,* 149–150.
[12] The committee included Matthew Woll of the A.F. of L., and a number of economists and manufacturers (*ibid.,* 156).
[13] *Congress. Rec.,* 72:1, Dec. 21, 1931, 1033–1036.

Fundamental and sweeping measures were now needed, LaGuardia insisted. "Near palliatives will not do; a major operation is necessary. . . . One thing I want to impress upon you is that the entire financial structure of the world has collapsed; the present economic system is not adequate to meet the industrial age in which we are living and it may be necessary to go into the very fundamentals of our system and bring about an economic readjustment." Unless this was done, LaGuardia warned, there might be serious trouble, not from professional radicals, but from ordinary Americans, "who have an intelligent understanding of economics and who simply resent going on the breadline and seeing their families in want." Shaking his head at objections by Majority Leader Rainey of Illinois, LaGuardia said, "Ah, Mr. Rainey, this is no time for ultra-conservatism." [14]

He saw the immediate need as a program of government relief, because private and local charities were not sufficient, and then a great public works program, which "may run into billions but would be worth it." He suggested as possible ventures a vast highway system or federal loans to municipalities to build five hundred commercial air fields. Furthermore, all appropriations for warships should be switched to merchant vessels, he suggested. Such a comprehensive program would require increased taxation, LaGuardia agreed, but the burden must be placed on the wealthy. Five per cent of the nation's citizens owned 80 per cent of its wealth, LaGuardia said, and "such a condition is unwholesome in any republic." [15]

The climax of his speech was the proposal for a national system of unemployment insurance. He alluded again to his favorite analogy on this subject: employers kept their idle machinery well oiled, housed, and insured against fire and theft, while the human beings who operated that machinery were ignored. In addition to unemployment insurance, LaGuardia said, the nation must move towards a five-day week to spread employment. When his speech met with the argument that his suggestions were unconstitutional, he replied with some impatience, "If the Constitution stands in the way, well, the Constitution will simply have to get out of the way." [16]

LaGuardia knew, as not all of his colleagues did, what distress

[14] *Ibid.*   [15] *Ibid.*   [16] *Ibid.*

was hidden behind the mottled brick walls of the tenement houses in East Harlem. As the blasts of winter grew icier in January and February of 1932, his mail was filled with tales of personal grief. One of his friends in the district wrote to him:

Every night our club is besieged by countless unemployed men and women and their children, all looking for relief from the sufferings of starvation, the dire need for clothing and the landlords threat of eviction for non-payment of rent. What can this organization do? Little or nothing. Major, in this battle to relieve human suffering we are with you to a man.[17]

In the Senate, La Follette, Jr., and Edward P. Costigan of Colorado were sponsoring a bill to appropriate $375,000,000 for relief, and the American Federation of Labor, noting that eight million people were unemployed, urged swift enactment of the measure. The A.F. of L.'s weekly news bulletin said: "Bitterness is developing. . . . Cynicism and resentment against society is growing." [18] However, Herbert Hoover had already told a press conference that "we cannot squander ourselves into prosperity." [19]

LaGuardia's feeling that something was fundamentally wrong with the economic system and his anxiety to find basic rather than merely temporary solutions were reinforced by his study of an article written for *Harper's Magazine* by Henry Pratt Fairchild, Professor of Sociology at New York University. It was entitled "The Fallacy of Profits." Fairchild sent LaGuardia a copy and summarized the article for him in these words:

There are two main points in the article. The first is that an economic system based on the assumption of general and unlimited profits is inherently self-contradictory and self-destructive. The second is that a

---

[17] Harding Republican Club to LaGuardia, Feb. 3, 1932, LaG. Papers. Seeking jobs for the unemployed was not unmixed with patronage, and it was often hard to separate the two aims. Vito Marcantonio wrote to LaGuardia Jan. 11, 1932: "I understand that the work on the new Post Office Building as well as the new Federal Court House will commence within a week or so. I think this is the place where we can employ a great number of people in our district. . . . If you could place about one hundred men through this medium, it would be doing not only a great deal to relieve the suffering in our district but at the same time would enhance our cause considerably" (*ibid.*).

[18] *American Federation of Labor*, Feb. 6, 1932.

[19] Myers and Newton, *op. cit.*, 162.

more even distribution of purchasing power is absolutely essential, not only in the interests of social justice, but also for the sake of economic stability and the maintenance of prosperity for each as well as all.[20]

Two weeks later LaGuardia delivered another long speech in the House of Representatives, stressing the need to bolster the purchasing power of the nation's low-income groups.[21] The occasion for his speech was a concentrated campaign in April by President Hoover for "economy" in government expenditures. Hoover held a series of meetings with the Economy Committee of the House of Representatives which led to proposals in the House for salary cuts for government employees.[22] On May 3, 1932, the House passed the Omnibus Economy bill, but the persistence of LaGuardia and others had reduced Hoover's proposed $250,-000,000 savings to $30,000,000.[23]

Early 1932 had seen the creation of the Reconstruction Finance Corporation with a half-billion-dollar pool to aid railroads, banks, and other commercial enterprises. On May 9, 1932, a number of senators joined Robert Wagner and Thomas Walsh in introducing a bill to permit the R.F.C. to lend three hundred million dollars of its funds to states for public works projects.[24]

LaGuardia believed that the usual expenditures for public works would not be sufficient to stimulate spending and provide employment. He saw a great opportunity now to tear down the festering slum areas of the nation and build decent homes, this providing jobs, purchasing power, and housing in one great undertaking. He broached his idea in a letter to Secretary of the Treasury Ogden Mills, the one cabinet member with whom he had friendly personal relations. Any plan sufficient to meet the existing crisis, he told Mills, "must necessarily be of enormous magnitude," and therefore the usual public works program should be supplemented by loans to limited-dividend corporations, which would construct rental apartments. "In this day and age," he wrote, "there should be no squalid, dismal, unhealthy tenements.

[20] Fairchild to LaGuardia, March 30, 1932, LaG. Papers.
[21] *Congress. Rec.*, 72:1, April 14, 1932, 8225–8229.
[22] Myers and Newton, *op. cit.*, 193–194.   [23] *Ibid.*, 200.
[24] *Congress. Rec.*, 72:1, May 9, 1932, Senate Bill no. 4755.

Right in the city of Washington, we have alley dwellings, shacks
and dilapidated hovels, in which human beings are living. Quite
a contrast to the monumental public buildings we are now erect-
ing." [25]

That spring of 1932, Progressives in the House of Representatives organized an unofficial committee of fifteen men, including five Republicans, five Democrats, and five Progressives, chaired
by James Mead of New York, to study relief legislation. LaGuardia
was one of the leading spirits of the committee. At the end of
May, as mutterings about adjournment began to grow in the
cloakrooms, Mead spoke for the committee, insisting that Congress should stay in session all summer, if necessary, to pass measures for relief of the unemployed. His position was supported
in even more forceful language by LaGuardia, who asked, "Can
we adjourn with millions of industrial workers walking the
streets, and hundreds of thousands—yes millions—of farmers
with the sheriffs marching upon their homes with foreclosure
papers?" [26]

The Progressive bloc issued a letter to fellow congressmen, asking a conference to consider relief legislation. Its position was
strongly backed by the magazine *Labor,* which declared: "It is
time to face the facts. Millions of Americans are not only jobless,
but they are hungry. They demand jobs or food. The resources
of states and cities and private charity have been exhausted. Only
the national government can deal with the situation." [27]

The introduction of a number of bills in the House calling
for great federal expenditures for relief and public works met
with a sharp rebuff by Hoover. He told a press conference on
May 27, 1932, "The urgent question today is the prompt balancing of the budget." Sharply attacking the proposed expenditure of $900,000,000 for public works, he said: "This is not un-
employment relief. It is the most gigantic pork barrel ever
proposed to the American Congress. It is an unexampled raid on the
public treasury." [28] He did, however, several days later, personally
address the Senate and approve the idea of R.F.C. loans to the
states for relief, while insisting that public works should not be

[25] May 14, 1932, LaG. Papers.   [26] *Labor,* May 24, 1932.
[27] *Ibid.,* May 31, 1932.   [28] Myers and Newton, *op. cit.,* 212–213.

further expanded and that the primary aim must be to balance the budget.[29]

A Democratic-Progressive bloc, after a stubborn battle in the House, finally passed a relief measure sponsored by Speaker Garner, appropriating over two billion dollars for relief to the unemployed. The New York Times commented, "But for the help of thirteen progressive Republicans led by Rep. LaGuardia of New York, Democratic support of the bill would have been defeated." [30] A companion bill was introduced in the Senate by Robert Wagner while the Progressive bloc in the House battled to stay in session. LaGuardia took the floor on June 11, 1932, with the House members obviously anxious to go home, and announced that the Progressive bloc had met that morning and resolved to resist any attempt to adjourn until passage of the Wagner-Garner relief measure by both houses, with enough time remaining to override a probable presidential veto.[31]

With the Wagner-Garner omnibus relief measure in conference, LaGuardia and Senator Costigan of Colorado co-operated on introducing a bill in both houses "to provide emergency financing facilities for unemployed workers, to relieve their distress, to increase their purchasing power and employment, and for other purposes." The measure proposed the creation of a United States Exchange Corporation with five hundred million dollars in capital to make loans up to five hundred dollars to individuals in distress.[32] It was a poor man's R.F.C.; LaGuardia's office was soon receiving letters from people all over the country applying for loans in the event of the bill's passage, but the proposal was buried in committee and never heard from again.

[29] *Ibid.*, 216. Local officials were beginning to take united action. In Detroit a conference of mayors was meeting to discuss unemployment, with Mayors James Curley of Boston and Frank Murphy of Detroit visiting Garner to urge a five-billion-dollar bond issue for public works (New York *Times,* June 7, 1932). And in Buffalo a conference of New York State mayors asked the national government to authorize direct federal loans to municipalities for work and relief purposes (Report on Buffalo conference June 7–9, LaG. Papers).

[30] New York *Times,* June 7, 1932.

[31] *Congress. Rec.,* 72:1, June 11, 1932, 12696.

[32] *Ibid.,* July 1, 1932, H.R. no. 12885.

As Washington sweltered in midsummer heat, the Wagner-Garner bill finally returned from conference to face final debate in the House. The Senate and House conferees had reached final agreement on the complex relief measure, only to be summoned to a conference with the President, who expressed his objection to certain parts of the bill. Hoover favored Title I in the bill, authorizing $300,000,000 in R.F.C. loans to states and cities. He strenuously objected, however, to Title III, which provided $322,-000,000 in public works expenditures, and was even more vehement in his opposition to Title II, which would add one and a half billion dollars to the two-billion-dollar lending power of the R.F.C. with the stipulation that this would be available not only to banks and corporations but to individuals, small business, states, and municipalities.[33]

Garner reported to the House on the presidential conference, denouncing Hoover's interference with the legislative function, which, he asserted, violated the separation of powers doctrine in the Constitution. The Texan had told Hoover that ordinary people should be aided by the R.F.C., just as four thousands banks had been relieved. To Hoover's statement that the money loaned to banks eventually helped everyone, Garner replied, "The drippings do not reach down to the earth," and added angrily that he was "through with class legislation." [34]

When Garner had finished his speech, staunch administration supporter Bertrand Shell of New York took the floor to answer what he called "the Democratic candidate for Vice President's speech of acceptance of the nomination" (Garner had, a week before, received the nomination of the Democratic national convention). Shell insisted that the basic issue was whether or not the United States was going to "go into the banking business and set up a super-banking organization in every state, county, town in the United States." To objections that the R.F.C. aided only the great financial institutions, he replied, "Who owns the railroads; who owns the life-insurance companies?" The ordinary man in the street owned these enterprises through his shares of stock and life-insurance policies, Snell argued.[35]

The exchange between Garner and Snell had been marked by

[33] *Ibid.*, July 6, 1932, 14684–14691.   [34] *Ibid.*   [35] *Ibid.*

acrimony, and now LaGuardia took the floor to deplore political partisanship "on the question of relieving human misery." He waved his arms in characteristic fashion and told the House:

There can be no compromise with hunger. If the president does not realize this now, accept a relief plan of heroic and gigantic size, he will unleash a tempest that will cost thousands of lives and hundreds of millions of dollars and write a page of everlasting shame in our country.

Misery, unemployment, hunger exist all over the country. My colleagues need go no farther than a few blocks from the National Capitol to see human beings degraded to the extent of publicly sleeping in makeshift hovels, kennels, and living off scraps of donated food. My God—that condition must not be permitted to continue! [36]

Hoover's opposition should not be taken into account in deciding upon approval of the conference report, LaGuardia told his colleagues, for this would constitute surrender of its prerogatives by the legislative branch of government. If Hoover wanted to veto the bill, that was his right, but Congress could override it. He attacked the Hoover philosophy of letting aid "drip down" from the wealthy corporations to the ordinary man and said:

I do not want to see my country come out of this crisis with just two classes of people; one a small property-owning class, and the other an impoverished mass of workers and tenant peasants at the mercy of the other class. No, I refuse to see the American people dragged down to a state of economic serfdom and forced to pay the whole cost of the dishonesty and blunders of the financiers who have brought this ruin to our country.[37]

The Wagner-Garner measure, LaGuardia reminded the House, was only a palliative, only first aid to a "suffering and, I fear, incurable economic system." Bold measures must be taken to change the economic mechanism, he asserted. "We must be courageous. We must prepare ahead of time for an economic readjustment that is inevitable. . . . Present machines, present means of production, are inconsistent with old theories of profits." [38]

Just before the final vote LaGuardia once again took the floor, asking for passage of the bill and taking the opportunity to speak for the buried LaGuardia-Costigan bill enabling small loans to individuals. If hundreds of millions of dollars could be loaned

[36] *Ibid.*, 14690–14692.   [37] *Ibid.*   [38] *Ibid.*

to large corporations, why not loans to the men whose labor ("Yes, exploited labor!") had created the property of those corporations. "Personally," he declared angrily, "I am sick and tired of hearing this patronizing, smug expression of help given in millions of dollars to powerful corporations 'percolating' or 'dripping down' to the individual." Once again he called for "a new industrial system in keeping with the machine age in which we are living." [39]

The House passed the Wagner bill by a vote of 202–157. It was approved in the Senate, too, and with Congress ready to adjourn went to the President. Hoover vetoed it on July 11, 1932, with a long message attacking the public works section of the bill but reserving his main fire for the grant of authority to the R.F.C. to make loans to individuals, small businesses, or localities. He invoked the same principle which he had cited in his veto of the Norris bill for Muscle Shoals, saying that this section of the bill "would place the government in private business" and would constitute "a gigantic centralization of banking and finance." The proposal, Hoover said, "violates every sound principle of public finances and of government. Never before has so dangerous a suggestion been seriously made to our country." [40]

Fiorello LaGuardia, disagreeing bitterly with Hoover's position, pointed in the closing days of the session to the barren stretch of land opposite the Capitol, called Anacostia Flats, where 20,000 veterans were encamped. These men were, he said, living reminders of the work still to be done.[41] All through the summer

[39] *Ibid.*, 14801.

[40] Myers and Newton, *op. cit.*, 226–229. Before adjourning on July 16, Congress passed and Hoover signed a relief bill which met his approval, eliminating the "pork barrel" and "centralized banking" provisions he had found objectionable (*ibid.*, 234–237).

[41] *Congress. Rec.*, 72:1, June 15, 1932, 13053. A year before, LaGuardia had voted with an overwhelming House majority to override Hoover's veto of a bill allowing veterans to borrow up to one-half the value of the Adjusted Credit Certificates voted them by the Congress in 1923 (*ibid.*, Feb. 26, 1931, 6171). However, on June 15, 1932, LaGuardia opposed the Patman Bill for a $2,400,000,000 bonus, on the ground that such huge sums should be spent on projects designed to aid everyone in need, not just veterans; 87 per cent of the unemployed, he said, were nonveterans, and they should not be excluded from any relief measure. The situation required, LaGuardia insisted, a total solution.

of 1932 the veterans had been arriving in Washington to press
their demands for the right to borrow on the total value of their
certificates. By July, 10,000 men, 700 women, and 300 children
were encamped in pup tents and flimsy shacks on the desolate
flats of Anacostia with no facilities for sanitation or water.[42]
Hoover refused to see their representatives, and a heavy military
guard began to patrol the White House.

On July 16, 1932, Congress adjourned, and bitterness grew.
Twelve days later the hurling of missiles at police by veterans led
to the killing of two veterans by a Washington policeman, and
Hoover called out contingents of cavalry, infantry, and tanks
under General MacArthur. Advancing with drawn bayonets under
a cloud of tear gas, the grotesquely masked soldiers dispersed the
men, women, and children on the Flats and then burned their
shanties.[43]

Hoover, charging that many of the bonus-seekers were Communists and hoodlums, announced (while soldiers patrolled the
charred ruins of the encampment): "A challenge to the authority of the United States Government has been met swiftly and
firmly." [44] The President's action was supported by the Washington *Post* [45] and the New York *Herald Tribune*,[46] but La-
Guardia wired Hoover: "Soup is cheaper than tear bombs and
bread better than bullets in maintaining law and order in these
times of depression, unemployment and hunger." [47]

The veterans straggled back to their homes all over the country, and by August, LaGuardia was back in East Harlem, watching the furniture of evicted families pile up in the streets and
beginning to think about the coming election campaign.

[42] W. W. Waters and W. C. White. *B.E.F.: The Whole Story of the Bonus
Army* (New York, 1933).

[43] Mitchell, *op. cit.*, 110.

[44] New York *Times,* July 30, 1932. Arthur M. Schlesinger, Jr., after a detailed examination of various arguments, concludes that Communist influence in the B.E.F. was insignificant (*The Crisis of the Old Order 1919–
1933* [Boston, 1957], 519).

[45] July 29, 1932.   [46] July 29, 1932.

[47] Undated copy of wire to Hoover, LaG. Papers.

15 * "Foul Birds of Prey": The Financiers

IN LaGuardia's long war against monopoly and special privilege, he had always reserved a special distaste for bankers and brokers. As Ernest Cuneo (a young lawyer on his staff in 1931–1932) saw it: "At the top of his hierarchy of iniquity the bankers roost, like foul birds of prey. In Fiorello's mind they were forever behind huge mahogany desks in vast vault-like offices, scheming." [1] It was natural, therefore, that LaGuardia, in fixing responsibility for the sorrows of the early 1930's, should turn upon the bankers. Stock-market speculation had helped bring on the depression, he firmly believed, and throughout 1932, in a campaign which came to center on the Reconstruction Finance Corporation, he insisted that the Stock Exchange be curbed and that the government redirect its financial aid from the vested interest to the common man.

The way in which stock-market speculation could ruin the lives of small investors was brought home to LaGuardia by the activities of the American Bond and Mortgage Company, which had marketed $150,000,000 worth of securities and was now bankrupt, leaving its investors ruined. LaGuardia received dozens of letters complaining about the loss of investments due to the peculiar operations of that company, which invested in mortgages on property about to be condemned. One man, fifty-nine years of age, wrote: "I can't go to work from auto accident six years ago.

[1] *Life with Fiorello* (New York, 1956), 49.

All my life savings are in this company. . . . I have no money
to fight the company. . . . God bless you Mr. LaGuardia. . . .
Only the fear of meeting my God keeps me from killing myself." [2]
LaGuardia asked the Department of Justice to investigate. Actually, the Department had already begun to probe and in the fall
of 1931 began prosecuting some of the important figures involved
in the American Bond and Mortgage transactions.[3]

One month following the 1929 crash LaGuardia had introduced
a bill, destined to be buried in the Judiciary Committee, making
it unlawful to use interstate communication or transport facilities to deal in commodities of securities for speculative purposes.[4]
Two years later, when the early optimism had dissipated, many
congressmen came around to the idea that speculation should be
curbed. Senator Watson of Indiana sponsored a bill to stop short
selling, and LaGuardia wrote to him: "I feel particularly elated
because in this instance my conservative friends are following
only two years after such a progressive step was suggested. The
time on other measures generally runs from ten to fifteen years." [5]
Actually, President Hoover and other conservatives were also
concerned about short selling and speculation.

Richard Whitney, president of the New York Stock Exchange,
defended short selling in a speech before the Hartford Chamber
of Commerce, and a New Yorker wrote to LaGuardia suggesting
he read the speech "before engaging in an effort to tinker . . .
with the law of supply and demand." [6] On the other hand, streams
of letters arrived from people in every state urging LaGuardia
to continue his assault against short selling, many of them blam-
ing "Wall Street" for the depression.

In December, LaGuardia's bill to outlaw short selling was introduced in the House and once again given to the Judiciary Committee.[7] Richard Whitney testified before the committee in February, 1932, against the bill. LaGuardia, for his argument, drew

[2] Letter of April 19, 1931, LaG. Papers.

[3] LaGuardia to William D. Mitchell, Oct. 16, 1930; Nugent Dodds to
LaGuardia, Oct. 20, 1930, *ibid.*

[4] *Congress. Rec.,* Nov. 21, 1929, H.R. no. 5412.

[5] LaGuardia to Watson, Oct. 5, 1931, LaG. Papers.

[6] Letter of Oct. 17, 1931, *ibid.* Whitney told a Senate committee later that
short selling "is not a matter of opinion; it is a matter of principle"
(Ferdinand Pecora, *Wall Street under Oath* [New York, 1939], 267).

[7] *Congress. Rec.,* 72:1, Dec. 8, 1931, H.R. no. 4.

upon the extensive knowledge of New York County Justice William Harman Black, author of *The Real Wall Street,* who made many helpful suggestions.[8] His stand against Whitney and against speculation drew a steady round of letters from people who had been ruined on the stock market, urging him to hold firm.[9]

Hoover's annual message to Congress on December 8, 1931, recommended the establishment of "an emergency reconstruction corporation" which would lend money to "agriculture credit agencies, . . . railways and financial institutions." [10] Acting upon this suggestion, administration spokesmen in Congress introduced the bill setting up the Reconstruction Finance Corporation. LaGuardia announced that he would try to hold up action on the proposed R.F.C. until he could get aid for the small depositors through a national system of deposit insurance.[11] He had gotten the idea from a similar law in Nebraska and introduced his bill in the house with the comment: "Anyone who deposits at a bank has a right to sleep nights." [12]

His bill was pushed aside, however, to make way for the administration measure, and LaGuardia took the floor on January 11, 1932, to argue against the establishment of the R.F.C.[13] He called the bill the result of a "ruthless, cruel coercion on the part of bankers." What it did, he said, was to put the cart before the horse, protecting the bankers rather than the depositors. His proposal for unemployment insurance, he noted, had been attacked as a dole, but what the administration was proposing now was a "millionaire's dole."

LaGuardia slammed hard at the greed of the bankers, comparing them with horse thieves of the old West, who, he noted, were often hung by irate citizens. Interrupted at this point by a colleague who asked if he proposed the same treatment for bankers, he replied, "Yes, I would hang a banker who stole from the people." These bankers were the ones responsible for the present crisis, he told the House, and yet the R.F.C. would aid them with hundreds of millions of dollars.[14]

8 Various letters February, March, 1932, LaG. Papers.
9 *Ibid.*   10 Myers and Newton, *op. cit.,* 149.
11 New York *Herald Tribune,* Jan. 4, 1932.
12 *Congress. Rec.,* 72:1, Jan. 4, 1932, 1246.
13 *Ibid.,* Jan. 11, 1932, 1742–1745.   14 *Ibid.*

Federal Reserve Board Chairman Eugene Meyer, who was being mentioned for a top post in the R.F.C., came in for sharp attack, as LaGuardia charged him with profiting personally from his chairmanship of the War Finance Corporation. He had, La-Guardia claimed, sold $70,000,000 of his own corporation's bonds to the government, and the transaction had been covered by alterations in the records. In spite of this last-minute effort, the R.F.C. bill passed both houses, and even before he signed it Hoover appointed Eugene Meyer as chairman and Charles G. Dawes as president of the new corporation.[15]

Incensed by what they considered outrageous favoritism, Progressives in Congress, aided by some Democrats, moved to bring the scales into better balance by proposing financial aid to ordinary people in need of loans. In the Senate, David Walsh of Massachusetts proposed that the government issue a billion dollars in fiat money,[16] but this was doomed to failure. LaGuardia suggested to the House an amendment to the R.F.C. bill, enabling the board of directors to sell fifty-dollar and one-hundred-dollar bonds directly to the public.[17] The amendment was quickly buried.

Congressional Progressives found themselves isolated on the R.F.C. issue. The measure was greeted warmly by the press, and Raymond Clapper, broadcasting to the nation after Hoover signed the bill, said:

With this, the federal government is now embarking upon a superlative effort to turn the course of business upward. It is a bold, gigantic conception of President Hoover. . . . This action . . . marks the first gigantic attempt actually to pump government money and government credit directly into business on a major scale.[18]

LaGuardia had also been calling for "bold, gigantic" moves, but his proposals were aimed at pouring purchasing power into

[15] Myers and Newton, *op. cit.,* 165. LaGuardia later attacked a loan of ninety million dollars made by the R.F.C. to a bank with which Dawes was connected. Jesse H. Jones says he and Herbert Hoover thought it was the proper thing to do in order to prevent a panic in other Chicago banks (*Fifty Billion Dollars* [New York, 1951], 72–81).

[16] Myers and Newton, *op. cit.,* 165.

[17] *Congress. Rec.,* 72:1, Feb. 19, 1932, 4382.

[18] Raymond Clapper Papers, Library of Congress, Washington, D.C.

the vast lower echelons of the population, whereas the R.F.C., he was convinced, would make even more top-heavy the unequal distribution of wealth.

LaGuardia soon began receiving letters from friends and supporters in various states, reaffirming his belief that the R.F.C. was not playing a constructive role. A memo from financial expert Max Lowenthal expressed the opinion that a pending R.F.C. loan to the New York Central Railroad would do nothing to increase employment. Lowenthal said that if the R.F.C., on the other hand, were given power to lend to states and municipalities, as the Progressives were asking, jobs would be created.[19]

A small-town probate judge in Alabama wrote to LaGuardia, praising his stand on the R.F.C. and saying:

This Finance Corporation is a dole to the big bankers. . . . Depositors of closed banks and farmers who . . . are losing their homes are getting no relief under this Hoover program. . . . We have a large tenant population who are suffering as never before. . . . They are running up and down our highways hunting shelter and support, but finding neither. They need a "dole." We have thousands of children out of school, having neither nourishing food or adequate clothing. They need a "dole." [20]

From Jacksonville, Florida, one man wrote: "I want to thank you for the plain, unvarnished truth and statement of fact which you gave in that last speech. . . . My whole opinion is . . . that this R.F.C. is the rottenest piece of stealing of taxpayers' money for the benefit of special interests and bankers that any civilized government ever put upon its statute books." [21] And a few days after this came a letter from Inspiration, Arizona: "I shudder when I think how easily the bankers and industrialists of the United States can get relief in this time of distress while it seems impossible to get relief for our millions of unemployed." [22]

[19] Lowenthal to LaGuardia, Feb. 27, 1932, LaG. Papers.

[20] Letter of Feb. 12, 1932, *ibid.*   [21] Letter of Feb. 10, 1932, *ibid.*

[22] Letter of Feb. 13, 1932, *ibid.* A different view of the R.F.C. is that of Jesse Jones, who was its chairman for seven years under both Hoover and Roosevelt. Jones believes that the R.F.C. was a major factor in pulling the nation out of the depression. "In its ministrations to the nation's sorely stricken people and their economy, the R.F.C. gave aid and comfort at first hand, or indirectly, to every person in the United States" (*op. cit.,* 6–9). The

The letters kept coming, from small towns and big cities in every part of the country. Many praised LaGuardia for his stand. Almost unanimously they asked that the government do something for the unemployed rather than for the bankers. Some writers gave specific information which LaGuardia filed for use. A Washington, D.C., man noted that the Florida East Coast Railroad, owned by the Flagler Estate, was applying for a million-dollar R.F.C. loan. The railroad was in the receivership, with $36,000,000 worth of bonds in default, while a car ferry company, also owned by the Flagler Estate and with the same directors and officers as the railroad, had a surplus of fourteen million dollars.[23]

LaGuardia learned of large R.F.C. loans to mortgage companies that had foreclosed on jobless tenants. One correspondent, noting a $1,500,000 loan to the Prudence Company of New York, reported that one of its affiliates had foreclosed the mortgage on his little house in Brooklyn after he lost his job as an accountant. "My wife, two children and I are living in a cold water flat in Brooklyn. I have worked for the past fifteen months as an elevator operator. . . . I started at $27 a week and they have reduced us to $21.60." [24]

After reading this letter, LaGuardia began his own private probe of the Prudence Company. He secured some inside information from his long-time friend in the Republican party Arthur W. Little, who told him, "They're pretty tough babies, and they are going to try to get the government's money to use for their own insiders profit." They had loaned Little $400,000, he told LaGuardia, and would be happy to foreclose on him. Little said that one of the officers of the corporation was one of the "big short sellers of the past few months." [25]

All of this information fitted in with LaGuardia's efforts to smoke out the men responsible for stock-market speculation. In April of 1932, while the Senate committee investigating short selling listened to the testimony of Stock Exchange President Richard Whitney, LaGuardia lashed out at Whitney and the Exchange

---

truth was that, after its original powers had been strengthened, and it could make loans to states and municipalities, it financed thousands of public works projects which boosted employment in depression days.

[23] Letter of March 28, 1932, LaG. Papers.

[24] Letter of April 5, 1932, *ibid.*   [25] Letter of April 18, 1932, *ibid.*

on the floor of the House. The Stock Exchange had permitted the flotation of $250,000,000 in Kreuger bonds, secured not by real property, but by worthless Austrian and other bonds, he charged, and those who had bought the Kreuger bonds lost all their money.[26]

LaGuardia now prepared to bring sensational evidence to the attention of the public. Raymond Clapper reported in his diary for April 23, 1932: "LaGuardia foned [sic] me to meet him at police hq. Norbeck and Brookhart only ones there besides us. Showed publicity clippings, some checks showing methods used by A. Newton Plummer in creating market for stocks." [27]

Three days after his meeting with Clapper, LaGuardia (who had been investigating stock-market activities for months appeared before the astonished Senate Banking Committee with two trunks full of evidence supplied by former Wall Street publicity man Plummer. The documents added up to the fact that Wall Street investment brokers had gone to unusual lengths to persuade prospective customers to invest in certain stocks. LaGuardia showed the committee hundreds of cancelled checks, paid to financial writers by Wall Street men who wanted them to "ballyhoo" certain stocks of dubious value. Stories were planted in the newspapers, he charged, and he gave the figures: 605 stories were circulated in 208 newspapers with circulations totaling 11,-000,000 in 157 cities.[28] Plummer himself was already implicated in alleged illegal pooling operations on the Exchange, and LaGuardia told the committee that Richard Whitney was aware of market irregularities.[29]

Several months later LaGuardia told a luncheon meeting of the Young Republican Club of New York:

If the security and commodity exchanges were closed like that [he snapped his fingers] the country would go on just the same, but many people would have to go out and earn an honest living. When I charge the stock peddlers, bondmongers, and all the rest of them with de-

---

[26] New York *Times,* April 19, 1932.   [27] Clapper Papers.
[28] New York *Evening Sun,* April 26, 1932; New York *Times,* April 27, 1932.
[29] On April 11, 1938, Richard Whitney, pleading guilty to charges that he had misappropriated funds amounting to six million dollars since 1932, was sentenced to five to ten years in prison.

ception, fraud, and larceny, I leave it to the jury of American suckers who lost millions to say whether I am right or wrong. If a grocer sold a can of beans with the deceit, fraud and misrepresentation that stocks and bonds are sold, he'd be in Atlanta under the pure food act.

The financial panic was brought about by dishonest financing in this country.[30]

His solution: put the stock and commodity exchanges under federal regulation. The Supreme Court, LaGuardia believed, would uphold the constitutionality of the law. Every corporation listing on the Exchange should be compelled, he asserted, to issue quarterly financial statements, lists of directors, the number of shares held by directors, and information on whether the directors were selling long or short on their own stock.[31] LaGuardia was anticipating by two years the Securities Exchange Commission of the New Deal.

In his customary hedge-hopping fashion, LaGuardia now leaped onto another issue which brought his antipathy to bankers into full view. Hoover's annual message had called for home loan discount banks, to bail out the distressed commercial banks by allowing them to discount home and farm mortgages for needed cash. The measure was introduced in the House on May 27, 1932, and LaGuardia was beside himself with rage. To him it was still more evidence that at a time when millions of Americans could not get enough to eat, the administration, deaf to pleas for a public works program, was determined to give large-scale aid to the nation's bankers. He exploded: "No dole for the millionaires! The bastards broke the People's back with their usury and now they want to unload on the government. No. No. No. Let them die; the People will survive." [32] He would rather, LaGuardia declared, see the government nationalize the banks.[33]

His chances to stop the bill were slim, so LaGuardia concentrated his attention upon an amendment "To Protect the Home Owner from Usurious Rates." It provided that the proposed Federal Home Loan Banks would refuse to discount mortgages if the total charges to the homeowner amounted to more than the maximum legal rate of interest. He knew that the addition of various extra charges, like title search fees, often raised the total

30 New York *Times,* Aug. 4, 1932.   31 *Ibid.*
32 Cuneo, *op. cit.,* 39.   33 *Ibid.*

interest rate on home loans to as high as 10 per cent. Speaking for his amendment on the floor, LaGuardia said, "In many cases, I fear, loan sharks are benefiting from government loans while the people Congress ought to help are exploited." [34]

When his mail bag began bulging with letters from loan companies protesting against his amendment and seeking to justify the fees they were charging, LaGuardia replied to one writer: "I do not care what explanations may be given. Any corporation which charges more than six percent interest on money is a hog and deserves no consideration." [35] He kept hitting at the "loan sharks" in public utterances and private letters [36] and compiled (from New Jersey newspapers over the course of one week) a list of 173 cases where loan associations "mercilessly and ruthlessly" foreclosed mortgages on homes. After much debate the House adopted LaGuardia's provision, but when the bill finally came out of conference it had been weakened, setting an 8 per cent maximum interest rate and then only in the absence of state legal limits. [37]

After the twelve Home Loan Banks began to operate, LaGuardia maintained his watchdog vigil over the administration of the law. In a radio speech delivered on the evening of August 18, 1932, he called the attention of his listeners to a provision in the law which read: "Any homeowner . . . who is unable to obtain mortgage money from any other source may obtain same from any bank organized under this act." This clause, LaGuardia insisted, made possible the direct granting of loans by the Home Banks to the home owner. "Will the Home Loan Bank Act benefit the home owner or the loan shark?" he asked. "The answer to that is anxiously awaited in a hundred thousand homes." [38]

The response to this speech was swift and gratifying, with many letters testifying to the urgent need of homeowners for financial aid. A number of writers wanted loans, and LaGuardia referred them to the Federal Home Loan Banks. It soon became apparent,

[34] *Congress. Rec.*, 72:1, June 10, 1932, 13003.
[35] Letter of June 28, 1932, LaG. Papers.
[36] Letter of June 3, 1932, *ibid.*
[37] Conference report, July 14, 1932, copy in LaG. Papers.
[38] New York *Herald Tribune*, Aug. 16, 1932; copy of speech delivered over WOR, LaG. Papers.

however, that the administration had no intention of interpret-
ing the law in such a way as to make it easy for homeowners to
get loans directly from the new lending agency. Franklin W.
Fort, appointed by Hoover as chairman of the Federal Home Loan
Bank Board, said that applications for direct loans would be referred back to local lending institutions. The New York *World
Telegram* commented: "While this policy does not definitely bar
direct loans, it is expected to involve such complications and delay as to render this provision of the act inoperative." [39]

LaGuardia's swelling resentment against the bankers, frustrated
time and again on the floor of Congress and in administrative
offices, found an outlet in an article he wrote for the October,
1932, issue of the magazine *Brass Tacks*. The article was entitled
"Usury—The Curse of Humanity." Usury, he said, was one of
the few great evils still plaguing the world.

Mankind has made great progress in the last twenty centuries. Pestilence, epidemics, scourges have been removed. . . . There are but
three scourges left, each in its turn playing havoc, causing destruction
and leaving sorrow and misery in its wake—cancer, war, and usury.
Science is making headway with cancer. War and usury remain. Both
are founded on greed, selfishness, and ambition of men.

As an example of usury at its worst, LaGuardia cited Russell Sage
as "one of the most unscrupulous, disreputable loan sharks that
ever lived. . . . A grafting alderman, a crooked Congressman,
a thieving loan shark, and an admitted perjurer." [40] Pointing
to the connection between "loan shark" agencies and Wall Street,
he singled out the Household Finance Company, with 149 offices
in 13 states, which had its preferred stock listed on Exchange.
"When the time comes to purge the stock exchange, I hope those
who have the job in hand will drive this loan-mongering crew,
not back to the curb, but to the gutter, where they belong." [41]

In the closing days of December, 1932, LaGuardia introduced
a resolution to reduce all interest rates in the nation, which was
immediately attacked as amounting to "the confiscation of capital." One banker defended existing interest rates, saying, "The

[39] Aug. 22, 1932.   [40] *Congress. Rec.,* 72:2, Appendix, Dec. 10, 1932.
[41] *Ibid.* LaGuardia also quoted a statement by Franklin D. Roosevelt in
Liberty Magazine: "When a free citizen with good security cannot borrow
money for legitimate purposes on fair terms there is something wrong."

law of supply and demand never was working more effectively than it is today." [42] Small homeowners and mortagees disagreed and sent LaGuardia hundreds of letters lauding his stand against the bankers. The letters were heartwarming reminders that he had more support in the nation at large than in Congress, and in that winter of 1932 LaGuardia, like the tenement dwellers huddling around their stoves in East Harlem, was grateful for a little warmth.

[42] Unidentified clipping from Cincinnati newspaper, Dec. 28, 1932, LaG. Papers.

16 · *Triumph on Two Fronts:*

Taxes and Labor Injunctions

IN the midst of the battles over relief, public works, and finance, LaGuardia did not lose sight of that most potent of weapons in the arsenal of the House of Representatives—the power to tax. If taxation involved class issues in the 1920's, it fairly bristled with them in the hard days of 1931 and 1932, and LaGuardia, seeing the growing ranks of apple-sellers as visible evidence of the failure of the Mellon philosophy, sprang into action.

The echoes of Wall Street's market crash in October, 1929, were still faintly audible when Congressman Willis C. Hawley of Oregon, discussing the raising of revenue for the coming year, expressed the belief that corporations were "relatively speaking, overtaxed. . . . It can hardly be denied that the way to give the greatest federal tax relief to the greatest number is through a reduction of the corporate rate." [1]

Progressives, on the other hand, maintained insistently that taxes on the higher-income brackets should be increased, and by spring of 1931, when it was becoming evident that the nation was in the grip of a serious depression, they began to plan the introduction of legislation for that purpose. In the House, LaGuardia and James Frear joined in a statement predicting that the nation would probably have to approach the "war-time level" of income taxes and that higher taxes on estates and large incomes were

[1] *Congress. Rec.*, 71:1, Dec. 5, 1929, 160–176.

the order of the day.[2] William E. Borah and George Norris made similar proposals in the Senate. Norris had been harping on this theme ever since World War I, and in the summer of 1931 he wrote to a constituent:

The danger which I see ahead for our country is in the enormous combinations of wealth. . . . To meet this danger a small group has advocated the levying of a progressive inheritance tax which would break up those immense fortunes and the increasing of income taxes on large incomes to prevent the accumulation of such large fortunes.[3]

"But," Norris said, "we are very much in the minority."

While very much in favor of a balanced budget, LaGuardia knew that behind the fiscal question of budget balancing lay the substantive issue of the distribution of wealth. How many of those who were "blabbing" about the balanced budget, he asked, would vote for increased inheritance and gift taxes "so that we can break up the accumulated wealth of this country?" [4] Responding in House debate to New York Congressman John Taber's proposal to levy taxes all down the line in order to have all groups share the expense of the government, LaGuardia cried:

Fine! Another idea of the discredited bankers. Put the burden on the poor fellow getting $25 a week; put more taxes on him; put more taxes on the man supporting a family on $35 a week. . . . My friends, let us trace the source of this drive to make the already exploited people who are compelled to work for a living now pay for the blunders of their exploiters.[5]

LaGuardia prepared in the early months of 1932 a frontal assault on the man whom he viewed as the spinal column holding together the heartless skeleton of presidential leadership since the war, Secretary of the Treasury Andrew Mellon. He had gathered a great deal of data on Mellon and now ordered his young secretary, Ernest Cuneo, to assemble a case for the impeachment of Mellon. Cuneo could find no specific statute which was violated by Mellon's stock-holding ventures (he had given up his directorships in order to comply with the law) and told LaGuardia so, but this was no deterrent. LaGuardia began a series of attacks

2 Washington *Herald,* March 29, 1931.
3 Norris to F. M. Richard, June 29, 1931, Norris Papers.
4 *Congress. Rec.,* 72:1, Jan. 23, 1932, 2585.   5 *Ibid.*

on Mellon in Congress.[6] He was beginning to get warmed up when Hoover suddenly smashed the underpinnings of his impeachment campaign by announcing, on February 3, 1932, the nomination of Andrew Mellon as Ambassador to England.[7] Two days later, Ogden Mills, who had been acting as Under Secretary, was appointed Secretary of the Treasury in Mellon's place.

Mellon was out of the way, but the real battle was yet to come. In the face of Hoover's declaration on Lincoln's Birthday, 1932, that he would favor a sales tax provided it excluded staple food and cheaper clothing,[8] LaGuardia issued his own tax plan. His proposal omitted the sales tax, but would favor $475,000,000 through increased income and inheritance taxes and another $100,000,000 through taxing stock transfers.[9] The issue had now been joined, and it was clear that the sales tax would be the focal point for the renewal of the old battle between progressives and conservatives on the distribution of wealth. The Social Darwinist argument against LaGuardia's plan was expressed concisely by a Westchester County man who wrote him angrily: "Your practice as a representative teaches forty-three millions . . . to expect the benefits of our government as a gift from the other two million, whose activity, energy, capacity and thrift you strive to penalize." [10]

When the House Ways and Means Committee reported the revenue bill to the House on March 10, 1932, it covered a provision, backed by both Republicans and Democrats,[11] for a 2¼ per cent sales tax, which would raise about $600,000,000. Hoover had called in leading congressmen to confer with him on the revenue bill, asking support for all its features, including the sales tax proposal. House Speaker John Nance Garner not only agreed to support the measure but volunteered to lead the fight for it in the House. Garner, the country-schooled veteran congressman from Red River County in Texas, had opposed Mellon

[6] Cuneo, *op. cit.*, 42–46.

[7] Hoover always maintained that Mellon had made a great contribution to the nation, and later, in his memoirs, wrote: "On the balance sheet of national welfare Andrew Mellon should be credited with having added to both the material and spiritual assets of America" (*Memoirs*, II, 60).

[8] Myers and Newton, *op. cit.*, 174.

[9] Press release, LaG. Papers.   [10] Letter of March 22, 1932, *ibid.*

[11] Myers and Newton say, "It was an example of what could be accomplished through united bi-partisan effort, and the country was encouraged" (*op. cit.*, 182).

and Coolidge consistently in fiscal legislation in the twenties and had indicated opposition to a sales tax.[12] In 1931 he had forced disclosure of huge tax refunds to corporations.[13] However, several weeks before, Garner, always concerned with budget balancing, had formed a Democratic Economy Committee and soon became convinced that a sales tax was needed to raise added revenue.

LaGuardia now made his preparations "like Nelson preparing for Trafalgar." [14] Tossing into the wastebasket the detailed document Cuneo had naïvely compiled in favor of the sales tax, he said he was going to base his fight on the idea of "Soak the Rich." [15] Within forty-eight hours of the committee report proposing the sales tax, LaGuardia was standing near his seat in the House, waving his hand frantically to get the floor. Then he told his colleagues that the sales tax was not suitable for a society where wealth was unevenly distributed. Perhaps in the coming generation, with the advance of industrial democracy, such a tax would be advisable, he said, but not in 1932. Replying to the boast of the Ways and Means Committee that its bill had bipartisan support, he said: "I will grant you that this demand for a sales tax is by no means partisan. There is no partisanship in anything that goes beyond $1,000,000." [16]

The alternatives suggested in his own tax plan, LaGuardia told the House, might be a nuisance but "not so much of a nuisance as to pay a tax on baby clothes and a pair of stockings and a pair of shoes, soap, or a can of beans." He had learned, through the Legislative Reference Service of the Library of Congress, that there were five million safety deposit boxes in the nation, and now proposed a 10 per cent tax on these, along with his previous suggestions for a stock transfer tax and increased taxes on income over $100,000.

The Washington *Herald,* in an editorial following LaGuardia's speech, asked that the Democratic party hold fast to the sales tax, saying: "When the Democratic Party has the sincerity to be democratic, when it has the patriotism to be American, it will substitute excise taxation and sales taxation for undemocratic, un-American and discriminatory income taxation." [17]

[12] Bascom M. Timmons, *Garner of Texas* (New York, 1948), 97, 140.
[13] Schlesinger, *op. cit.,* 62.   [14] Cuneo, *op. cit.,* 42.   [15] *Ibid.,* 43.
[16] *Congress. Rec.,* 72:1, March 12, 1932, 5888–5889.
[17] March 13, 1932.

LaGuardia sought the support of Ogden Mills, who had a number of times spoken of the difficulty of administering a sales tax, but Mills replied that the administration bill was fundamentally sound. "The main objective is a balanced budget," he wrote, and noted that LaGuardia's revenue proposals would leave a shortage of $530,000,000.[18]

The only member of the House Ways and Means Committee to vote against the administration revenue bill was Robert L. Doughton of North Carolina,[19] and now he joined the tiny group of "Allied Progressives" in the House, which, led by LaGuardia, took the floor repeatedly to denounce what they called an attempt to soak the poor at a time when the poor could barely keep alive. Support came from the American Federation of Labor,[20] from the Railroad Brotherhoods, and from correspondents throughout the country. A.F. of L. President William Green, in a press release, asked: "How can men and women who are unable to buy the bare necessities of life be expected to pay a sales tax upon the limited merchandise which they are able to buy?"[21] Sentiment within the House began to crystallize behind LaGuardia's arguments, and those who had counted on an easy victory for the bipartisan bill became alarmed. This alarm spread rapidly when, on March 18, 1932, a near riotous House session adopted an amendment to the tax bill providing for a maximum surtax of 65 per cent on incomes exceeding $5,000,000. The Washington *Herald* called it a "Soak the Rich Stampede,"[22] and other newspapers now began hurling a barrage of shells at LaGuardia. In an editorial called "Killing the Golden Goose" the New York *Daily News* said:

The soak-the-rich movement comes mainly, as always, from the South and West. . . . We are much puzzled, therefore, to see Rep. LaGuardia of New York, always interesting and often right, side with the soak-New York crowd. . . . Soak Rockefeller 72% of all he makes over $5,000,000 and two thirds he makes under $5,000,000 and how can he go ahead with Radio City, not to mention his vast philanthropic activities all over the world.[23]

[18] Mills to LaGuardia, March 17 and March 9, 1932, Mills Papers.
[19] New York *Times,* March 17, 1932.
[20] Wire from William Green, LaG. Papers.
[21] Release of March 16, 1932, *ibid.*
[22] March 19, 1932.   [23] March 20, 1932.

The New York *Times* chided LaGuardia: "All was serene a few days ago. . . . Then Mr. LaGuardia tossed a nice, new shiny monkey wrench." [24]

John Nance Garner, trying to salvage what was left of the great bipartisan coalition backing the bill, issued a statement to the press which coincided with Hoover's arguments:

The supreme purpose of the pending tax bill is to enable the government to balance the budget. . . . If the people lack confidence in the financial stability of their government, they will lack confidence in all forms of corporate and individual enterprise. It is therefore of the highest importance that the budget should be balanced. . . . As for myself, I say now that if the need be, I am ready to yield temporarily every economic opinion I have ever held to reach that goal— the financial salvation of my country.[25]

LaGuardia stood firm. Hailing his fellow progressives, "who know what this tax will mean to the struggling workers, to the unemployed, to the small business man, and to the small manufacturer," he announced their determination to resist the demand, from powerful quarters, for the sales tax. "We refuse to be stampeded and to be threatened." [26]

Attention began to center on LaGuardia as the key figure in the startling House turnabout. One newspaper commented:

For the moment, at least, F. H. LaGuardia, one of the interesting characters in American politics, is booted and spurred and riding strongly in the saddle in the House of Representatives. It is his leadership, more than that of anyone else, that the House has been following since last Friday while it tore to shreds the tax bill so carefully drawn up by its more conservative ways and means committee.[27]

The *Daily News* continued, as the LaGuardia forces kept growing in strength in the House, its series of editorials based on the theme that LaGuardia and his friends were killing the goose that laid the golden egg. The very force which gave multitudinous cheap products to the American population, that is, the wealthy

[24] March 27, 1932.
[25] *Ibid.*, March 20, 1932. Garner's relationship with LaGuardia was always a cordial one. He could not pronounce the New York congressman's first name, and called him "Frijole" (Timmons, *op. cit.*, 136).
[26] Copy of N.B.C. radio speech, LaG. Papers.
[27] *Evening Tennessean*, March 22, 1932.

group in America, would be crippled, the *News* said, by the "confiscatory taxation" of the progressives.[28] And the New York *Evening Journal* declared: "For outright demagoguery the fight of Congressman LaGuardia, of New York, against the sales tax in behalf of the income tax breaks all recent records. . . . If he persists in this course at the expense of his country, his country will demand an accounting from him—AND IT OUGHT TO" [*Journal*'s emphasis].[29] LaGuardia was "alien in mind and spirit from Americanism," the Chicago *Tribune* said.[30]

When the New York *Evening Post* attacked LaGuardia's tax proposals, one of its readers came to LaGuardia's defense, saying: "Once more you will probably brand him a fraud, a radical, a disciple of Moscow. . . . When will the *Post* (so sportsmanlike and fair in respect of most matters except those pertaining to economics) stop taking orders from the House of Morgan and discover that the American public is in revolt against unequal distribution of wealth and privilege." [31]

As the House prepared to vote on the tax bill, the Brooklyn *Daily Eagle* perceptively summarized the situation:

The fact that Rep. F. H. LaGuardia of New York occupies a position of practical dictatorship in the House of Representatives, as far as the manufacturers sales tax is concerned, is due to an uprising of deep resentment against the hitherto prevailing conservatism of both the Democratic and Republican parties in this session of Congress. To dismiss Mr. LaGuardia's performance as mere perverse radicalism is to miss the point. The movement, in its deepest significance, far from being a manifestation of Communism, is an expression of resentment at the failure of Congress to provide relief for the mass of the population, while billions have been appropriated for the relief of banks, railroads, and corporations.[32]

On March 24, 1932, the House, by a vote of 211–178, rejected the sales tax feature of the revenue bill. For LaGuardia it was one of the most gratifying victories of his congressional career, climaxing his gradual emergence as the leading spirit and master organizer of the progressive bloc in the House of Representatives. As in dozens of instances throughout the twenties, he had chal-

---

[28] March 21, 1932.   [29] March 24, 1932.   [30] March 21, 1932.
[31] March 22, 1932.   [32] March 22, 1932.

lenged a Republican-Democratic coalition which appeared invincible. In the twenties, one defeat followed another. This time, however, hunger and unemployment, representing no particular district, had joined the roll call on the side of the progressives. The Chicago *Tribune,* the New York *Evening Journal,*[33] and other leading newspapers lashed LaGuardia mercilessly. A small newspaper in Sandusky, Ohio, perceived, in a kind of helpless rage, the crucial significance of that combination of economic radicalism and political independence personified by LaGuardia. Its editorial said:

Chaos reigns in Congress. The nation is starting to pay dearly for the primary system of government, whereby all party allegiance is absolved . . . the blatant and irresponsible members of Congress, led by such men as LaGuardia of New York City, a product of the steerage and Ellis Island of a few years back, have dipped their fingers in the gore of confiscation and gone on an orgy which they themselves call 'soak the rich'. . . . Congress is rushing this nation to the edge of the precipice by its hysterical onslaught against party discipline and national integrity. . . . Back to party government. Congressmen must get in step now, this year, or else assume full responsibility for the sovietization of the land once ruled by freemen.[34]

But there was praise too. The Portland *Evening News* called the House vote "A victory for the American People" and said, "The guiding spirit of the revolt in the House was the intrepid Fiorello LaGuardia of New York, Republican." [35]

While the effects of LaGuardia's brilliant sales tax victory on the political situation in the election year of 1932 cannot be measured fully, it seems clear that the defeat of the sales tax bill was a serious blow to the conservative wing of the Democratic party, led by Garner in Congress and Chairman John J. Raskob and Executive Secretary Jouett Shouse of the Democratic National Committee. The St. Louis *Post-Dispatch* reported:

After ten days of bitter fighting over the billion dollar revenue bill, the House adjourns tonight in an atmosphere of profound uncertainty. Both parties were split wide open. . . . Among the strange aspects of a

33 Both papers, March 25, 1932.
34 Sandusky, Ohio, *Register,* March 24, 1932.
35 Clipping in LaG. Papers.

confusing situation it appeared that virtually the only member who still exerted an effective influence on both sides of the chamber was Representative LaGuardia, an uncompromising Republican Progressive from the Harlem District of New York City. . . . The only leader who appears to have a program and a plan for carrying it out is LaGuardia. . . . The disappointment felt by Bernard Baruch, John J. Raskob, and other large contributors to Democratic campaign funds over the rejection of the sales tax voiced tonight in a nation-wide radio broadcast by Jouett Shouse, executive secretary of the Democratic committee.[36]

The New York *Herald Tribune* referred to the outcome of the revenue battle as a "decisive overturn in the political situation" which sent Garner "into total eclipse as a Presidential possibility." It added: "Reports from about the country indicate that, of all the Presidential possibilities this year, none of those who stand a chance to be nominated makes a greater appeal to the 'radical' or liberal elements than does Governor Franklin D. Roosevelt of New York. . . . The Governor himself remains unscathed in the present debacle of Congress, while his principal opponents, the Shouse-Raskob group, stand defeated in their advocacy of the sales tax." [37]

The revenue bill, finally passed by the House at the end of March, 1932, embodied all the major proposals LaGuardia had made at the start of the session, and he happily wired Marcantonio in New York that he had won a "complete victory in every respect." [38] There was one more attempt before adjournment to reintroduce the sales tax, and LaGuardia arose, held up his hands like a football player about to punt, then drew back his right foot and kicked vigorously at an imaginary football. "That, gentlemen," he shouted to his colleagues, "is the way the sales tax will be booted out of this house." [39] He sat in the chamber, day after day, in the front row, refusing to leave for lunch, munching on peanuts instead, until he was certain that the sales tax was dead beyond revival.

The victory over the sales tax coincided with another triumph, the passage of the Norris-LaGuardia Anti-Injunction bill. The

[36] March 26, 1932.   [37] March 25, 1932.
[38] March 30, 1932, LaG. Papers.   [39] Washington *Post*, April 18, 1932.

enactment of this measure may rightfully be considered as launching the legislative "new deal" for labor, which emerged fully in the Wagner Act under Roosevelt.

Throughout the nation's history organized labor had been traveling across long barren stretches of governmental indifference or hostility, relieved only tantalizingly by a brief shower of reform laws in the first Wilson administration. Throughout the journey, attacks from the business interests, often aided by government, were unremitting, with one of the chief instruments of the attackers being the injunction.

LaGuardia had seen the debilitating effects of the injunction on labor unions as far back as the garment strikes before World War I. He had denounced its use against railroad workers in the Harding administration and against Pennsylvania coal miners in the Coolidge administration. Starting in 1924, at every House session he introduced anti-injunction legislation, which was always carefully buried in the files of the Judiciary Committee.

In the Senate, George Norris had been working on a similar program. As chairman of a Senate subcommittee in 1928, Norris studied the Shipstead bill to outlaw yellow-dog contracts (the bill had been prepared by seaman Andrew Furuseth, long active in the campaign for progressive labor legislation). Deciding to substitute a more comprehensive and workable bill, Norris' subcommittee held extensive hearings. In order to ensure that the bill would withstand constitutional objections, Norris sought the advice of Felix Frankfurter of the Harvard Law School, attorney Donald Richberg of Chicago, Professor Herman Oliphant of Johns Hopkins, Edwin E. Witte of the University of Wisconsin, and Francis B. Sayre of Harvard.[40] After a number of revisions,[41] the completed bill was introduced in the Seventieth Congress in 1929, with LaGuardia introducing a companion measure in the House,[42] but it failed to pass.

Early in 1932, as the Seventy-second Congress convened,

[40] *Fighting Liberal: The Autobiography of George Norris* (New York, 1945), 311–313.

[41] Richberg to Norris, May 18, 1928, Norris Papers.

[42] "He was always working with Senator Norris," says Marie Fischer LaGuardia. "Anything that was in the Senate and going to the House, or vice-versa, Norris would speak to him about it" (interview with Marie Fischer LaGuardia, Oral History Project, Columbia University).

Frankfurter wrote to Norris that the time was opportune for re-introducing the bill.[43] Accordingly, Norris and LaGuardia, con-ferring often and working closely together, did so in their respective chambers. The Norris-LaGuardia bill, seeking to rectify the ineffectual wording of the Clayton Act, specifically barred the use of injunctions to prevent strikes or union organiza-tion, limited the application of any injunction to the charges specified in the complaint (in order to bar the catch-all injunc-tion), provided jury trials for those charged with violating in-junctions,[44] barred yellow-dog contracts, and stipulated that the judicial voiding of any section of the measure would leave other sections intact.[45]

Section Two of the bill declared as a matter of "public policy" that since individual unorganized workers were "commonly help-less" they had the right to organize into unions, to bargain col-lectively with the employer, and to be free from coercion in these activities. It was a direct forerunner of the Wagner Act of 1935.

Debate opened in the Senate on February 23, 1932, with Norris taking the floor in a forceful defense of the bill. Anticipating at-tacks on its constitutionality, he asserted that Congress had the right to declare public policy on any subject where it had the right to legislate. The aim of the bill, he said, was to "have the same rule of law apply to the poor as to the rich." Without opening avenues of escape for real criminals, Norris said, the bill "pre-vents great aggregations of capital from combining against the weak and the poor in any way which would deprive them of the ordinary rights of free citizens." [46] A week later, after voting down a number of amendments designed to weaken the bill, the Senate adopted it, by a vote of 75–5.[47]

[43] Jan. 5, 1932, Norris Papers.

[44] Aiding Norris and LaGuardia, and in at least one instance offering helpful advice, were the members of the National Committee on Labor Injunctions, headed by Arthur Garfield Hays and Roger Baldwin. Baldwin wrote to Norris, Feb. 23, 1932, suggesting that the provision for jury trials in contempt cases be broadened, beyond injunction cases, to include all cases of criminal contempt outside the courtroom, such as newspaper editors cited for contempt for criticizing court orders. This was approved in the Senate, but the House version won out (ibid.).

[45] Congress. Rec., 72:1, Dec. 10, 1931, H.R. no. 5315.

[46] New York Times, Feb. 24, 1932.

[47] Ibid., Feb. 27 and March 3, 1932.

The crucial battle in the House of Representatives remained however, and here Fiorello LaGuardia assumed the leadership of the campaign to assure passage. On March 8, 1932, the House debate reached its climax, with Congressman James M. Beck of Pennsylvania delivering a long attack on the bill. He defended the use of injunctions in labor disputes on the ground that labor should not be given privileges denied to others. "What could be more humane and beneficent," Beck asked, "than this method of dealing with a labor controversy? The court . . . only commands him [the laborer] to refrain from interfering with his employer's property and from the liberty of other workmen to work for his employer." [48] In passing the bill, he charged, Congress would be "making a long march toward Moscow." [49]

There was little doubt in the House about who would deliver the chief rebuttal to Beck's arguments. LaGuardia rose, and after thanking Speaker Garner, Majority Leader Rainey, and the Rules Committee for sending the bill to the floor, began his discussion of its provisions. He said:

Gentlemen, this bill does not—and I cannot repeat it too many times —this bill does not prevent the court from being used as an agency for strike-breaking purposes and as an employment agent for scabs to break a lawful strike.[50]

This bill was made necessary, he charged, by the fact that a few federal judges had sought to win the favor of financially powerful interests. Important declarations of policy, he said, should be made by the elected representatives of the American people and not by a politically appointed federal judge.

In order to take the phrase "yellow-dog contract" out of abstract debate and bring its significance vividly to the minds of his colleagues, LaGuardia read the provisions of an actual yellow-dog contract and then asked, "Do you call that American liberty?" Winding up his argument, he quoted Abraham Lincoln in defense of labor and the right to strike. The House passed the bill that day by an overwhelming vote of 362–14,[51] and the New York *Times* reported: "Today's victory was the climax of an eight-year effort by Mr. LaGuardia." [52]

[48] *Congress. Rec.*, 72:1, March 8, 1932, 5478–5480.
[49] New York *Times*, March 9, 1932.
[50] *Congress. Rec.*, 72:1, March 8, 1932, 5478–5479.
[51] *Ibid.*, 5511.   [52] March 9, 1932.

President Hoover, after discussing the bill's constitutionality with Attorney General Mitchell (who said the constitutional questions were too difficult for the executive branch to decide), signed the bill on March 23, 1932. His motives in approving the bill were debated for some time. Administration supporters pointed out that Hoover had "protested vigorously" Daugherty's sweeping injunctions against railroad workers in 1922.[53] George Norris, on the other hand, said that Hoover had signed reluctantly in the face of certain repassage in the event of a veto.[54] The decisive pressure on Hoover in favor of the bill, Norris maintained, came from the American people, who were gaining a new consciousness of "the inequalities which then existed in the economic structure." [55]

The newspaper *Labor,* expressing the sentiments of organized labor throughout the country, hailed the Norris-LaGuardia Act. In the face of spirited attack, it noted, Fiorello LaGuardia "was always on guard," cutting down one by one the many weakening amendments offered by Beck of Pennsylvania and Blanton of Texas and seeing the bill through to final passage.[56]

Whatever else the session might produce before it ended in the summer of 1932, one thing was clear: LaGuardia had emerged as one of the national leaders of a new, dynamic, depression-based progressivism, which had won dramatic victories on the sales tax and on labor injunction and which now awaited the grace of a catch title, the responsibility of attachment to a major party, and the unifying effect of a great personality to become the New Deal.

[53] R. L. Wilbur and A. M. Hyde, *The Hoover Policies* (New York, 1937), 134.

[54] Statement of March 24, 1932, Norris Papers.

[55] Norris, *op. cit.,* 314. Alfred Lief points out that by this time both parties were pledged to do something about the use of injunctions in labor disputes, and this fact helped passage of the bill (*Democracy's Norris* [New York, 1939], 386). After the Supreme Court, for the first time, in 1895, passed on the scope and validity of injunctions in labor disputes, the Democratic party was the first to take up labor's demand for limitations on such injunctions; after the Republican party expressed a favorable attitude in 1908, the Clayton Act of 1914 represented a futile attempt to put into effect this seemingly bipartisan sentiment. In the 1928 campaign both parties committed themselves to anti-injunction laws (Felix Frankfurter and Nathan Greene, *The Labor Injunction* [New York, 1930], 1).

[56] Clipping in LaG. Papers.

17 · Communism, Nativism,

and Foreign Policy

NATIONAL crisis in the United States, whether domestic or foreign in origin, has often produced punitive expeditions in search of heretics and radicals, and the depression of the thirties was no exception. No sooner did it become evident that the nation was in a state of economic collapse that hostility to radicalism began to accumulate.

While the Red scare of the early 1930's was clearly directed at symptoms rather than cause, its supporters could point, at least, to symptoms which were genuinely alarming. Communists and Socialists found in the depression a perfect opportunity to convince Americans of the hopelessness of the capitalist system and to take the lead in demanding immediate solutions for the problems of hunger and joblessness. LaGuardia kept insisting, nevertheless, that the job of Congress was not to hunt Communists but to destroy the economic insecurity on which their movement fattened itself.

His first clash in this issue was with the dapper Grover Whalen, who had been appointed police commissioner of New York by Jimmy Walker. Whalen was convinced, as early as 1929, that "New York was becoming a hotbed of communism."[1] When a bomb addressed to Governor Roosevelt was found in the main

[1] *Mr. New York: The Autobiography of Grover Whalen* (New York, 1955), 150.

post office of New York City, Whalen's suspicions immediately fell upon the labor movement.[2]

Early in 1930 a huge crowd of New Yorkers jammed Union Square to participate in a Communist-organized demonstration for relief, and Whalen responded with riot squads and night sticks. Amos Pinchot, a leader of the American Civil Liberties Union, urged that Whalen be dismissed from his post because, Pinchot said, his actions revealed "a low grade of intelligence" and because "he resorts unnecessarily to violence." Whalen seemed, Pinchot declared, "unable to realize that an idea is a thing of a peculiar nature, in that it cannot be destroyed by the naive and simple means of striking it with a club." [3]

On May 2, 1930, Grover Whalen appeared before the House Immigration Committee to testify about Communist activities and released to the newspapers photostats of documents, in Russian, which appeared to indicate that the Soviet government was giving orders to American Communists through its trading company, Amtorg. Whalen refused to say where he obtained the documents, on the ground that the disclosure might interfere with investigations of Communist activities.[4] The photostats were given sensational treatment in the press, but a week after Whalen's testimony LaGuardia received a letter from the managing editor of the New York *Evening Graphic* that turned the whole episode on its ear. The letter informed him that a *Graphic* reporter named John Spivak, after intensive investigation, had discovered that the "Moscow" letters were in reality the product of a small print shop on East 10th Street in Manhattan.[5] LaGuardia soon had in his possession a list of twenty-one instances of clumsy errors in the alleged Soviet documents, proving conclusively that they had been forged; he also had an affidavit signed by the printer who had done the letterheads for the "documents." [6]

Wasting no time, LaGuardia took this evidence to the floor of

2 Bellush, *op. cit.,* 195.

3 March 21, 1930, Amos Pinchot Papers, Library of Congress, Washington, D.C.

4 *The Nation,* May 28, 1930.

5 H. Swain to LaGuardia, May 10, 1930, LaG. Papers.

6 The printer noted, for instance, that the type used on the letterhead claimed to have come from Moscow was exactly the same as that used on a Workmen's Circle leaflet advertising a meeting in New Brunswick, N. J

the House. He pointed out to his colleagues that even before Grover Whalen went to Washington he had been informed by the *Evening Graphic* editor of Spivak's discoveries, but Whalen went anyway and released the photostats.[7] At the same time Secretary of State Henry L. Stimson discovered that the Department of State had known for some time of the falsity of these documents, having refused to deal with the owners, who were trying to sell them at a fancy price.[8]

Undeterred by LaGuardia's evidence, Congressman Bertrand Snell of New York moved for a sweeping congressional investigation of Communist activities, asking (in line with another proposal by Hamilton Fish) that Congress set up a committee to investigate the Amtorg corporation, Communistic propaganda in the schools, and the *Daily Worker*.[9] Snell received a sharp letter of protest from Benjamin C. Marsh, speaking for the People's Lobby [10] (John Dewey was the Lobby's chairman) and asking: "Is your own fear of communism due to the fact that you have devoted much of your time here to helping wealthy looters legally to mulct weak workers? Your committee's hearings will doubtless serve as a political requiem for the most verbose incompetent who ever tried to be Police Commissioner of Wall Street." [11]

One month later the House took up a bill to grant $25,000 to a committee headed by Hamilton Fish "to investigate Communist propaganda in the United States." [12] LaGuardia attacked the resolution, asking that Congress uphold the right of free speech and urging that the economic roots of communism be eradicated by welfare legislation.[13] He compared the hysteria engendered by the Bolshevik Revolution to the Alien and Sedition Acts brought on by the French Revolution. Recalling that the House in 1917 had cheered the end of the Romanoff dynasty, LaGuardia declared: "I for one do not hesitate to say that any kind of government they may have in Russia is better than the crude, autocratic,

[7] *Congress. Rec.*, 71:2, May 12, 1930, 8769–8770.

[8] New York *Evening Graphic*, May 13, 1930.

[9] New York *American*, May 13, 1930.

[10] On the Advisory Committee of the People's Lobby were Oswald Garrison Villard, Rexford Guy Tugwell, Broadus Mitchell, Lewis Gannett, Morris L. Ernst, Harry Elmer Barnes, and Roger Baldwin.

[11] May 13, 1930, LaG. Papers.

[12] *Congress. Rec.*, 71:2, June 13, 1930, 10652.   [13] *Ibid.*, 10654–10655.

despotic government of Czar Nicholas and the Monk Rasputin."

Americans, he argued, should have the right to express their opinions. "Gentlemen," he said, "let me tell you the history of the world discloses that ideas cannot be suppressed, expression of views cannot be crushed; communication and exchange of views cannot be stopped by any law or investigation." Referring to Grover Whalen's testimony on the Communist menace in New York, LaGuardia said: "We have radicals and communists in New York but we are in no danger of having the city or the state or the national government overturned. I do not believe that we are in danger because some Communist furrier in New York is going to take a needle and stick it into the fleshy part of Grover Whalen's anatomy. Social revolutions are not brought about in that way."

Refusing to yield the floor, LaGuardia concluded with a demand for positive action. "Let us do something constructive; let us pass the Wagner Bill before we adjourn. Study my resolution for uniform labor laws, unemployment insurance, and other necessary legislation . . . and in that way we will stop all need for a Congressional investigation of Communist activity." [14]

However, the House passed the resolution appropriating $25,-000 for the Fish committee,[15] and the committee went to work. LaGuardia never missed an opportunity to belabor Fish on this issue, and eight months later told his colleagues in the House:

I am sure we all have the highest regard for our colleague from New York as a great football player in his day on his college team. He is the scion of a distinguished family. We also have the highest regard for him as a gallant soldier who rendered signal service to his company in action . . . but as a statesman—*jamais!* (Laughter and applause).[16]

When, in the winter of early 1931, Congressman William R. Wood of Indiana delivered a long speech to the House on the menace of Communist propaganda, asking that action be taken to stop it, LaGuardia retorted: "He suggests as a remedy the extermination of the vultures of the continuing of misery. He waxes fervent in his fury against the active radicals but offers no relief or help to the patient, suffering, hungry people who are in need." [17]

---

[14] *Ibid.*, Jan. 9, 1931, 1885.   [15] New York *World,* June 14, 1930.
[16] *Congress. Rec.*, 71:3, Feb. 2, 1931, 3784.   [17] *Ibid.*, Jan. 9, 1931, 1885.

Throughout 1931 and 1932 LaGuardia, in the midst of crowded days and hectic conflicts over economic legislation, kept one eye on the Bill of Rights.[18] He attempted repeatedly to repeal the Espionage Act, battled attempts to broaden the deportation power of the government over radicals, and criticized the State Department's refusal to protect the rights of a radical American newspaperman in China. The case of Tom Mooney caught La-Guardia's interest, and after the report of the Wickersham committee, criticizing the conduct of the trial in which Mooney was sentenced to death, he and Congressman Sirovich of Michigan introduced resolutions asking Governor Rolph of California to pardon Mooney immediately. The move failed, with LaGuardia's resolution losing out by one vote in the House Judiciary Committee.[19] Later, Congressman Blanton of Texas praised the California governor for refusing to pardon Mooney and called Mooney a "murderous dynamiter." LaGuardia suggested that Blanton read the Wickersham report and said: "I am sure that instead of taking the floor and glorifying the continued incarceration of an American citizen who has been proved to be innocent, after reading it he will hang his head in shame at the content, surroundings, and perjury of that trial." [20] As on many other issues, LaGuardia's pleas would not be heeded until the advent of a new national climate.

The nativist ideas that had flourished in the twenties were strengthened as the depression grew worse and demands began for further restrictions on immigration, with the unemployment figures used as supporting evidence. LaGuardia, in attempting to stop these proposals, had to face bitter hostility, with the economic crisis sharpening the emotionalism that already accompanied the issue. Throughout the nation, his name was linked with immigration, and the Denver *Post* wrote in the summer of 1930:

It goes against the grain of real Americans to have anybody by the name of LaGuardia telling the American people how to run their

[18] Correspondence between Roger Baldwin and LaGuardia, Feb. 2, 1931, and letter from John Haynes Holmes, Feb. 5, 1931, LaG. Papers; *Congress. Rec.*, 72:1, June 6, 1932, 12097–12107; New York *Times*, Aug. 4, 1932.

[19] New York *Times*, Feb. 13, 1932; New York *World Telegram*, Feb. 23, 1932.

[20] *Congress. Rec.*, 72:1, April 22, 1932, 8712–8715.

government. If he doesn't like our laws, he ought to go back to the country whence his ancestors came. . . . No state but New York would disgrace itself by sending such a man as LaGuardia to Congress and keeping him there. New York has been a cesspool into which immigrant trash has been dumped for so long that it can scarcely be considered American any more.[21]

Late in 1930 a "committee of experts" conducted extensive research for the American Eugenics Society into the effects of immigration and concluded that the national origins formula should stand. This was echoed by the influential *Saturday Evening Post,* which said of the national origins system: "It is the one system which preserves from generation to generation the relative proportions of our racial composition. . . . Its whole tendency is to check any sudden or violent change of racial values." The *Post* approved the committee's recommendation of a system for the registration of resident aliens and found in the committee's reports "a scientific spirit, a temperate tone, and a broad humanity which are too often lacking in the findings of zealots, amateur reformers or professional theorists." [22]

LaGuardia wrote despairingly to a supporter that the House "in its present mood" would be willing to vote for legislation completely suspending immigration. "You can realize," he said, "what we are up against with every restrictionist taking advantage of the unemployment situation and using that as a lever for the legislation they have been trying to get for many years." [23]

A bill to suspend immigration for two years was reported favorably to the House in January, 1931, with the majority report pointing to the great numbers of immigrants from the West Indies and the Philippines. "How many realize that a great part of the black colony in Harlem, New York, is from Jamaica, Haiti, and other islands of the West Indies. . . . Who knows how long it will be when these new elements shall choose to elect three or four members of the House of Representatives from their group?" [24]

In the face of a flood of bills restricting or suspending immigration for various periods of time, LaGuardia took the floor

[21] June 9, 1930.   [22] Nov. 1, 1930.
[23] LaGuardia to Read Lewis, Dec. 9, 1930, LaG. Papers.
[24] *Congress. Rec.,* 71:3, Jan. 28, 1931, Majority Report on H.R. no. 473.

to protest against the speed with which one of these bills was being rushed through the House. The Chamber was proceeding, he said, "under mob rule and not under parliamentary procedure." Angrily he told his colleagues:

It is almost incredible that when a bill that deals with human beings . . . is before the House any human being can be so inhuman as to gloat over the misery you are inflicting by this bill. Oh what a different performance it is around October when you go down on your knees and you come around and say: "LaGuardia, will you come in my district and tell my people what a good Congressman I am."

I say that the procedure this afternoon is a blot on the history of the American Congress. You would not dare bring out a bill at this time under this mob rule dealing with pigs in the Agriculture Department. . . . You ought to be ashamed of yourselves. . . .[25]

The House, with New York's Samuel Dickstein delivering a long and powerful speech in opposition, voted to cut immigration by about 50 per cent.[26]

Foreign affairs did not seem terribly important to a people concerned with food, clothing, and shelter, but they intruded, nevertheless, into the nation's consciousness. LaGuardia retained his keen interest in overseas developments, and spoke out whenever he could on behalf of his favorite ideas: peace, disarmament, and removing the profits from war.

The Kellogg-Briand Pact of 1928 had done little to calm the fears of the world, and the demands of patriotic groups for preparedness were not halted by the depression. In April of 1930 the House considered a proposal, backed by the American Legion, empowering the President to take steps for total mobilization in the event of war. A Legion bill for universal conscription had failed, and this new proposal was an attempt to achieve the same result in a more circuitous fashion. The resolution spoke of con-

---

[25] *Ibid.,* March 2, 1931.

[26] *Ibid.,* 6744; New York *Herald Tribune,* March 2, 1931. In mid-1932, LaGuardia introduced a bill, sponsored by attorneys for the International Labor Defense, permitting the voluntary departure of aliens about to be deported, allowing them to go where they pleased rather than just to their country of origin. This was intended to replace the procedure of arbitrary deportation to a country where the deportee's life might be endangered (like Fascist Italy) (Marcantonio to LaGuardia, May 13, 1932, LaG. Papers).

scripting property as well as men, but the trade unions were wary, and the 1929 national convention of the American Federation of Labor resolved unanimously to oppose the measure.

LaGuardia spoke against the bill in the House.[27] He poked fun, first, at its authorship: "Mr. Chairman, this bill presents a very interesting question on eugenics. It is known as the Snell-Wainwright-McSwain-Johnson resolution; and no off-spring with such a multitudinous variety of fathers can be a wholesome child." When the laughter subsided he continued. The bill, he charged, "doesn't mean what it says and it doesn't say what it means." He noted that the provision for conscription of wealth would never be carried out because of constitutional objections, while the drafting of men would certainly take place. He said:

Gentlemen, something is wrong in a system which permits the government to reach out in one family, take a boy, put a uniform on him, and send him to fight and die, and to reach out to another family and hand it a cost-plus contract to make profits out of a war. . . . If our Constitution protects one citizen's property and dollars but renders another liable to military service which may cost him his life, let us prepare now to change the Constitution.[28]

The Legion proposal did not pass, and several months later, LaGuardia was in London, speaking in the lavish chamber of the House of Lords to the Inter-Parliamentary Union. In what the New York *Times* called the "most outspoken of the day's speeches," he said:

Let's stop talking about overproduction and stress more the lack of ability to purchase the necessities of life. Let's be frank enough to say that this lack of ability to purchase could in great measure be removed if nations would have the good sense to direct to useful and beneficial purposes a portion of the enormous sums now expended annually for armies and navies in preparation for war. Isn't it possible in this age to build as powerful and effective machines for the preservation of life and the promotion of happiness as in the past it was possible to create machines for the destruction of life and property? I think it is, and at much less cost.[29]

[27] *Congress. Rec.,* 71:2, April 1, 1930, 6307–6319.   [28] *Ibid.*
[29] New York *Times,* July 19, 1930. LaGuardia's opposition to militarism extended to an attempt to take away from the armed forces funds used to finance compulsory drill activities in civil schools, but he lost out (*American Teacher,* Feb., 1931).

LaGuardia was incensed at the reluctance of House members to appropriate money for American participation in the Geneva Disarmament Conference of 1932. Stung by charges that the futility of the conference was proved by the failure of the League to halt the Japanese invasion of China in 1931, LaGuardia replied that the ten Commandments had often been violated but were still appropriate. He caustically compared the $450,000 required for delegates to the conference to the Army-Navy budget of $644,650,000. The House passed the resolution.[30]

While criticizing Hoover's action in declaring a moratorium policy on foreign debts before Congress had a chance to act, La-Guardia strongly urged that the moratorium be extended to all European countries. He pointed to Germany as particularly in need of such aid because "there is a political party in Germany right now that is hoping this Congress turns down this moratorium. Why? Because the Hitlerites will move in and take control of the government." [31]

He had been pleading for peace and disarmament, but, when the Japanese attacked Shanghai and invaded China in 1931, La-Guardia was dismayed and angered. According to Ernest Cuneo, LaGuardia was "for forcing war then and there" and even made preparations for a return to the army. The news that American women and children were marooned in Shanghai led him to urge Stimson to land marines to evacuate them.[32]

Unlike the Japanese, Mussolini had not yet committed any large-scale act of aggression, but it was becoming more and more evident, even to Italian-Americans who had initially sympathized with Il Duce on nationalist grounds, that liberty was dying in Italy. LaGuardia's attitude toward the Fascist regime seemed to be crystallizing about this time. When Italy's foreign minister Dino Grandi visited New York, LaGuardia declined an invitation extended by Mayor Walker to be a member of the reception committee.[33] In private, it seems, LaGuardia made no secret of his distaste for Mussolini. Cuneo says: "I remember very clearly how scathing he always was in his references to Mussolini, whom he considered a pitiful caricature of a man, a local barbershop bully involved in a game far beyond his capacities." [34]

---

[30] *Congress. Rec.*, 72:1, Jan. 18, 1932, 2196.
[31] *Ibid.*, Dec. 18, 1931, 826–827. [32] Cuneo, *op. cit.*, 130.
[33] New York *Times*, Nov. 14, 1931. [34] Cuneo, *op. cit.*, 129.

In January, 1933, LaGuardia had just enough time, in the midst of the frantic activities in the lame-duck session, to read the news that Adolf Hitler had become the Chancellor of Germany. What he had spoken of fearfully had come to pass but, like most of the world's leaders, he was busy at this time with immediate political problems at home.

18 · *Political Defeat and Moral*

Victory, 1932-1933

AFTER his win in the 1930 election, LaGuardia did not imagine that he would wage only one more congressional campaign or that his defeat in 1932 would usher in an era of victory for all the proposals he had been making throughout the decade. He went about his usual political shenanigans, exasperating the Republicans, teasing the Democrats, perplexing the Socialists, and delighting his supporters. It was noted in the Brooklyn *Eagle* that the congressman from the Twentieth District "had become the leader and spokesman for the so-called Progressives in the House and as such a favorite of the galleries." The *Eagle* said:

An experienced and clever parliamentarian and debater, he is much more active than either Bertrand H. Snell or Henry T. Rainey, leaders of the regular Republicans and Democrats respectively. So quick is his wit and so devastating his sarcasm that few members of the House will venture to cross swords with him, though he frequently baits Republicans as well as Democrats. As leader of the Progressives, he is their chief sponsor of so-called Progressive legislation.[1]

The Republicans, needing every vote in order to organize the new Congress, wheedled and cajoled to get LaGuardia's support, while he remained by turns aloof or intransigent. Invited to attend a Republican "caucus" in early 1931, LaGuardia insisted on a clear definition of whether this was a "caucus," binding its members, or an informal "conference." He replied: "I am quite will-

[1] Jan. 16, 1931.

ing to attend a conference, but could not consistently attend a caucus because I do not believe in them. Kindly advise me." [2] The answer coming from an anxious caucus chairman, who seemed to be perspiring at every pore in attempting to eat his caucus and have it too, was equivocal,[3] and LaGuardia stayed away.[4]

Progressive-minded Americans at this time were scattered in tiny groups working on various levels, often with divergent ideas. Progressive congressmen, middle-class intellectuals, and trade union representatives would pool their efforts on many economic and civil liberties issues, but questions of political tactics brought disagreement. In early 1931, John Dewey was ready to help organize a third party. George Norris, on the other hand, considered the prospect "practically impossible at this time." Under existing circumstances, he maintained, any new party would become controlled by wealth.[5]

Accordingly, when Progressives decided to hold a conference in Washington in March of 1931, it was called an "Economic Conference" and specifically disavowed any intention of starting a third party. Called by Norris, Costigan, Bronson Cutting, Wheeler, and La Follette, Jr., the meeting aimed to exchange ideas for a legislative program. William Green, Sidney Hillman, Donald Richberg, Charles Beard, E. A. Ross, and Joseph Bristow were among those attending.[6]

LaGuardia at this time was in the hospital, being treated for a sudden recurrence of his old spinal injury, and wrote to Norris expressing his regrets that he could not come. The three-page letter summarized LaGuardia's economic philosophy and outlined a program of action for progressive congressmen. His general appraisal of the nation was expressed in a terse paragraph:

There is a tendency on the part of leaders in both of the major parties to continue to legislate on fundamentals laid down in the age of the stage coach, the spinning wheel and tallow candles. This tendency has resulted in the concentration of great wealth under the control of a few families in this country with the large masses of workers

---

[2] LaGuardia to Hawley, Feb. 23, 1931, LaG. Papers.
[3] Hawley to LaGuardia, Feb. 24, 1931, *ibid.*
[4] Washington *News*, Feb. 24, 1931.
[5] Letter of Feb. 7, 1931, Norris Papers.   [6] MacKay, *op. cit.*, 254.

entirely at their mercy for their very existence. Legislation has not kept abreast with the progress in mechanics, electricity, chemistry, transportation and the sciences. The result is that we find ourselves with an unprecedented wealth, with warehouses full and millions of willing workers out of employment and large numbers dependent upon private charities for relief. It would seem that the fortunate few who own the present modern means of production are even anxious to keep control of charities. When millions of workers through no fault of their own are thrown out of employment it is the duty of the government to give them relief and not force them to apply for private charity.[7]

Reviewing the accomplishments of the Hoover administration in the first seventeen months of the economic crisis, LaGuardia noted bitterly that "threats of vetoes, pronouncement of platitudes, states' rights slogans, met every constructive program offered or even suggested by Congress." The one relief measure passed, for the benefit of drought-stricken farmers, merely enabled them to borrow, thus placing them deeper in debt.

Bold measures were needed, he said, to meet the needs of the new industrial society. A shorter workday and unemployment insurance would help, and he suggested a study of the rate of interest, which he called "the value of money not accompanied by effort or labor." He would, LaGuardia told Norris, try to get out of the hospital in time to attend at least one of the conference sessions, but, he concluded, "If I am not, know that my heart is in the work and that I have not become discouraged and still hope that we may be able to do something for the American people." [8]

Out of the hospital, LaGuardia began talks with Norris and told newspapermen that House Progressives, commanding fifteen to eighteen votes would seek passage of unemployment insurance, an anti-injunction bill, a Muscle Shoals bill, and revision of the House rules to permit proposals to be pulled out of committee by petition of one hundred members.[9]

The New York *Times* tried to dismiss the Progressive bloc with humor but was obviously annoyed:

Without some sort of Progressive conference, no week can take more than a drab and unregretted place in the calendar of time. In that of

[7] March 10, 1931, LaG. Papers.   [8] *Ibid.*
[9] New York *Times*, March 24, 1931

virtue, it is but a blank. So it is good to know that the eight Wisconsin Progressive Republicans in Congress are to call at Madison a confabulation of themselves and six other statesmen, including our own Mr. La-Guardia and Mr. Kvale, the Farmer-Labor Party of the House. The fourteen, provided all the invitations are accepted, will lay down the policies that ought to be followed by the 72nd Congress. This is very kind of them and should be instructive to Congress.[10]

Norris and LaGuardia pledged co-operation between House and Senate Progressives in the new Congress.

A meeting of Progressives in and out of Congress was held in the office of North Dakota Republican Senator Lynn Frazier, with Norman Thomas and Benjamin C. Marsh attending, along with representatives from the Fellowship of Reconciliation, the American Civil Liberties Union, and the Women's League for Peace and Freedom.[11] The immediate outcome of the meeting was a demand for a special session of Congress, and a delegation visited House Speaker Longworth to press this upon him. LaGuardia said: "We are in the midst of a crisis which I consider as serious as a war. The welfare of our six million unemployed is far more important than the political fortunes of any individual. It is our purpose to demand action. . . ." The special session should launch a three-billion-dollar public works program, the Progressives said, and give five million dollars for relief, to be matched by communities.[12]

It was the last demand made by the Progressives upon Longworth, for several weeks later, the old Republican war horse died of lobar pneumonia. Once again they determined to use their bargaining power in the contest over the Speakership, in order to get support for progressive legislation.[13] This meant that La-Guardia again became a source of great irritation for the Republicans, and his name was conspicuously absent from the invitation list for a dinner given by the Republican Committee of New York County in honor of Sam Koenig. Lowell Limpus, editor of the *News,* reported the imminence of a "complete break" between LaGuardia and the party.[14]

[10] *Ibid.,* Oct. 29, 1931.   [11] New York *Herald Tribune,* March 24, 1931
[12] *Ibid.*   [13] New York *Daily News,* April 14, 1931
[14] *Ibid.,* May 11, 1931.

As Congress prepared to convene in November of 1931, House Progressives met and announced a campaign to liberalize the House rules. LaGuardia and Paul Kvale of Minnesota said they would seek a new rule permitting bills to be discharged from committee by a vote of 100 members rather than the 218 then required.[15] This time, their stratagem worked, and a new rule was put into effect, enabling one-third of the House members—145 signatures—to discharge a bill.[16]

The Seventy-second Congress started its sessions with LaGuardia having attained a new stature as the leader of the Progressive group in the House. Robert S. Allen reported from Washington: "One of the many sweeping changes in the new House of Representatives, one of the very most important and dramatic, is the emergence of a militant progressive leader." Since the death of La Follette, Allen observed, the Progressives had disintegrated, but about 1930 "there stepped forward and definitely assumed the role of commander of the progressive sentiment in the House one of the most picturesque and independent figures in both branches of Congress." LaGuardia had "singlehandedly," Allen said, forced a vote on the Wagner Relief bill, which was subsequently vetoed by Hoover.[17]

LaGuardia was still nominally a Republican, but the New York *Times* noted that when a colleague in Congress asked LaGuardia, "Is your party in favor of granting subsidies to corporations?" LaGuardia replied, "Which party?" [18] By the spring of 1932 his two-fisted attacks on the Hoover administration were beginning to bring results. He had won victories on Muscle Shoals, on the sales tax, on the House rules. His power had to be reckoned with seriously now by men of both parties. Heywood Broun ably described the situation in one of his columns:

The real leadership in the House has come into the hands of a man who has won that position wholly by his own driving force. The orthodox members of the Republican Party are not in sympathy with his political views. He is, in the eyes of many, a Socialist in sheep's clothing, and today, in spite of all opposition, he stands as the most power-

[15] New York *Herald Tribune,* Nov. 23, 1931
[16] New York *Times,* Oct. 25, 1931.
[17] Washington *Times,* Dec. 11, 1931.   [18] March 27, 1932.

ful and persuasive member of the lower House, if not of the entire Congress. Naturally you have guessed by now that I mean Fiorello LaGuardia.[19]

Broun quoted a conservative Senator as having told him privately: "Down here we recognize the fact that LaGuardia is the fellow we've got to fight. He's always on the job, and he's one of the few men in Washington with a definite political philosophy." This philosophy, Broun said, was a radical one, despite the fact that LaGuardia was not "the darling of organized radicalism."

Political courage had been demonstrated by LaGuardia on many occasions, Broun noted. He had challenged both Democratic and Republican hierarchies in his battle against the sales tax and dared to defy the man who was, Broun said, the real author of that proposal—William Randolph Hearst. "Undoubtedly, La-Guardia will have to pay for his temerity. . . . From now on the hand of every boss is against him. . . . Attaboy Fiorello!" [20]

As the hot New York summer of 1932 drew to an end, with the remnants of the Bonus Army straggling to their homes throughout the country and the election leaning close, it seemed clear to LaGuardia that a Democratic upsurge was on its way. Mindful of his close victories in past congressional races, he began to maneuver toward a daring objective, the winning of both Democratic and Republican nominations. His hopes were lifted by the backing of Robert F. Wagner, William Green, and John L. Lewis. He visited Greenpoint Democratic boss John McCooey, who told him: "Mr. LaGuardia, I'd like to see you made Ambassador to Australia; but failing that, I'll try to send you back to Washington. Anywhere, just so long as you're kept out of New York City." [21] McCooey's sentiments were in line with the long-time Democratic-Republican "gentleman's agreement" giving Republicans the national offices and Tammany the city spoils. However, the final decision on whether LaGuardia would get Democratic support had to come from Tammany Hall, and Jimmy Hines refused his request.[22] The Democrats nominated James Lanzetta,[23]

---

[19] New York *World Telegram*, May, 1932.   [20] *Ibid.*

[21] Cuneo, *op. cit.*, 147–149.

[22] Ironically, as Cuneo notes, this move led LaGuardia to the mayoralty and Hines to the penitentiary.

[23] New York *Times*, Aug. 24, 1932.

an engineer and lawyer who had been elected to the Board of Aldermen the year before, and LaGuardia prepared for the toughest campaign of his career.

As usual, he had little money, but he counted heavily on the fierce enthusiasm of his supporters, climbing the long flights of stairs in the tenements and talking to the depression-ridden families of East Harlem. When LaGuardia made his annual report at the Star Casino on September 21, 1932, the hall was packed tight with over five thousand people, while a thousand more stood in the street outside. He mentioned the prohibition issue briefly, and devoted most of his speech to the depression, stressing the need for a shorter work week as part of a fundamental "economic readjustment." [24]

Labor came to LaGuardia's support. William Green wrote, "No member of Congress has served more faithfully, loyally, and devotedly than Congressman LaGuardia." [25] Twenty-one railroad unions announced they were behind LaGuardia, and Edward Keating, editor of *Labor*, who was campaigning for Franklin D. Roosevelt nationally, addressed a trade union rally for LaGuardia in the Twentieth District.[26] Progressives throughout the country urged his re-election. Norris sent a letter saying, "The good you have done for the common, ordinary citizen often under difficult and trying circumstances, certainly marks you as one of the advance leaders in honest government and progressive legislation." [27] Hiram Johnson also gave notice of his backing.[28]

Street-corner campaigning was different in 1932. The microphone and amplifier had replaced the old soapbox, and it was possible for LaGuardia to reach large numbers of people at each street meeting. Two thousand people crowded the corner of Lexington Avenue and 106th Street to hear him talk on unemployment insurance. "Call it a dole if you want," he shouted. "You're not going to scare me by that any more. . . . Political freedom and universal suffrage are of no value without economic security." A thirty-hour week was necessary, said LaGuardia, under the new economic conditions. The economic system has

[24] *Ibid.*, Sept. 22, 1932. [25] *Ibid.*, Oct. 4, 1932.
[26] New York *Evening Journal*, Oct. 4, 1932.
[27] New York *World Telegram*, Oct. 27, 1932.
[28] *Home News*, Oct. 28, 1932.

"got to get in line," he declared. "The people will refuse to be poor." [29]

In charge of LaGuardia's campaign was Vito Marcantonio, who had taken an increasingly active part in each campaign since 1924 and had become a close friend of the man who was his idol. In 1926 he had lived for a while with LaGuardia in the University Heights apartment,[30] and all the time LaGuardia was in Washington, Marcantonio had kept the local political organization in top fighting shape. Ernest Cuneo, who worked with "Marc" in the 1932 campaign, describes him as "one of the smartest cookies I ever encountered, one who could trade political punches blow for blow with any comer. He was a really tough guy." [31]

Cuneo said later of his association with LaGuardia in the 1932 campaign: "I was with him a great deal during the whole of it, and a more shrewd, knowing, intuitive, and consciously artful politician I never hope to see. There was always method to his madness, from grand strategy to a minor skirmish." [32] LaGuardia's constituents, Cuneo found, were amazingly well informed on the political issues of the day and proved this by the questions they asked at street meetings. LaGuardia knew his slum dwellers, never underestimated their intelligence, and rested his campaign strategy on the basic premise that, if presented with the facts, the voters would make an intelligent choice. Cuneo reported:

Fiorello was a dynamo throughout the campaign—absolutely tireless. People waited to see him in long lines, and he saw every one of them. He kept tabs on the smallest detail, but could switch from a trivial registry question to a fiery speech concerning basic issues on no notice at all. He was everywhere at once, encouraging, strengthening, and inspiring us all.[33]

Noted Democrats coolly snubbed Tammany and asked for LaGuardia's re-election. Letters of endorsement came from Senator Edward P. Costigan of Colorado and from Frederic C. Howe, secretary of the National Progressive League for Franklin D. Roosevelt. Helping out in the LaGuardia campaign was Edward

---

[29] New York *World Telegram*, Oct. 22, 1932.
[30] Interview with Miriam Marcantonio, August, 1956.
[31] Cuneo, *op. cit.*, 155–156.   [32] *Ibid.*, 151–152.   [33] *Ibid.*, 171.

McBrady, attached to the Roosevelt campaign headquarters as a labor representative.[34]

The imminence of election day brought emotions to a boil, and violence broke out in the last week of the campaign. While LaGuardia was speaking to a large crowd in the Puerto Rican section of his district, at 113th Street and Madison Avenue, a barrage of bricks, bottles, and other missiles came flying down from a nearby roof, and two of the listeners had to be sent to the hospital.[35] LaGuardia's personal vigilantes—the faithful Ghibonnes—dashed to the roof top to find the culprits, and the meeting ended in a flurry of fist fights. At another street-corner rally, a baby carriage was hurled from a roof top and landed on the cab of the sound truck.[36]

LaGuardia's final speech of the night before the election is described by Cuneo as "unforgettable." He says:

The finale of every LaGuardia campaign was a great ceremony. It always took place at his Lucky Corner, 116th Street and Lexington. Thousands of people were on hand, a moving demonstration of faith by people who regarded Fiorello not only as their own champion, but as the champion of humanity as a whole. There was almost a religious fervor about it. Fiorello spoke, and his soul was in every word. Never had his integrity, all his gifts, found better expression. He was a charging lion. As he concluded, a searchlight played down on him from somewhere above. And at the end the tumult of the crowd was such as must have toppled the Walls of Jericho.[37]

Election day belonged completely to the Democratic party and its dynamic presidential candidate. Franklin D. Roosevelt reversed the huge Republican majorities of the twenties, with 22,-000,000 votes to Hoover's 15,000,000, carrying 42 states.[38] In the Twentieth District, Roosevelt won by a smashing 20,000 vote majority. It was miraculous that LaGuardia lost the election by only 1,200 votes.[39]

---

[34] New York *Evening Journal*, Oct. 22, 1932.

[35] New York *Sun*, Oct. 27; New York *Herald Tribune*, Oct. 27, 1932.

[36] Cuneo, *op. cit.*, 166.   [37] *Ibid.*, 173.

[38] Roy V. Peel and Thomas C. Donnelly, *The 1932 Campaign: An Analysis* (New York, 1935), 215.

[39] Lanzetta received 16,326 votes, LaGuardia 15,051, and Socialist Candidate Porce 464, New York *Times*, Nov. 10, 1932.

"Exit One Gadfly" was the headline over the editorial in the New York *Times* after the election.[40] LaGuardia had been, the *Times* said, "in many ways, the most effective leader in the House. His influence was sought; the House hung upon his words." His defeat, the editorial pointed out, "will be a source of relief to many of them who often found themselves unable or fearful to answer him when he was in the full flight of oratory." No longer would his opponents have to face "his colossal energy and industry." [41] From all over the country came letters and wires from friends and supporters, expressing their sadness.[42]

From the larger, national view, however, LaGuardia's defeat was an unpleasant but minor blemish on an otherwise cheering situation. A progressive-minded Democrat had been elected; Franklin D. Roosevelt had called for a "new deal" and seemed to mean it. Also, there were still three months of the lame-duck Congress before the victorious candidates took office, and LaGuardia, suppressing the disappointment inside his stocky frame, prepared for his last congressional fling at the ramparts of traditionalism.

The opening of the lame-duck session in December, 1932, coincided with a much publicized "hunger march" on Washington by three thousand jobless persons. Admittedly, the Communist party had played a large part in organizing and leading the demonstrators, although there was little doubt that the marchers had genuine grievances. The group, including many Negroes, paraded for six miles through the capital, under what the New York *Times* called "the most rigid police supervision on record in Washington." [43] The term "supervision" was somewhat euphemistic since the police maneuvered the marchers into a dead-end street where they were forced to halt, boxed in by an embankment railroad on one side and cordons of police armed with tear gas and night sticks on the other. Representatives of the demonstrators presented petitions to Vice President Curtis and Speaker Garner, asking unemployment insurance legislation and a direct bounty of fifty dollars for every jobless family, to help it get food and fuel for the winter.

40 *Ibid.*, Nov. 15, 1932.   41 *Ibid.*
42 Various letters, Nov., 1932, LaG. Papers.   43 Dec. 7, 1932.

LaGuardia denounced the handling of the "hunger march" by Washington police [44] and told the House of Representatives that "exaggerated" police precautions had been taken because some official got "panicky." It was true, he said, that the demonstration and march were under Communist auspices (he disagreed, he emphasized, with Communist philosophy and methods) but the constitutional right of petition should apply to all groups, regardless of their political beliefs. Twelve to thirteen million Americans were jobless, he observed, meaning that, with families, thirty-six to forty million people were affected, outside of the indigent farm population. "The unemployment situation," LaGuardia declared, "is not going to be solved by a policeman's night stick." [45]

If it took more than a policeman's night stick to solve the unemployment situation, LaGuardia was prepared to say what was necessary. In a radio address from Washington at a New York luncheon of the League for Industrial Democracy, he hit out at the "privileged classes and the small minority who have caused the financial debacle" and pointed to "the collapse of their economic system" as proof of their failure. Now these same groups were invoking constitutional arguments to prevent legislation which would repair the economic system, but neither states' rights arguments nor other constitutional obstructions should be allowed to halt economic progress, he insisted.[46]

LaGuardia coupled his vocal demands for nationwide measures with action on a local level to alleviate distress. He brought together New York's Emergency Employment Relief Committee and unemployed garment workers. The committee bought surplus cotton for the needleworkers to make into clothes. In this way, several thousand New Yorkers were given employment for eight to ten weeks.[47]

"The farmers and the industrial workers have been kept apart by the stock ticker long enough," LaGuardia had told the League for Industrial Democracy,[48] and the following month he showed

[44] Washington *News*, Dec. 7, 1932.
[45] *Congress. Rec.*, 72:2, Dec. 7, 1932, 134–135.
[46] New York *Times*, Dec. 11, 1932.
[47] *Congress. Rec.*, 72:2, Dec. 19, 1932, 712.
[48] New York *Times*, Dec. 11, 1932.

in practice on the House floor that he was not simply a spokesman for narrow urban interests. The farm bloc was waging the
climactic campaign of its decade-long battle to convince Republican administrations that farm relief legislation was needed. At
issue in January of 1933 was the "farm domestic allotment plan"
to subsidize producers of cotton, wheat, tobacco, and hogs, who
agreed to limit their cultivated acreage by 20 per cent.[49] The
subsidy would be paid for by a processing tax. It was a preview
of the later Agricultural Adjustment Act. Representatives from
urban areas, in general, lined up against the bill, with Pennsylvania's Congressman Beck saying that the plan was similar to
Stalin's.[50]

LaGuardia took the floor for a long, vigorous defense of the
plan. Pointing to Hoover's campaign speeches, he said that a
fundamental conflict of philosophies was involved and proceeded
to deliver a blistering attack on the doctrine of "rugged individualism."

How can we talk about the equal opportunity of the individual when
our economic, industrial, and agricultural system has destroyed individuality? . . . If the American system of equal opportunity, equity,
square deal, and the right of living decently is to be conserved, then
we naturally must make some very drastic changes in an economic
system which has outlived its usefulness. . . . We cannot abandon the
individual when economic and industrial conditions have stripped
all semblance of individuality from the citizen. The only semblance of
individuality that is left is the affliction, the misery, and the poverty
that surround the individual when he loses his place in the ranks of
his industrial regiment and the farmer when his unit is destroyed by
the tickertape and the adding machine.[51]

In a spirited defense of the farmer, LaGuardia went farther
than he had ever gone in laying aside a narrow sectional view.
Even if the farm subsidies brought high prices to the city, he was
prepared to support the bill, for high prices, he said, were a necessary part of prosperity. What would the workers do if prices rose?
"We will demand increased wages," LaGuardia declared. Banks,

[49] The plan is discussed in detail in John D. Black, *Agricultural Reform
in the United States* (New York, 1929), 271–301.
[50] Washington *Post*, Jan. 11, 1933.
[51] *Congress. Rec.*, 72:2, Jan. 10, 1933, 1489–1493.

industries, and railroads had come to the government for aid. "Why not the farmer?" [52]

To the argument of Congressman Robert Luce of Massachusetts that the bill favored "a minority," LaGuardia retorted by placing the blame on another minority, the nation's corporate interests: "That is the minority, Mr. Luce, that is threatening the country; that is the group that has long obtained class legislation. The minority that owns the wealth of the country has ruined our country, and not the minority that produces the food." He added a confident prediction: "We have arrived at a time, I want to say to the gentleman from Massachusetts, when those who owned and controlled the finances and wealth of the land are to be stripped of their arrogance. They are to be controlled instead of controlling." [53]

LaGuardia did not disguise his own feeling that the domestic allotment plan was a limited one and that, unaccompanied by more drastic measures, it would not really be effective. Personally, he told his colleagues, he would have preferred to avoid circumvention and to have "straight price-fixing for all surplus agricultural commodities. . . . The habit of thinking along constitutional lines makes many timid." In lieu of that, however, the present plan merited approval, he said.[54] The farm bill passed the House by a vote of 204–151,[55] but failed in the Senate.[56]

In one of his exchanges with Luce on the farm bill, LaGuardia made unmistakably clear what had been implicit in his speeches for some time—the need for national economic planning. When Luce objected that he had not used the term "planning," LaGuardia replied stubbornly, "Future production planning under proper governmental supervision is one of the necessary factors in an economic readjustment that some of us are shaping." [57]

The lame-duck session saw the beginning of the end of the long battle against prohibition. In December, 1932, both houses of Congress approved the Twenty-first Amendment by the neces-

[52] *Ibid.*   [53] *Ibid.*   [54] *Ibid.*   [55] *Congress. Rec.*, 72:2, 1694.

[56] Russell Lord, *The Wallaces of Iowa* (Boston, 1947), 311, views the lame-duck session from the farmer's viewpoint and calls it "a sad show." He gives credit to Marvin Jones and to LaGuardia for fighting "coolly and ably through infinite intricacies to assert and clarify a defensible principle for sustaining the general welfare by farm relief."

[57] *Congress. Rec.*, 72:2, Jan. 10, 1933, 1489–1493.

sary two-thirds vote, and LaGuardia hailed the result. "Congress will now," he said, "be able to give its undivided attention to economic matters, less controversial but far more important." [58]

The depression had brought the urban dweller face to face with the farmer's perennial problem—paying off debts in a period of plummeting prices. LaGuardia moved to relieve the plight of both groups by a joint resolution reducing all interests rates in the nation to 3 per cent or lower. He had deliberately worded his resolution in simple language, he told the House, "so that the bankers of the country can understand it." [59] His colleagues laughed, but his resolution was kept bottled up in the Ways and Means Committee until the session ended.

In the days of the lame-duck session, no representative from the prairie country battled more stubbornly than did Fiorello LaGuardia to ease the burden of farmers whose homes and lands were falling by the thousands under the auction hammer. He had been receiving letters from all parts of the country telling pitiful stories of foreclosures after years of painful scrimping to maintain payments. He took the House floor early in February to link the problem of the farmer with a broader question, the concentration of landed wealth in the nation. The depression, LaGuardia said, "has created a new class of profiteers, a small group of people who are able to exploit the misery of the American people and who are slowly but gradually increasing their holdings of the property of this country. Every foreclosure means that property is being concentrated into fewer hands in this country." [60]

The newspapers had been full of stories of farmers resisting the attempts of sheriffs to seize their property. LaGuardia compared the Iowa farmers who had recently resisted foreclosure to the participants in the Boston Tea Party, who had also commited illegal acts for just cause. He noted bitterly that the Home Loan Bank Act enacted by Congress in the last session had done nothing for the individual homeowner. "To date it has relieved only the money lenders—the high interest sharks." [61]

He had long been investigating the Prudence Corporation of New York, which held many mortgages, and now noted that it

[58] *Ibid.*, Feb. 20, 1933, 4514.   [59] *Ibid.*, Dec. 7, 1932, 995.
[60] *Ibid.*, Feb. 3, 1933, 3321–3323.   [61] *Ibid.*

had received $18,000,000 in R.F.C. loans "and there is not a more despicable, lower gang of loan sharks and usurers in the whole country." With nine and a half billion dollars held in mortgages throughout the nation, there should be a gigantic refinancing at interest rates of 2 to 3 per cent, LaGuardia said. When someone expressed doubt that businessmen would invest in 2 per cent mortgages, his reply was, "The capitalist, if he does not invest his money, cannot eat it." [62]

In translating these sentiments into practical legislative proposals, LaGuardia now found reinforcements at hand. Adolf A. Berle, Jr., was in Washington, representing the advance guard of the Roosevelt administration and anxious for the passage of legislation which would put the New Deal into action even before Roosevelt took the oath of office. [63] Berle, a young, Columbia professor, selected as an early member of F. D. R.'s "Brain Trust," had just written (with Gardiner Means) *The Modern Corporation and Private Property,* which LaGuardia had read with enthusiasm.

Upon his arrival in Washington, Berle sought out the House Speaker and Vice President-elect John Nance Garner for advice on how to get Roosevelt's program into the legislative hopper. Garner thereupon told him that "there is only one man who can make the House do anything." This was LaGuardia. Berle approached LaGuardia, and the two men worked closely together for the rest of the session. Berle was at first dismayed by the "pure chaos" of that lame-duck session, but found LaGuardia "a pint of liquid dynamite." [64]

LaGuardia and Berle, with the aid of research done by the Legislative Drafting Bureau of Columbia University and the advice of Cordell Hull, drew up a bill designed to stop the flood of foreclosures. [65] It proposed a Farm and Home Credit Bank,

[62] *Ibid.*

[63] Marie Fischer LaGuardia tells of LaGuardia and Berle working together in the lame-duck session, and notes that LaGuardia and F. D. R. had come to know one another in the twenties, when Roosevelt was convalescing from his polio attack. "Roosevelt would come down to Washington and stay at the Continental Hotel. Fiorello was living there at the time" (Oral History Project, Columbia University).

[64] Comments made by Adolf A. Berle, Jr., on N.B.C. radio program, 1957

[65] Press release, Feb. 18, 1933, on H.R. no. 14,710, LaG. Papers.

with $200,000,000 of government capital, to refund farm and
home mortgages at interest rates of 3 per cent.[66] The proposal
was sent to the House Finance Committee, where it remained
bottled up for the rest of the session.

More successful was another measure on which LaGuardia and
Berle collaborated in the lame-duck session. This was an amendment to the Federal Bankruptcy Act relieving debtors by allowing a federal judge to grant credit extensions on the basis of
petitions filed by debtors. An accompanying amendment took
the reorganization of defunct railroads from the hands of private
bankers and gave it to trustees appointed by the Interstate Commerce Commission. On the first of March the bank panic was
in full swing, and banks all over the nation were closing. La-
Guardia told the House that day:

Within the next few days several railroads—it is now no secret—will
be in the hands of receivers. This is your choice. Are you going to
leave the management of the reorganization and receivership of these
railroads in the hands of the gang that has ruined the railroads, or are
you going to take it out of the hands of that gang . . . and put such
control and supervision in the hands of a government agency, the
Interstate Commerce Commission? [67]

On the last day of the Hoover administration, this proposed
amendment to the bankruptcy statutes became law.[68]

While working with Berle and other New Deal emissaries,
LaGuardia proposed to Congress on February 25, 1933, that,
because of the severity of the economic crisis and the dangerous
situation that existed, Roosevelt and his cabinet should be invited to Washington to begin working immediately with the out-
going administration. There was no time to lose, he said. With
financial panic on its way and millions of Americans going hungry,

[66] New York *Times,* Feb. 19, 1933.

[67] *Congress. Rec.,* 72:2, March 1, 1933, 5357–5358, H.R. no. 14,359.

[68] The co-operation between LaGuardia and Norris in trouble shooting
is illustrated in connection with this bill. *Labor* editor Edward Keating discovered some phraseology in the bankruptcy amendment, while it was being
debated in the Senate, which would impair labor contracts. He hurried to
LaGuardia in the House, who scrawled an amendment which was vague
enough not to excite suspicion, whereupon Keating brought it to Norris,
who wrote it out explicitly, introduced it, and saw it through to passage
(Alfred Lief, *op. cit.,* 410).

Congress should be ready for morning, afternoon, and night sessions.[69] His colleagues listened attentively to the suggestion, but it was not taken up.

To the very end of the session LaGuardia remained one of the watchdogs of the American Civil Liberties Union, closely scrutinizing every bill believed to threaten the Bill of Rights. A.C.L.U. Director Roger Baldwin kept in constant touch with him on various bills punishing the advocacy of revolutionary doctrines, deporting alien Communists, and setting up investigations of Communist activities. He was able to assure Baldwin that the session would end without repressive legislation going through.[70] LaGuardia's interest in the campaign to free Tom Mooney never lessened, and in the last days of the session he telegraphed Fremont Older and Lincoln Steffens in San Francisco that he would not be able to come to the West Coast on Mooney's behalf, as had been requested, because he was working on important legislation. He added: "Will be glad to help cause in any way I can from here." [71]

Despite the urgency of domestic problems, LaGuardia did not ignore foreign affairs, and stood fast against the swelling power of isolationist sentiment in the early days of the depression. He fought in vain in February of 1933 to get the House to appropriate $150,000 for delegates to attend the international monetary and economic conferences in London. Texas Congressman Blanton suggested that the United States "stay at home for a while and attend strictly to our own business." LaGuardia's reply, in support of the conference, also revealed how definite had become his change of heart about the First World War. "The time to have kept out of Europe," he told Blanton, "was in 1917." [72]

The lame-duck session ended on the fourth of March, 1933.[73]

---

[69] *Congress. Rec.*, 72:2, Feb. 25, 1933, 5050.

[70] LaGuardia to Baldwin, Feb. 27, 1933, LaG. Papers.

[71] Wire of March 3, 1933, Tom Mooney Papers, University of California, Berkeley, Calif.

[72] *Congress. Rec.*, 72:2, Feb. 20, 1933, 4533.

[73] This was the last lame-duck session. In January the required number of states had ratified George Norris' Twentieth Amendment to the Constitution. LaGuardia had played an important part in getting the amendment through the House after a number of near misses (Lief, *op. cit.*, 310–311; Norris, *op. cit.*, 342).

While Franklin D. Roosevelt was being sworn in, Fiorello and Marie LaGuardia were preparing for their departure from the nation's capitol. The pain of defeat was eased somewhat by letters and telegrams that had been piling up in the office since November, signed by senators and miners, judges and garment workers, expressing deep regrets that LaGuardia was leaving his congressional post and wishing him good luck wherever he was going. Heading for New York, he had, alongside aching thoughts about what-might-have-been, the satisfaction of knowing that a new administration, and perhaps even the promised "new deal," were in the offing for the nation.

19 ⋆ *Fiorello LaGuardia in*

Congress: An Appraisal

THE concept of an "age of reform," encompassing approximately the past sixty years, gives to American progressivism a continuity which is obscured when one studies only its two peaks—the Progressive movement and the New Deal. That this is a real continuity and not one artificially imposed by historians is proved by the activities of Fiorello LaGuardia, whose congressional leadership in the period 1917–1933 makes him a vital link between the Progressive and New Deal eras. LaGuardia entered Congress as the Bull Moose uproar was quieting and left with the arrival of the New Deal; in the intervening years no man in national office waged the Progressive battle so long, so consistently, or so vigorously. In a decade marked by lustreless leadership, he generated an inexhaustible supply of excitement.

Chronologically LaGuardia's position as a transitional figure between Progressive and New Deal movements is clear. In terms of political ideology, the relationship is more complex. He was the herald of a new kind of progressivism, borne into American politics by the urban-immigrant sections of the population. In many ways he was a scout and reconnaisance man for the New Deal. And yet, even the New Deal did not venture as far as LaGuardia in thought and action. This ambivalent position of his, both foreshadowing the New Deal and going beyond it, deserves some elaboration.

LaGuardia represented a gradual departure from the atmosphere of a respectable middle-class reformism that characterized the Progressive movement [1] and toward the less genteel working-class elements that helped form the New Deal coalition. Although both the Progressive movement and the New Deal [2] were essentially middle class in leadership, the New Deal had stronger ties with the labor movement. There was no Progressive-era relationship, for instance, to match the New Deal–C.I.O. liaison, and the New Deal not only was in more intimate touch with labor leaders but received greater support from working people.[3] In the earlier period the I.W.W. and the Socialist party had drained off a good deal of working-class backing.

As the son of a financially harassed musician (who had to join

[1] Virtually all recent historical studies of the Progressive movement agree on the middle-class nature of Progressive leadership. Hofstadter, *Age of Reform*, 5, defines Progressivism as the enlargement and redirection, after 1900, of agrarian discontent "by the growing enthusiasm of middle-class people for social and economic reform." This is affirmed by: George Mowry, "The California Progressive and His Rationale: A Study in Middle Class Politics," *Mississippi Valley Hist. Rev.*, XXXVI (Sept., 1949), 239–250; William E. Leuchtenburg, *Mississippi Valley Hist. Rev.*, XXXIX (Dec., 1952), 483–504; Richard Ravitch, "Progressive Reactions of 1912," *King's Crown Essays*, Winter, 1955; and Harry J. Carman and Harold C. Syrett, *A History of the American People* (New York, 1952), 338–339. It is not the validity, but the significance of the characterization that may seem open to question. See note 4.

[2] The New Deal has been similarly characterized, as by Samuel Lubell, *op. cit.*, 80, who says that "the Roosevelt Revolution appears to have strengthened rather than weakened the traditional middle-class basis of American politics." This was seen very early, and welcomed, by Arthur N. Holcombe, *The New Party Politics* (New York, 1933), 133. This would seem to be challenged by C. Wright Mills, *White Collar: The American Middle Classes* (New York, 1953), 351, who denies the possibility today (and there is no clear indication how far back in recent history he would extend "today") for any middle-class political movement, on the grounds that the very diversification of this group provides "no homogeneity of base among them for common political movement." But it is this very heterogeneity which characterizes American political parties. A good part of the apparent disagreement may stem from the lack of clear definition in the terms "party," "movement," and "middle class."

[3] The Progressive movement coincided with some of the most militant labor struggles in American history (and, indeed, may owe much to them), but these constituted pressure on the movement from the outside, whereas the C.I.O. was at least partly inside the New Deal cluster of forces.

the army in order to assure his family a regular livelihood and who nurtured them on the rather meager pay of an enlisted man), Fiorello LaGuardia can probably be characterized as "lower-middle class" in his background.[4] He was in the Foreign Service, but only as a minor official. He was a lawyer, but never a successful one in terms of money, and he certainly never shared that conservative brand of progressivism espoused (as Hofstadter puts it) by "corporation lawyers on a moral holiday."[5] Even more significant is the fact that LaGuardia established ties with the trade union movement as early as 1912, and this connection became closer during the twenties and early thirties. Throughout the lengthy twentieth-century courtship of labor and progressive politics, which reached its most intimate stage under Franklin Roosevelt, LaGuardia played the part of a persevering Cupid.

[4] This writer is skeptical about the analytical significance of such an imprecise definition as "middle class." The series of sociological studies in class stratification conducted by W. Lloyd Warner and associates in their "Yankee City Series" finds that the most numerous group in the population, 60–70 per cent, occupies the "lower-middle" and "upper-lower" classes. Further, sociologists say: "The American system of stratification is vague and loose with much blurring and overlapping of strata. . . . Traditionally, the line between the middle and lower classes is between white collar occupations and labor. Even this distinction is blurred in America" (Leonard Broom and Philip Selznick, *Sociology* [New York, 1955], 177–178). Characterizations of people in political life as "middle class" may, therefore, take in such a broad area as to be without much significance, for once the very rich and very poor are eliminated the rest may be called middle class (79.2 to 88 per cent of the American people consider themselves "middle class," according to a 1940 Fortune survey and an Institute of Public Opinion poll). In view of this, the characterization of political movements in terms of their leadership may be meaningless, since all political movements, from the Liberty League to the Socialist party, are "middle class"–led for the most part. (David Shannon, "The Socialist Party before the First World War," *Mississippi Valley Hist. Rev.*, XXXVIII [Sept., 1951], 279–288, notes the extent of middle-class leadership in the Socialist party.) It would seem more useful to characterize movements in terms of program than the background of their leaders, since the basic aim in pointing out the "middle-class" nature of the Progressive and New Deal movements seems to be recognition of their moderate, limited, compromise objectives.

[5] *Age of Reform*, 163. C. Wright Mills distinguishes those lawyers serving in "corporate law factories" from those in "political offices, mainly in the northeast and in big cities, where politics often centers on immigrant levels" (Mills, *op. cit.*, 127).

The Progressive movement developed an urban quality [6] which
distinguished it from its Populist antecedents, but one which was
still largely native-born and Midwestern,[7] while the urbanism
of the New Deal was based to a great extent on the new immigrant-descended populations of the large Eastern cities (although
"Eastern" should probably include Pittsburgh and Chicago).[8]
LaGuardia emerged in the twenties as the advance agent of these
new urban-immigrant groups. Others joined him later: Democrats Samuel Dickstein and Emanuel Celler of New York, and
Adolph Sabath of Chicago. But he was the first important national
spokesman of the urban-immigrants and their constant champion,
at a time when fellow progressives from the West supported restrictionist legislation.[9] Al Smith is often mentioned as the pro-
genitor of the New Deal in this regard,[10] but (without minimizing
his contribution) it should be noted that, unlike LaGuardia (who
was the first Italian-American in Congress), he did not represent
the new immigration from southern and eastern Europe. Moreover, the Happy Warrior was a local figure, appearing on the
national scene only as a presidential candidate, while LaGuardia
brought the new groups directly into the main stream of national
politics.

LaGuardia's urbanism managed to escape some of the narrow
sectional bias of other representatives from city districts. In his

[6] This is attested to by Carman and Syrett, *op. cit.*, 346; Hofstadter, *Age of
Reform*, 131; and others. Holcombe calls it a new, "urbane" politics. Hofstadter says: "Populism had been overwhelmingly rural and provincial. The
ferment of the Progressive era was urban, middle-class and nationwide."
Carman and Syrett say: "Progressivism was to a considerable extent an
urban counterpart of Populism." George Mowry, *Theodore Roosevelt and the
Progressive Movement* (Madison, 1947), says the new nationalism appealed
mostly to the cities.

[7] Hofstadter, *Age of Reform*, 11, sees both Populist and Progressive movements as aiming to "maintain a homogenous Yankee civilization."

[8] Lubell, *op. cit.*, 28–29, says the "submerged, inarticulate urban masses
. . . became the chief carriers of the Roosevelt Revolution."

[9] Goldman, *op. cit.*, 235, says: "By the Twenties, urban influences had
marked reform so deeply that the progressive who spoke Anglo-Saxonism
was rare." But LaGuardia stood almost alone among Progressives in Congress as a foe of restrictive quotas.

[10] Holcombe, *op. cit.*, 111; Hofstadter, *Age of Reform*, 296.

view, farmers and city workers were both victims of the monopolies, and he consistently supported farm relief legislation even when, as in the McNary-Haugen and domestic allotment plans, they seemed to point to higher prices for city consumers. LaGuardia was as much a product of the Arizona desert as of the sidewalks of Manhattan and could never wholly identify himself with the carping provincialism of some of his colleagues.

It was in keeping with this breadth of view that LaGuardia found his own solution to the problem which perplexes every congressman under our political system: how to fulfill his duty as national legislator while maintaining the good will of the local voters and politicos on whom he depends for re-election. La-Guardia's overwhelming concern was with the national issues,[11] and after spending his time and energy on them in Washington he went home to explain to his constituents how these problems affected them. Thus he fought for public power at Boulder Dam and Muscle Shoals as well as in upstate New York. He supported striking miners in Pennsylvania as well as garment workers in Manhattan. The pages of the *Congressional Record* show that he introduced extremely few private bills as compared to his colleagues and took the floor more often than any other legislator of his time on issues of national importance. He believed that, ultimately, the living conditions of his constituents depended on the social and economic state of the union, and he acted accordingly.

This is not to say that the people and problems of the Twentieth District did not have a tremendous influence on LaGuardia's actions. In fact, they supplied the motive force for his fierce attacks on immigration restriction and on what he considered the rapaciousness of the wealthy. He saw this district as a microcosm of the national state of affairs and translated local needs into national legislation.

In his intense preoccupation with economic issues LaGuardia was, again, a nascent New Dealer. The Progressive movement, in a time of relative prosperity, had devoted a good part of its

[11] Marie Fischer LaGuardia says: "His mail was terrific. I think the people outside New York City knew him as well, if not better, almost, than some of them here" (Oral History Project, 1950).

program to political reform,[12] but the New Deal, in a time of severe crisis, was willing to overlook and even use corrupt local political machines to gain desired economic ends.[13] Although it was LaGuardia's early revulsion against Tammany Hall that turned him to the Republican party, he soon became involved in Republican party politics. Of course, he fought the machine, deserted it from time to time, formed his own organization in the Twentieth District, and was always in difficulty with regular Republicans. Yet he could not afford to ignore the machine's usefulness at election time and thus was never completely a free agent. He had to support Harding in 1920; he had to be silent in the 1928 campaign although he favored Al Smith; he spoke for many local Republican candidates purely as political favors (while insisting that his speeches follow his own platform and not the party's); and made many temporary liaisons when they were useful. He sometimes played politics at its lowest levels [14] in order to achieve desired objectives on the highest levels. He was often in the position of officiating at a shotgun wedding of power and morality.

The Progressive movement had never really welcomed the Negro. Theodore Roosevelt courted Southern whites in building the Progressive party,[15] and Woodrow Wilson favored segregation in government departments.[16] It was a movement largely of native-born whites with more than a trace of chauvinism and snobbery. LaGuardia's attitude to the Negro anticipated the more friendly approach of the New Deal. There were few Negroes in his district in the 1920's, and the anti-Negro attitudes of many of the new immigrant groups have often been noted. Yet, without making it one of his major points, he spoke out for racial equality on a number of occasions, clashing with Southern congressmen and federal judges on different issues.

Another distinctive quality of the New Deal seems to be that

[12] Mowry, "California Progressive," notes the Progressive stress on political reform, and so do many other students of the Progressive movement.

[13] Hofstadter, *Age of Reform,* 308.

[14] Cuneo, *op. cit.,* 141, cites some examples.

[15] Mowry, *Theodore Roosevelt.*

[16] Arthur S. Link, *Woodrow Wilson and the Progressive Era* (New York, 1953).

it dropped the moralistic-religious overtones of the Progressive movement.[17] Wilson's moralism has often been noted,[18] and George Mowry has found in the California Progressives the characteristics of religiosity and piety.[19] Hofstadter comments that in the New Deal period the resort to moralizing was mostly on the conservative side. Of course, moral attitudes are usually implicit even when not stated, and this is true of the New Deal; [20] the difference is probably that its morality was couched in human rather than divine terms. In this regard, too, LaGuardia presaged the New Deal. He was an Episcopalian, but never an ardent churchgoer.[21] Unlike many congressmen, he was not given to pious (and pompous) allusions to the Almighty, though he could not resist, on occasion, quoting from the Bible when it supported some of his political points. His moralism was humanistic and utilitarian rather than narrowly religious.[22]

In examining the idea that the New Deal was less ostentatiously moralistic, but intrinsically more moral than the Progressive movement, foreign affairs seem a fair testing ground. Expansionism has been a persistent national trait since the 1890's (indeed, since the Revolution, if we include continental expansion), and it would not be correct to polarize the positions of Progressive movement and the New Deal in this regard. Both were nationalistic interventionist. Entrance into world war sidetracked the progressive programs of both Wilson and Franklin Roosevelt. The rebuff to the London Economic Conference stands as a symbol of economic nationalism under the early New Deal, and while the New Deal did not intervene in Latin America in the manner of Wilson and Teddy Roosevelt, it intervened more quickly and more seriously in both Europe and Asia. The difference is not,

[17] Hofstadter talks of progressivism's aim to "bring back a kind of morality and civic purity" (*Age of Reform,* 5, also 323).

[18] H. C. F. Bell, *Woodrow Wilson and the People* (New York, 1945), stresses this aspect of Wilson's outlook.

[19] "There was but one law for him—that of the church-going middle class" (Mowry, "California Progressive").

[20] James MacGregor Burns, *The Lion and the Fox* (New York, 1956), 476, finds the moral concept of "man's responsibility for the well-being of his fellow man" at the core of F. D. R.'s subsurface beliefs.

[21] Cuneo, *op. cit.,* x, says he saw Heaven as "achievable on earth."

[22] His stand on prohibition would seem to reflect this.

it would seem, in the decision to take part in world affairs; both (though Wilson hesitated until 1917 and Roosevelt until 1937) ended up as active participants. Yet two points of distinction should be noted. One is the greater degree of bellicosity and of unashamed jingoism on the part of an important group of Progressives, like Theodore Roosevelt and Beveridge, who find no real counterpart among New Dealers.[23] Another is the fact that (allowing for real analytical difficulty), when the New Deal did intervene in Europe, it did so on more clear-cut moral ground than existed in World War I, so much so that New Dealers went along with Roosevelt almost 100 per cent in joining the fight against the Axis, whereas Progressives had split almost fifty-fifty on World War I.[24] LaGuardia heralded a definite movement away from the flagrant aggressiveness of Teddy Roosevelt.

As a youth, he was caught up in the Rough Rider spirit that accompanied the Spanish-American War. In 1917 he was more hesitant but, once war was declared, plunged loudly into the fray.[25] The postwar period brought disillusionment, both as a result of Italy's humiliation at the peace table and because of the unsolved economic problems in America after the war. By the early 1930's, LaGuardia was saying bitterly that our entrance into the conflict was a mistake. However, his readiness to go to war when he saw crucial principles at stake is shown by his quick reaction to the Japanese invasion of China in 1931.

After his brief aberration on Mexican affairs in 1919, LaGuardia strongly opposed American imperialism in Latin America, thus foreshadowing the "good neighbor" policy of the New Deal (as well as the gentler attitude of the late Coolidge and Hoover years). His opposition to both marine and dollar diplomacy in Nicaragua revealed how far behind he had left his old hero, Teddy Roosevelt.

[23] Leuchtenburg, "Progressivism and Imperialism."

[24] Mowry, *Theodore Roosevelt,* notes that the war split the Progressive party.

[25] His flair for the dramatic may have played a part here, for any congressman donning the uniform was certain to be watched and publicized. Also (and this, too, is hard to prove) there may have been a conscious or subconscious desire to demonstrate the patriotism of the new immigrant-descended groups. Once his stature as a patriot was established, LaGuardia was in a better position to risk an anti-imperialist position abroad, as well as a radical stand at home.

Never an isolationist,[26] he was in favor of exercising American influence abroad so long as it was clearly on behalf of democracy or for national independence or against autocracy. His support of the Russian Revolution of 1917 [27] and of the Irish independence movement are examples of this. Unlike a number of progressive colleagues, he consistently backed attempts at international organization, from the League and the Inter-Parliamentary Union to the various peace and disarmament conferences. In matters of foreign policy, as in other matters, he believed that, if the economic roots of the trouble were excavated, the poisonous growths of war and depression would wilt and die.

Besides presaging the New Deal in his background and ideology, LaGuardia's specific legislative program was an astonishingly accurate preview of the New Deal. The battle for Muscle Shoals and Boulder Dam led to the T.V.A., the domestic-allotment plan to the A.A.A., and so on, in the areas of unemployment insurance, wage-hour legislation, child labor, debtor relief, securities regulation, and other issues. The impressive legislative structure of the famed first hundred days of the New Deal owed much to the foundation dug earlier by LaGuardia, Norris, Wagner, Costigan, Mead, and a handful of others. If the New Deal was born before Roosevelt took his oath of office, a political paternity test would probably attribute parentage, not to Herbert Hoover (as Walter Lippmann suggests in *The New Imperative*) or to Al Smith (as Bernard Bellush says) but to the little group of congressional progressives who jabbed at the conscience of the twenties.

We have thus a fairly substantial case for depicting LaGuardia as a man who neatly marks the transition from Progressivism to the New Deal, and we might confidently close on this theme. However, several things about LaGuardia jar the smoothness of the contours on the graph and create a more complex picture;

[26] Here too the term may not be truly significant, since most so-called "isolationists" usually support intervention under conditions which they favor.

[27] While LaGuardia did not favor the Lenin-Stalin policies that followed the Bolshevik Revolution, he believed that no regime could be worse than that of the Tsar, so that his initial enthusiasm for the February Revolution in Russia was dimmed, not extinguished, by the events that followed October. In April of 1929 he was part of a small congressional group which supported recognition of Soviet Russia (William A. Williams, *American-Russian Relations 1781–1947* [New York, 1952], 223).

they reveal that LaGuardia refused to stay in place and dashed ahead of the New Deal in a number of significant ways.

There is, first, the fact of his political independence, which was by far the dominant streak in the complex mixture of expediency and insurgency which marked his career in politics. The New Deal was a monopoly of the Democratic party in the thirties, gaining thereby both the advantage of nationwide support and the handicap of a conservative ballast which could not be easily jettisoned. This created the necessity of going along with Democratic machines in the large cities and also with the South.[28] LaGuardia had a great deal more political mobility, maneuvering back and forth across party lines, if not with the greatest of ease, at least often enough to exasperate the machines and pressure them into desired actions. Undoubtedly this was aided by the nature of the American political system, with its single-member congressional districts subject more to the slack tactics of local politics than to any responsible national party organization. La-Guardia's experience offers no clear argument either for third-party activity or for pressure-from-within tactics, a problem which has plagued American liberals from Locofocoism to the Americans for Democratic Action. His tactics were flexible and pragmatic.

Second, LaGuardia's plans for economic reform were far bolder than those of the New Deal. Both the Progressive movement and the New Deal, it has been observed, were reform movements of limited objectives.[29] Faced by the elephantine growth of corporatism, both stalked the prey nervously and uncertainly, poking here and there at the thick hide, investigating with apparent bravado, but hesitating at drastic action. Hence the sweeping probes of the Pujo committee and the Temporary National Economic Committee, the first culminating in the ineffectual Clayton Act and Federal Trade Commission, the second forgotten in the excite-

[28] Burns, *op. cit.*, 154. Of course, this was fundamentally due to the nature of our political structure, which gives to every party a built-in gyroscope stabilizer to thwart radical turns.

[29] This is the consensus of opinion in all studies of both movements. Leuchtenburg, in "Progressivism and Imperialism," says that the Progressive movement was middle-class and traditional. Daniel Fusfeld, *The Economic Thought of Franklin D. Roosevelt and the Origins of the New Deal* (New York, 1956), 251, tells of F. D. R.'s adherence to the retention of private enterprise and private profit.

ment of war. Not wanting to go as far as nationalization, the only thing left was to retreat to dreams of a free-enterprise past.[30] Roosevelt himself epitomized this in his summary of the T.N.E.C. recommendations: "It is a program whose basic thesis is not that the system of free enterprise has failed in this generation, but that it has not yet been tried." [31]

For LaGuardia there was no such hesitation. He was willing, even anxious, for the government to regulate the production and distribution of food and other necessities, in peace as well as war.[32] When certain industries, like the railroads or mines or telephone system, appeared to him to be either rapacious or inefficient, he declared in favor of nationalizing them.[33] His stubborn fight on taxes was not just a bread-and-butter expedient but was based on the desire for a fundamental redistribution of the nation's wealth.

When his congressional colleagues accused LaGuardia of being a socialist, they were close to the truth. Without being a member of any organized socialist movement,[34] without subscribing to any specific body of socialist theory,[35] he thought in socialist terms and even used socialist terminology. He kept speaking of a "new economic order" to match the new industrial age, which was really a less sophisticated version of the Marxian insistence that capitalism must depart the scene because it no longer adequately matches the gigantic "productive forces" of today. LaGuardia showed a certain pride in being considered a radical.[36]

[30] Hofstadter, *Age of Reform*, 5, says that the "general theme" of progressivism was "the effort to restore a type of economic individualism and political democracy that was widely believed to have existed earlier in America." Carman and Syrett, *op. cit.*, 338–339, point to the romanticism of the Progressives. Ravitch, *op. cit.*, says the New York Progressive party "looked to the past for guidance."

[31] Mitchell, *op. cit.*, 365.

[32] Fusfeld, *op. cit.*, 254, says F. D. R. in 1932 accepted the principle of planning, but in an experimental, partial way.

[33] The T.V.A. shows the New Deal was willing to create new national enterprises; nationalizing existing ones was a more radical step.

[34] Cuneo, *op. cit.*, 94, says LaGuardia found the Socialist party too dogmatic.

[35] Marie Fischer LaGuardia, in her interview with this writer, said LaGuardia had not read Marx, Engels, or other socialist theoreticians.

[36] It would be useful to compare the radicalism of his congressional period with his policies as a mayor, indicating thereby the different spans of political

However, if he was close to being a socialist, he was not a doctrinaire one. His theoretical framework was confined to a few simple principles, like the welfare of the majority and the inherent right of all human beings to a share of the earth's wealth, rather than any cumbersome and complex body of socialist theory. This, while keeping him out of socialist organizations, gave him the kind of operational freedom he craved. His was (if any descriptive phrase can capture his elusive ideology) a kind of pragmatic radicalism.[37]

Finally, in any assessment of LaGuardia's contribution to American reform, it should be noted that he advocated programs beyond those of the New Deal at a time when economic conditions did not seem to warrant bold measures. While important sections of the American lower classes were suffering throughout the twenties—and LaGuardia never took his eyes from their situation—there was also basis in fact for the general aura of prosperity in the period: the high level of employment, the wide distribution of new products, the luxuries enjoyed by an expanding middle class, and the fact that even the poor were not as poor as they would find themselves after 1929. In this context, LaGuardia's battle on behalf of economic justice for the voiceless

---

freedom of a legislator and a chief executive and revealing perhaps to what extent various pressures induce executives to compromise and conciliate rather than boldly lead.

[37] This pragmatism is perhaps best revealed in a lack of any clearly defined LaGuardia approach to social planning on a national scale. When he encountered immediate localized situations where private enterprise was inadequate, he was ready at a moment's notice to declare for nationalization and government planning for specific industries, like mining, the railroads, or communications. However, he never expressed publicly (nor, so far as is known, privately) any predisposition to over-all national planning. The depression led more conservative, but less pragmatic individuals and groups to espouse the idea of national planning. Herbert Hoover's own Research Committee on Social Trends, headed by economist Wesley C. Mitchell, concluded, after a monumental sociological survey of the nation in the early 1930's, that "to deal with the central problem of balance, or with any of its ramifications, economic planning is called for." The committee made clear that it was not urging that the planning be done completely, or even in great part, by the government, but was emphatic in its demand for a planned reorganization of social, economic, and political life in America, rather than "a policy of drift" (President's Research Committee on Social Trends, *Recent Social Trends in the United States* [New York, 1934], xxxi-lxxi).

part of the population required acute perception and courage. More than that, he was in his own way demanding that the nation analyze its "prosperity" through a subsurface examination. He tried to tell his countrymen that they were living in an era when the dominant jazz motif muffled the faint but unmistakable lament of the blues. LaGuardia was sounding the warnings about the "prosperity" of the twenties with as much futile desperation as a few lone observers of Fascism were warning of the "peace" of the thirties.

Beyond his political philosophy (although inseparable from it), LaGuardia deserves recognition as a human being of epic proportions. He possessed a store of driving power that seemed inexhaustible and which kept him going at top speed throughout his ten years in Congress.[38] Strong enough to withstand the impact of overwhelming personal tragedy—the premature deaths of his father, his first wife, his child—LaGuardia was also sensitive enough to be profoundly affected. He did not let these experiences gnaw destructively at his insides, but utilized them to harden his anger at the social conditions which he held responsible: profiteering, in the case of his father; the city slums, in the case of his young bride and child.

LaGuardia's mind was quick, his memory deep. He was fluent in a half-dozen languages, a master of parliamentary rules, and an indefatigable worker (although the heat of his argument sometimes drove him to oversimplify facts and made him careless with figures). He rarely wrote out a speech, but usually spoke extemporaneously, with sheaves of notes and statistics before him. He spoke simply and forcefully, in language that tenement dwellers could understand, constantly repeating phrases that appealed to him, sacrificing grammar for vitality, coupling invective with humor and anger with irony.[39] Sometimes his speeches had the

[38] "Fiorello lived hard every minute, reveled in every second. The overall atmosphere he created was one of tremendous vitality" (Cuneo, *op. cit.*, 9). "The secret of his galvanic energy is that it can be shut off at will. He rests as intensely as he works" (Spalding, *op. cit.*, 237). "Fiorello LaGuardia is in a class by himself. . . . He is happy only when he is on the floor in the midst of a furious battle. Once in the chamber he never leaves until adjournment. He sends out for peanuts and munches them so as not to miss a chance to object or to offer a pertinent amendment" (Pearson and Allen, *op. cit.*, 246).

[39] His political rival Jimmy Walker commented admiringly on LaGuardia's

flavor of demagoguery, but he always meant what he said, and his actions matched the vigor of his language.[40]

Not a sophisticated analyst of contemporary society, LaGuardia hammered away crudely, repetitively, at a few major themes: in economics, his enemy was corporate wealth; in politics, it was party regularity; in the social sphere, it was racial and national egoism. He was often tactless, obstinate, abusive,[41] and overdramatic and could intersperse bold schemes for national reform with huge expenditures of anger at petty grievances. Through these traits, however, ran a profound honesty which made even his political enemies respect him.[42]

As a participant in Washington's social life he was a failure. When other congressmen were spending Sunday mornings making dignified appearances at church and Sunday afternoons (sometimes less dignified) at cocktail parties, LaGuardia was reading

---

linguistic skill and noted that "even when he speaks English, he speaks two kinds to suit his audience of the moment—the King's English or just English" (Fowler, *op. cit.*, 245–246).

[40] LaGuardia has sometimes been called a demagogue, as by Reinhard H. Luthin, *American Demagogues* (Boston, 1954), 212. *Webster's Collegiate Dictionary* (5th ed.) defines a demagogue as: "A speaker who seeks to make capital of social discontent and gain political influence." The word has come to have pejorative connotations, but it seems doubtful that any important reformer of past or present could escape falling within that definition. The difficulty in characterizing people this way seems to derive from the fact that both personal aggrandizement and lofty social aims are often intertwined so closely that it is difficult to say which the politician in question values more highly. It is impossible, in reviewing LaGuardia's record of both talk and action, to ignore the fact that, while he was certainly a showman and reveled in the spotlight, he had an unquenchable passion for social justice and in pursuance of this took the kind of political risks that no mere opportunist would be willing to face.

[41] He wrote, once, in a letter to the editor of the New York *Evening Graphic*, protesting the emasculating of one of his articles: "To arrange one's editorial expressions to meet the desire of big advertisers is to my mind journalistic pimping of the lowest degree. For a writer to adjust himself to such a condition is nothing less than intellectual prostitution" (LaGuardia to Emil H. Gauvreau, Aug. 7, 1928, LaG. Papers).

[42] Gene Fowler says that LaGuardia had a "truculent hunger for office" (Fowler, *op. cit.*, 245–246). But this is true of every politician. One would have to go further and inquire how many hungry office seekers were willing to risk political starvation by defying party leaders and party programs as often as LaGuardia did.

bills and poring over the legislative calendar, preparing for the Monday session. His distaste for social pretensions was matched by his enjoyment of small, informal gatherings with friends. He loved music, attended operas and concerts as often as he could, and had a rather poignant need for the fellowship of creative people. His adoration of children was boundless, and this was symbolic of his general feeling for the underprivileged. His marvelous sense of comedy made some people view him as a clown, but there was no more serious figure on the national political scene.

If, out of all this, there is one quality which may be singled out as crucial, it is perhaps that LaGuardia combined a profound sense of social responsibility with an irrepressible individualism. He was a rebel, but not a nihilist, a man who smashed wildly through party and organizational walls, but only to follow his principles wherever they led. In a time of conformity and irresponsibility, when so many minds are imprisoned by rigid loyalties and so many others luxuriating in the freedom of indecision, the recollection of LaGuardia's untamed but conscience-stricken spirit seems a precious gift to those in our generation who will receive it.

* *Bibliography* *

MANUSCRIPTS

The Papers of William E. Borah. Library of Congress, Washington, D.C.

The Papers of Nicholas Murray Butler. Columbia University, New York City.

The Papers of Raymond Clapper. Library of Congress, Washington, D.C.

The Papers of Calvin Coolidge. Library of Congress, Washington, D.C.

The Papers of Fiorello LaGuardia. Municipal Archives, New York City.

Note: The LaGuardia Papers are now (1959) roughly indexed in various file folders, some of the folders arranged chonologically and others topically, as they were when the research for this book was done.

The Papers of Ogden L. Mills. Library of Congress, Washington, D.C.

The Papers of Tom Mooney. University of California, Berkeley, Calif.

The Papers of George Norris. Library of Congress, Washington, D.C.

The Papers of Amos Pinchot. Library of Congress, Washington, D.C.

The Papers of Franklin D. Roosevelt. Hyde Park, New York.

The Papers of Oswald Garrison Villard. Harvard University, Cambridge, Mass.

NEWSPAPERS

Bronx *Home News,* Brooklyn *Daily Eagle,* Chicago *Tribune, The Day, Harlem Home News, The Harlemite, Il Giornale Italiano, Labor,*

New York *American,* New York *Call,* New York *Daily Mirror,* New York *Daily News,* New York *Evening Graphic,* New York *Evening Journal,* New York *Evening Telegram,* New York *Evening World,* New York *Globe,* New York *Herald,* New York *Herald Tribune,* New York *Journal of Commerce,* New York *Mail,* New York *Post,* New York *Staats-Zeitung,* New York *Sun,* New York *Times,* New York *Tribune,* New York *World,* New York *World Telegram,* Pittsburgh *Sun-Telegraph,* Washington *Herald,* Washington *News,* Washington *Post,* Washington *Star,* Washington *Times.*

PERIODICALS

American Mercury, The Annals, Atlantic Monthly, Business Week, Collier's, Congressional Digest, Current History, Literary Digest, The Nation, Outlook, Review of Reviews, Saturday Evening Post, Scribner's Magazine, Time Magazine.

ARTICLES

American Mercury, June, 1927.

Business Week, March 30 and April 6, 1932.

Collier's, Nov. 5, 1927, June 1, 1929, and May 7, 1932.

Congressional Digest, Dec., 1929, and May, 1932.

Fitzgerald, F. Scott. "Echoes of the Jazz Age," *Scribner's Magazine,* XC (Nov., 1931).

Hutchinson, Edward P. "Immigration Policy Since World War I," *The Annals,* CCLXII (March, 1949).

LaGuardia, Fiorello H. "The National Origins Quota System," *The Nation,* March 21, 1928. "Government Must Act," *The Nation,* April 4, 1928. "Lobbying in Washington," *The Nation,* May 23, 1928. "The National Origins Quota System," *Current History,* Nov., 1928. "Usury: The Curse of Humanity," *Brass Tacks,* Oct., 1932.

Leuchtenburg, William E. "Progressivism and Imperialism," *Mississippi Valley Historical Review,* XXXIX (Dec., 1952).

Literary Digest, July 13, 1918, and Oct. 19, 1929.

Mowry, George A. "The California Progressive and His Rationale: A Study in Middle Class Politics," *Mississippi Valley Historical Review,* XXXVI (Sept., 1949).

The Nation, Oct. 23, 1929.

Neibuhr, Reinhold. "Awkward Imperialists," *Atlantic Monthly,* CXLV (May, 1930).

North American Review, Nov., 1929.

Outlook, Nov. 12, 1919, May 22, 1929, and Sept. 4, 1929.

Plain Talk, Aug., 1929.

Ravitch, Richard. "Progressive Reactions of 1912," *King's Crown Essays,* Winter, 1955.

Saturday Evening Post, Nov. 1, 1930.

Time, Jan. 26, 1925.

Weekly People, Feb. 28, 1931.

Williams, William A. "The Legend of Isolationism in the Twenties," *Science and Society,* XVIII (Winter, 1954).

INTERVIEWS

"The Reminiscences of Henry Bruere." (Oral History Project.) Columbia University, 1949.

"The Reminiscences of Samuel S. Koenig." (Oral History Project.) Columbia University, 1950.

Personal Interview with Marie Fischer LaGuardia, Aug., 1956, New York City.

"The Reminiscences of Mrs. Marie Fischer LaGuardia." (Oral History Project.) Columbia University, 1950.

Personal Interview with Mrs. Miriam Marcantonio, Aug., 1956, New York City.

"The Reminiscences of Newbold Morris." (Oral History Project.) Columbia University, 1950.

"The Reminiscences of Norman Thomas." (Oral History Project.) Columbia University, 1950.

UNPUBLISHED DOCTORAL DISSERTATIONS

Bagby, Wesley Marvin. "Progressivism's Debacle: The Election of 1920." Columbia University, 1954.

Ewald, Peter Kenneth. "Congressional Apportionment and New York State." New York University, 1954.

Hubbard, Preston J. "The Muscle Shoals Controversy 1920–1932: Public Policy in the Making." Vanderbilt University, 1955.

McKenna, Marian Cecilia. "The Early Career of William E. Borah, 1865–1917." Columbia University, 1953.

Reynolds, William Robinson. "Joseph Pulitzer." Columbia University, 1950.

Shideler, James H. "The Neo-Progressives: Reform Politics in the United States, 1920–1925." University of California at Berkeley, 1945.

GOVERNMENT PUBLICATIONS AND DOCUMENTS

City of New York. *Annual Report of the Department of Public Charities of the City of New York for 1917.* New York: O'Connell Press, 1918.

Congressional Record.

Personnel Folder of Fiorello LaGuardia in United States Immigration Service. Federal Records Center, St. Louis, Mo.

Pension Application File for Achilles LaGuardia. National Archives, Washington, D.C.

Records of the Foreign Service Posts of the Department of State. Record Group no. 84, National Archives, Washington, D.C.

Regular Army Enlistment Register for Achilles LaGuardia. Adjutant General's Office Record Group 94, National Archives, Washington, D.C.

Report of the Commission Appointed by the President to Investigate the Conduct of the War Department in the War with Spain. Senate Doc. no. 221, 56th Congress, 1st sess., 1899–1900.

United States Department of Commerce, Bureau of the Census. *Fifteenth Census of the United States: 1930. Metropolitan Districts— Population and Area.* Washington: Government Printing Office, 1932.

United States Department of Commerce, Bureau of the Census. *Fifteenth Census of the United States: 1930. Unemployment,* Vol. II. Washington: Government Printing Office, 1932.

United States Department of Labor, Bureau of Labor Statistics. *Retail Prices 1890–1928.* Washington: Government Printing Office, 1929.

United States Department of State. *Relations between the United States and Nicaragua.* Washington: Government Printing Office, 1928.

United States Senate, Committee on Foreign Relations. *Hearings on Treaty of Peace with Germany, Sixty-sixth Congress, First Session.* Washington: Government Printing Office, 1919.

GENERAL WORKS AND MONOGRAPHS

Adams, Samuel Hopkins. *Incredible Era—The Life and Times of Warren Gamaliel Harding.* Boston: Houghton, 1939.

Ahearn, Daniel J. *The Wages of Farm and Factory Laborers 1914– 1944.* New York: Columbia University Press, 1945.

Albrecht-Carrié, René. *Italy at the Paris Peace Conference.* New York: Columbia University Press, 1938.

Allen, Frederick Lewis. *Only Yesterday.* New York: Harper, 1931.

Bailey. Thomas A. *A Diplomatic History of the American People.* New York: Appleton-Century-Crofts, 1950.

——. *Woodrow Wilson and the Lost Peace.* New York: Macmillan, 1944.

Baker, Ray Stannard. *Woodrow Wilson and World Settlement.* New York: Doubleday, Page, 1922.

Bartlett, Ruhl. *The Record of American Diplomacy.* New York: Knopf, 1954.

Benedict, Murray R. *Farm Policies of the United States 1790–1950.* New York: Twentieth Century Fund, 1953.

Berle, Adolf A., Jr., and Means, Gardiner C. *The Modern Corporation and Private Property.* New York: Macmillan, 1937.

Bernard, William S., ed. *American Immigration Policy.* New York: Harper, 1950.

Black, John D. *Agricultural Reform in the United States.* New York: McGraw-Hill, 1929.

Borgatta, Edgar F., and Meyer, Henry J. *Sociological Theory.* New York: Knopf, 1956.

Buell, Raymond Leslie. *Isolated America.* New York: Knopf, 1940.

Chafee, Zechariah, Jr. *Free Speech in the United States.* Cambridge, Mass.: Harvard University Press, 1941.

Chase, Stuart. *Prosperity: Fact or Myth.* New York: Albert & Charles Boni, 1930.

Cline, Howard F. *The United States and Mexico.* Cambridge, Mass.: Harvard University Press, 1953.

Coleman, McAlister. *Men and Coal.* New York: Farrar & Rinehart, 1943.

Collier, John. *Indians of the Americas.* New York: New American Library, 1947.

Commager, Henry Steele. *Documents of American History.* New York: Appleton-Century-Crofts, 1949.

Council on Foreign Relations. *Survey of American Foreign Relations.* New Haven: Yale University Press, 1929.

Curti, Merle. *The Growth of American Thought.* New York and London: Harper, 1943.

Cushman, Robert E. *Leading Constitutional Decisions.* New York: Appleton-Century-Crofts, 1955.

Denny, Harold Norman. *Dollars for Bullets.* New York: Dial Press, 1929.

Douglas, Paul H. *Real Wages in the United States 1890–1926.* Boston: Houghton, 1930.

Dulles, Foster Rhea. *America's Rise to World Power 1898–1954.* New York: Harper, 1954.

———. *Labor in America.* New York: Crowell, 1949.

Epstein, Ralph C. *Industrial Profits in the United States.* New York: National Bureau of Economic Research, 1934.

Federal Writers' Project. *The Italians of New York*. New York: Random House, 1938.

Feis, Herbert. *The Diplomacy of the Dollar 1919–1932*. Baltimore: Johns Hopkins Press, 1950.

Ferrell, Robert H. *Peace in Their Time*. New Haven: Yale University Press, 1952.

Frankfurter, Felix. *The Case of Sacco and Vanzetti*. Stanford, Calif.: Academic Reprints, 1954.

Frankfurter, Felix, and Greene, Nathan. *The Labor Injunction*. New York: Macmillan, 1930.

Franklin, John Hope. *From Slavery to Freedom*. New York: Knopf, 1956.

Galbraith, John Kenneth. *The Great Crash: 1929*. Boston: Houghton, 1955.

Garis, Roy L. *Immigration Restriction*. New York: Macmillan, 1928.

Gerth, H. H., and Mills, C. W. *From Max Weber: Essays in Sociology*. New York: Oxford University Press, 1946.

Goldman, Eric F. *Rendezvous with Destiny*. New York: Knopf, 1952.

Gruening, Ernest. *The Public Pays: A Study of Power Propaganda*. New York: Vanguard Press, 1931.

Hapgood, Norman, ed. *Professional Patriots*. New York: Albert & Charles Boni, 1927.

Hofstadter, Richard. *The Age of Reform*. New York: Knopf, 1955.

———. *The American Political Tradition*. New York: Knopf, 1948.

Holcombe, A. N. *The New Party Politics*. New York: Norton, 1933.

Joughin, Louis, and Morgan, Edmund M. *The Legacy of Sacco and Vanzetti*. New York: Harcourt, Brace, 1948.

Kelly, Alfred H., and Harbison, Winfred A. *The American Constitution*. New York: Norton, 1948.

Kepner, Charles David, Jr., and Soothill, Jay Henry. *The Banana Empire: A Case Study of Economic Imperialism*. New York: Vanguard Press, 1935.

Kyrk, Hazel. *Economic Problems of the Family*. New York: Harper, 1933.

Leighton, Isabel, ed. *The Aspirin Age 1919–1941*. New York: Simon & Schuster, 1949.

Leuchtenburg, William E. *Flood Control Politics: The Connecticut River Valley Problem 1927–1950*. Cambridge, Mass.: Harvard University Press, 1953.

Lindley, Ernest K. *The Roosevelt Revolution*. New York: Viking Press, 1933.

Lindner, Robert. *Must You Conform?* New York: Rinehart, 1956.

Lubell, Samuel. *The Future of American Politics*. New York: Harper, 1951.

Lundberg, Ferdinand. *America's 60 Families*. New York: Citadel Press, 1937.

Luthin, Reinhard H. *American Demagogues*. Boston: Beacon Press, 1954.

Lynd, Robert S. and Helen M. *Middletown: A Study in American Culture*. New York: Harcourt, Brace, 1929.

MacKay, Kenneth Campbell. *The Progressive Movement of 1924*. New York: Columbia University Press, 1947.

Mellon, Andrew W. *Taxation: The Peoples Business*. New York: Macmillan, 1924.

Mencken, Henry L. *Notes on Democracy*. New York: Knopf, 1926.

Merz, Charles. *The Dry Decade*. New York: Doubleday, 1930.

Millis, Walter. *The Martial Spirit*. Cambridge, Mass.: Literary Guild, 1931.

Mills, C. Wright. *White Collar: The American Middle Classes*. New York: Oxford University Press, 1953.

Mills, Frederick C. *Economic Tendencies in the United States*. New York: National Bureau of Economic Research, 1932.

Mitchell, Broadus. *Depression Decade*. New York: Rinehart, 1947.

Mumford, Lewis. *Technics and Civilization*. New York: Harcourt, Brace, 1934.

Murray, Robert K. *Red Scare: A Study in National Hysteria 1919–1920*. Minneapolis: University of Minnesota Press, 1955.

Myers, Gustavus. *History of Bigotry in the United States*. New York: Random House, 1943.

Myers, William Starr, and Newton, Walter H. *The Hoover Administration—A Documented Narrative*. New York: Scribner, 1936.

National Conference of Social Work. *Proceedings of the National Conference of Social Work*. Chicago: University of Chicago Press, 1925.

National Industrial Conference Board. *The Cost of Living in the United States 1914–1929*. New York: National Industrial Conference Board, 1930.

Paxson, Frederic L. *Postwar Years: Normalcy 1918–1923*. Berkeley and Los Angeles: University of California Press, 1948.

Pearson, Drew, and Allen, Robert S. *Washington Merry-Go-Round*. New York: Liveright, 1931.

Pecora, Ferdinand. *Wall Street Under Oath*. New York: Simon & Schuster, 1939.

Peel, Roy V., and Donnelly, Thomas C. *The 1928 Campaign: An Analysis*. New York: Richard Smith, 1931.

Peel, Roy V., and Donnelly, Thomas C. *The 1932 Campaign: An Analysis*. New York: Farrar & Rinehart, 1935.

Radomski, Alexander L. *Work Relief in New York State 1931–1935*. New York: King's Crown Press, 1947.

Riis, Jacob. *How The Other Half Lives*. New York: Scribners, 1890.

Schlesinger, Arthur M. Jr. *The Crisis of the Old Order 1919–1933*. Boston: Houghton, 1957.

Schriftgiesser, Karl. *This Was Normalcy*. Boston: Little, 1948.

Seldes, Gilbert. *The Years of the Locust*. Boston: Little, 1933.

Shannon, Fred A. *America's Economic Growth*. New York: Macmillan, 1940.

Shaw, Frederick. *The History of the New York City Legislature*. New York: Columbia University Press, 1954.

Shotwell, James T. *At the Paris Peace Conference*. New York: Macmillan, 1937.

Slosson, Preston William. *The Great Crusade and After 1914–1928*. New York: Macmillan, 1930.

Soule, George. *Prosperity Decade: From War to Depression 1917–1929*. New York: Rinehart, 1947.

Stimson, Henry L. *American Policy in Nicaragua*. New York: Scribner, 1927.

Stuart, Graham H. *Latin America and the United States*. New York: Appleton-Century-Crofts, 1955.

Thomas, Norman, and Blanshard, Paul. *What's the Matter with New York*. New York: Macmillan, 1932.

Ware, Caroline F. *Greenwich Village 1920–1930*. Boston: Houghton, 1935.

Waters, W. W. *B.E.F.—The Whole Story of the Bonus Army*. New York: Day, 1933.

Wecter, Dixon. *The Age of the Great Depression 1929–1941*. New York: Macmillan, 1948.

Weinberg, Arthur K. *Manifest Destiny*. Baltimore: Johns Hopkins Press, 1935.

Werner, Maurice R. *Tammany Hall*. Garden City, N.Y.: Doubleday, 1928.

Wilbur, Ray Lyman, and Hyde, Arthur M. *The Hoover Policies*. New York: Scribner, 1937.

Williams, William A. *American Russian Relations 1781–1947*. New York: Rinehart, 1952.

Wisan, Joseph. *The Cuban Crisis as Reflected in the New York Press 1895–1898*. New York: Columbia University Press, 1934.

Wish, Harvey. *Contemporary America: The National Scene Since 1900*. New York: Harper, 1945.

Yellen, Samuel. *American Labor Struggles.* New York: Harcourt, Brace, 1936.

BIOGRAPHIES AND MEMOIRS

Bellush, Bernard. *Franklin D. Roosevelt as Governor of New York.* New York: Columbia University Press, 1955.

Burns, James MacGregor. *Roosevelt: The Lion and the Fox.* New York: Harcourt, Brace, 1956.

Butler, Nicholas Murray. *Across the Busy Years.* New York: Scribner, 1939. Vols. I, II.

Coolidge, Calvin. *The Autobiography of Calvin Coolidge.* New York: Cosmopolitan Book Corp., 1929.

Corsi, Edward. *In the Shadow of Liberty.* New York: Macmillan, 1935.

Cuneo, Ernest. *Life With Fiorello.* New York: Macmillan, 1955.

Flynn, Edward J. *You're The Boss.* New York: Viking Press, 1947.

Fowler, Gene. *Beau James: The Life and Times of Jimmy Walker.* New York: Viking Press, 1949.

Franklin, Jay. *LaGuardia: A Biography.* New York: Modern Age Books, 1937.

Freidel, Frank. *Franklin D. Roosevelt: The Triumph.* Boston: Little, 1956.

Fuess, Claude M. *Calvin Coolidge—The Man from Vermont.* Boston: Little, 1940.

Furman, Bess. *Washington By-Line.* New York: Knopf, 1949.

Fusfeld, Daniel R. *The Economic Thought of Franklin D. Roosevelt and the Origins of the New Deal.* New York: Columbia University Press, 1956.

Ginger, Ray. *The Bending Cross.* New Brunswick, N.J.: Rutgers University Press, 1949.

Hoover, Herbert. *The Memoirs of Herbert Hoover: The Cabinet and the Presidency 1920–1933.* New York: Macmillan, 1952. Vol. II.

Howe, Frederic C. *The Confessions of a Reformer.* New York: Scribner, 1925.

Ickes, Harold. *The Secret Diary of Harold Ickes: The First Thousand Days 1933–1936.* New York: Simon & Schuster, 1953.

Johnson, Claudius O. *Borah of Idaho.* New York: Longmans, 1936.

Jones, Jesse H. *Fifty Billion Dollars.* New York: Macmillan, 1951.

Josephson, Matthew. *Sidney Hillman.* New York: Doubleday, 1952.

Kerney, James. *The Political Education of Woodrow Wilson.* New York: Century, 1926.

La Follette, Belle Case and Fola. *Robert M. La Follette.* New York: Macmillan, 1953.

LaGuardia, Fiorello H. *The Making of an Insurgent: An Autobiography 1882–1919.* Ed. by M. R. Werner. Philadelphia and New York: Lippincott, 1948.

Lief, Alfred. *Democracy's Norris.* New York: Stackpole, 1939.

Limpus, Lowell, and Leyson, Burr. *This Man LaGuardia.* New York: Dutton, 1938.

Link, Arthur S. *Woodrow Wilson and the Progressive Era 1910–1917.* New York: Harper, 1954.

Longworth, Alice. *Crowded Hours.* New York: Scribner, 1933.

Lord, Russell. *The Wallaces of Iowa.* Boston: Houghton, 1947.

Marsh, Benjamin C. *Lobbyist for the People.* Washington: Public Affairs Press, 1953.

Mason, Alpheus Thomas. *Brandeis—A Free Man's Life.* New York: Viking Press, 1946.

Moskowitz, Henry, ed. *Progressive Democracy: Addresses and State Papers of Alfred E. Smith.* New York: Harcourt, Brace, 1938.

Mowry, George E. *Theodore Roosevelt and the Progressive Movement.* Madison: University of Wisconsin Press, 1947.

Norris, George. *Fighting Liberal: The Autobiography of George W. Norris.* New York: Macmillan, 1945.

O'Connor, Harvey. *Mellon's Millions.* New York: Day, 1933.

Pesotta, Rose. *Bread Upon the Waters.* New York: Dodd, 1945.

Pringle, Henry F. *Alfred E. Smith: A Critical Study.* New York: Macy-Masius, 1937.

Pusey, Merlo J. *Charles Evans Hughes.* New York: Macmillan, 1951.

Rosenman, Samuel, ed. *The Genesis of the New Deal 1928–1932.* (*The Public Papers and Addresses of Franklin D. Roosevelt,* Vol. I.) New York: Random House, 1938.

Rubinstein, Annette T., and associates, eds. *I Vote My Conscience: Debates, Speeches and Writings of Vito Marcantonio.* New York: Vito Marcantonio Memorial, 1956.

Spalding, Albert. *Rise to Follow.* New York: Holt, 1943.

Speranza, Florence C., ed. *The Diary of Gino Speranza 1915–1919.* New York: Columbia University Press, 1941. Vol. II.

Timmons, Bascom N. *Garner of Texas.* New York: Harper, 1948.

Villard, Oswald Garrison. *Fighting Years.* New York: Harcourt, Brace, 1939.

Wald, Lillian D. *Windows on Henry Street.* Boston: Little, 1934.

Whalen, Grover A. *Mr. New York: The Autobiography of Grover Whalen.* New York: Putnam, 1955.

White, William Allen. *A Puritan in Babylon: Calvin Coolidge.* New York: Macmillan, 1938.

Ybarra, T. R. *Caruso.* New York: Harcourt, Brace, 1953.

* Index *

AMERICAN HISTORY TITLES IN THE NORTON LIBRARY